Jonathan Bygrave

**STARTER**

# Total English

## Students' Book

PEARSON

Longman

# Contents

| LESSON 3 | COMMUNICATION | FILM BANK |
|---|---|---|
| **Do you know ...?** page 8   Grammar: useful language | | |
| **Grammar:** *Where are you from?* **Vocabulary:** common phrases **Can do:** introduce someone; start a conversation | **Can do:** understand and say phone numbers | Saying hello **page 116** |
| **Grammar:** *his/her; a/an* **Vocabulary:** jobs **Can do:** give information about other people; write a short personal profile | **Can do:** talk about favourite people and things | Favourites **page 117** |
| **Grammar:** *Yes/No questions with to be* **Vocabulary:** days of the week **Can do:** ask for tourist information | **Can do:** have an extended phone conversation | A journey across Canada **page 118** |
| **Grammar:** possessive *'s* **Vocabulary:** irregular plurals **Can do:** ask about things and make simple transactions | **Can do:** ask for and give locations | The flowers **page 119** |
| **Grammar:** *can/can't* **Vocabulary:** telling the time **Can do:** talk about general abilities | **Can do:** check into a Bed and Breakfast | Holiday places **page 120** |
| **Grammar:** Present Simple (3) *he/she/it* **Vocabulary:** verbs of routine **Can do:** talk about the routines of people you know | **Can do:** ask and answer questions about a friend | The interview **page 121** |
| **Grammar:** *would like* **Vocabulary:** ordinal numbers **Can do:** welcome a visitor to your place of work | **Can do:** understand and give directions in a building | The company **page 122** |
| **Grammar:** *question words* **Vocabulary:** food **Can do:** suggest a restaurant; book a restaurant; order food in a restaurant | **Can do:** ask for and give information about people | Change your life **page 123** |
| **Grammar:** *Can/Could you ...?; Can/Could I ...?* **Vocabulary:** housework **Can do:** make a simple request and ask permission | **Can do:** talk about school days | 100 years ago **page 124** |
| **Grammar:** *going to* **Vocabulary:** future plans **Can do:** talk about immediate and long-term plans | **Can do:** talk about past and future holidays | Cucumber sandwiches **page 125** |

Pronunciation bank page 130

# Welcome to Total English!

## To the teacher

### What is *Total English*?

*Total English* is a six-level general English course for adults and young adults who want to learn to communicate effectively.

### Clear goals and objectives

Every input lesson begins with a *Can do* objective to give learners a clear sense of where they are going. These objectives mean the students know why they are studying that lesson and how they can use the new language. The flexible and clearly-structured units also make teaching and learning transparent and easy to follow.

### Engaging learners' interests

Learners need to be genuinely engaged in coursebook content. *Total English* texts have new and fresh angles on the topics students need, and provide frequent opportunities for personal response. In addition, each *Total English* Students' Book has a DVD which contains a rich variety of authentic extracts from film and TV.

### Helping learners catch up

Learners have busy lives and attending English classes on a regular basis is not always possible. If students miss lessons, the *Reference* and *Review and practice* pages at the end of each unit provide a summary of the main points covered. Also, the *Total English* Workbooks have free-standing CD-ROMs that include self-study 'catch-up' material to present and practise language from any lesson the learner has missed.

### Complete package

*Total English* provides a comprehensive range of resources: the Teacher's Book not only includes lesson-by-lesson teaching notes, but also extra photocopiable activities and progress tests plus a Test Master CD-ROM with extra editable tests. The *Total English* website provides Teacher tips, downloadable worksheets and a *Total English* CEFR Portfolio document.

## To the learner

*Total English* has six levels.

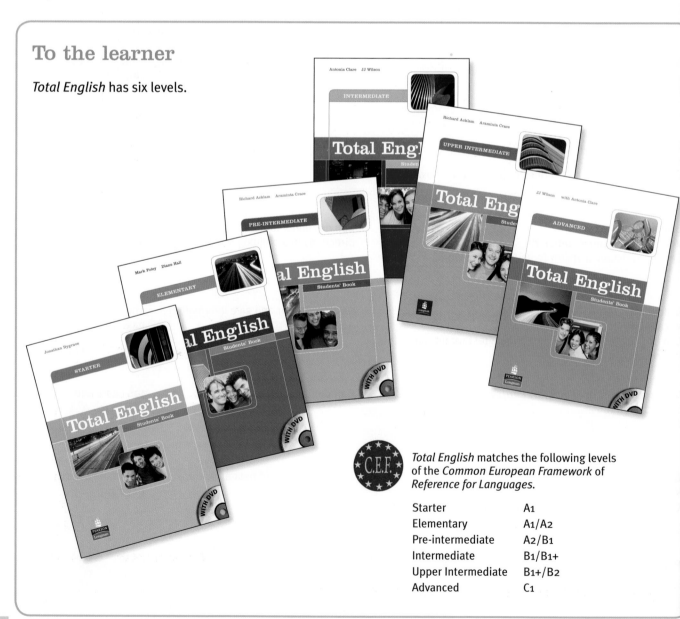

*Total English* matches the following levels of the *Common European Framework* of *Reference for Languages*.

| | |
|---|---|
| Starter | A1 |
| Elementary | A1/A2 |
| Pre-intermediate | A2/B1 |
| Intermediate | B1/B1+ |
| Upper Intermediate | B1+/B2 |
| Advanced | C1 |

# Total English Starter

*Total English Starter* has ten units. Each Students' Book unit has ten pages.

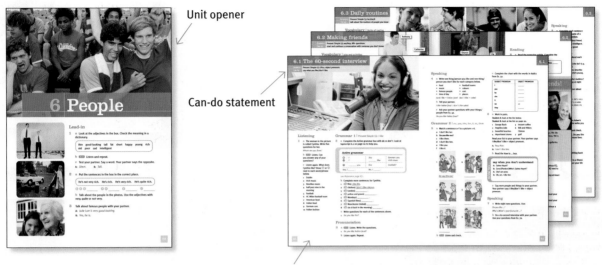

Unit opener

Can-do statement

There are three double-page lessons in each unit.

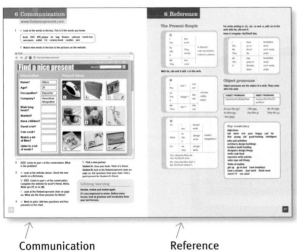

Communication

Reference

Review and practice

## Back of Students' Book

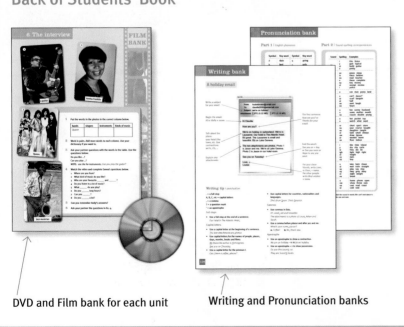

DVD and Film bank for each unit

Writing and Pronunciation banks

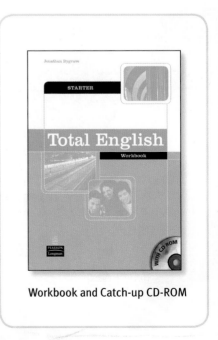

Workbook and Catch-up CD-ROM

# Do you know...?

## International words

1 **DYK1** Do you know these words? Match a word in the box to a picture 1–15. Then listen and check.

> football   television   police   bus   ~~supermarket~~   camera
> tennis   doctor   telephone   pizza   hotel   restaurant   cinema
> taxi   university

1   *supermarket*

3 _____

4 _____

5 _____

7 _____

8 _____

9 _____

10 _____

12 _____

13 _____

14 _____

## Numbers and alphabet

1 **DYK2** Do you know numbers 0–9? Listen and repeat.

| 0 | 1 | 2 | 3 | 4 |
|---|---|---|---|---|
| zero | one | two | three | four |
| 5 | 6 | 7 | 8 | 9 |
| five | six | seven | eight | nine |

2 **DYK3** Do you know the English alphabet? Listen and repeat.

| a | b | c | d | e |
|---|---|---|---|---|
| A | B | C | D | E |
| f | g | h | i | j |
| F | G | H | I | J |
| k | l | m | n | o |
| K | L | M | N | O |
| p | q | r | s | t |
| P | Q | R | S | T |
| u | v | w | x | y |
| U | V | W | X | Y |
| z | | | | |
| Z | | | | |

# Useful language

**1  a** Do you know classroom instructions? Match the instructions in the box to the pictures 1–7 below.

> ~~Listen~~   Look   Read   Write   Speak   Repeat   Match

**1**

*Listen*

**2**

_____

**3**

_____

**4**

_____

**5**

_____

**6**

_____

**7**

_____

**b** `DYK4` Listen and check your answers.

**2** `DYK5` Learn these useful phrases. Listen and repeat.

| English | Translation |
| --- | --- |
| Sorry, I don't understand. | _____ |
| What's '*Hola*' in English? | _____ |
| Can you say that slowly, please? | _____ |
| Excuse me, can you help me? | _____ |

A

# 1 Arrivals

## Lead-in

**1**  **a** Match a conversation below to a photo A–D.

B

A: Good morning.
B: Good morning.
A: Welcome to Easton Hotel.
B: Thank you.
**Photo** ___

A: Hello. I'm Alonzo Moreno.
B: Hello. I'm Camila Diaz. Nice to meet you.
A: Nice to meet you, too.
**Photo** ___

A: Hi, Nina.
B: Hi, James.
**Photo** ___

A: Hello. I'm Maria Hofmann. What's your name?
B: I'm Helga Peters.
**Photo** _C_

**b**  🔊1.1 Listen and check your answers.

C

**2**  🔊1.2 Listen. Reply to each person.

*Good morning.*
**You:** *Good morning.*

**3**  Introduce yourself to other students.

A: *Hello. I'm Adelina Garza.*
B: *I'm Nahid Golovina. Nice to meet you.*
A: *Nice to meet you, too.*

D

# 1.1 Hotel check-in

| Grammar | *I'm/you're* |
|---------|--------------|
| Can do | check in to a hotel |

## Vocabulary | numbers 0–9

**1 a** **1.3** Listen and repeat.

**b** Write the numbers next to the words.

four ___  eight ___  one ___  two ___

five ___  seven ___  six ___

three ___  zero ___  nine ___

**2** Point to a number. Your partner says the number.

**3 a** Read the How to ... box. Write the room numbers.

**HOW TO ...**

### say hotel room numbers

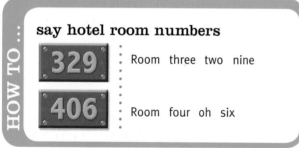

329 : Room three two nine

406 : Room four oh six

**1** 129 — Room *one* *two* *nine*

**4** 209 — Room ___ ___ ___

**2** 438 — Room ___ ___ ___

**5** 608 — Room ___ ___ ___

**3** 517 — Room ___ ___ ___

**6** 345 — Room ___ ___ ___

**b** Say the room numbers.

## Listening

**4** **1.4** Listen. Choose the correct information.

**1**

| NAME: | Cristina Bally |
|-------|----------------|
| ROOM: | 329 |

**2**

| NAME: | Cristina Branco |
|-------|-----------------|
| ROOM: | 329 |

**3**

| NAME: | Cristina Branco |
|-------|-----------------|
| ROOM: | 239 |

**5** Work in pairs. Read the How to ... box. Repeat the conversation in Ex. 4 with your name.

**HOW TO ...**

### say names

Mr Smith           Mrs/Ms/Miss Jones

A: Hello.

B: Hello. I'm Leonardo Gallo.

A: Welcome to Bally Hotel, Mr Gallo. You're in room ...

B: Thank you.

## Grammar | *I'm/you're*

**6** Complete the Active grammar box with *'m* or *'re*.

> **Active grammar**
>
> | ➕ | *I* | *am* | *Cristina Branco.* |
> | | *I* | ___ | |
> | | *You* | *are* | *in room 329.* |
> | | *You* | ___ | |

*see Reference page 17*

**7** **a** Complete the conversations with *'m* or *'re*.

1 **A:** Good morning. *I'm* Mateo Alvarez.
**B:** Good morning, Mr Alvarez. You___ in room 121.

2 **A:** Hello. Welcome to Hotel Lux.
**B:** Thank you. I___ Britney Black.
**A:** You___ in room 820, Ms Black.

3 **A:** Good morning. I___ Mi Lei Ling.
**B:** I___ Walter Mann. Nice to meet you.

4 **A:** Hello, Ms West. You___ in room 320.
**B:** Thank you.

5 **A:** I___ Paul Wolf.
**B:** Nice to meet you, Mr Wolf. I___ Konrad Nowak.
**A:** Nice to meet you, too, Mr Nowak.

**b** Work in pairs. Practise the conversations with the information below.

**A:** *I'm Scott Wilson.*

**B:** *Hello, Mr Wilson. You're in room two three five.*

1 Scott Wilson
**2 3 5**

2 Jasmine Dudek
**4 0 9**

3 Carlos Santos
**1 2 6**

4 Elsa Richter
**9 0 8**

5 Luca Rosa
**2 1 7**

6 Marisa Gonzales
**3 4 1**

7 Jane Cross
**7 3 6**

8 Lara Bezmel
**1 0 8**

## Vocabulary | greetings

**8** **a** Complete the conversations with the words in the box.

> evening   afternoon   morning   night

**1**
**Alfred:** Good _____ .
**Betty:** Good _____ .

**2**
**Alfred:** Good _____ .
**Camilla:** Good _____ .

**3**
**Alfred:** Good _____ .
**Daniel:** Good _____ .

**4**
**Alfred:** Good _____ .
**People:** Good _____ .

**b** **1.5** Listen and check your answers.

**c** Practise in pairs.
**A:** *Good afternoon.*   **B:** *Good afternoon.*

## Speaking

**9** Choose Student A or Student B.

**Student A:** you are a receptionist. Think of a name for your hotel. Find four guests for your hotel. Write their names below.

**Student B:** you are a guest. Find four different hotels. Check in to the hotels.

| ROOM | NAME |
|------|------|
| 504 | |
| 319 | |
| 428 | |
| 716 | |

**A:** *Good evening. Welcome to Hotel California.*

**B:** *Thank you. I'm Gerik Pawlak.*

**A:** *Mr Pawlak. You're in room 504.*

**B:** *Thank you.*

## Vocabulary | letters

**1**  **a**  `1.6` Listen to the alphabet.

**a** b c d e f g **h i** j **k** l m n
o p q r s t u v w x y z

**b** Listen again and repeat.

**c** Work in pairs. Say the alphabet.

**2**  **a** How do you say the sounds below? Match the letters of the alphabet to the <u>underlined</u> sounds.

/eɪ/ (<u>eigh</u>t) = <u>a</u> ___ ___ ___
/iː/ (thr<u>ee</u>) = <u>b</u> ___ ___ ___ ___ ___ ___ ___
/e/ (t<u>e</u>n) = <u>f</u> ___ ___ ___ ___ ___ ___
/aɪ/ (f<u>i</u>ve) = <u>i</u> ___ ___
/əʊ/ (zer<u>o</u>) ___
/uː/ (tw<u>o</u>) <u>q</u> ___ ___ ___
/ɑː/ (<u>are</u>) ___

**b**  `1.7` Listen and check your answers.

**3** Say the flight numbers on the Arrivals board.

**A:** *HD three four seven.*

**B:** *Delhi.*

### Arrivals

| Flight number | From | Arrival time | Comments |
| --- | --- | --- | --- |
| HD347 | Delhi | 14.00 | landed |
| AR191 | Sydney | 14.05 | landed |
| CT248 | Buenos Aires | 14.05 | delayed |
| WG506 | Tokyo | 14.10 | |
| MO793 | New York | 14.15 | |
| JF820 | Rio de Janeiro | 14.15 | on time |
| ML145 | London | 14.25 | |
| PE706 | Berlin | 14.25 | |
| IS003 | Rome | 14.30 | cancelled |
| YI449 | Warsaw | 14.30 | |

## Vocabulary | countries

**4**  **a** Match a city on the Arrivals board to a country in the box below.

> Argentina  ~~India~~
> Germany  Japan  Italy
> Poland  the UK
> Australia  Brazil  the US

| | City | Country |
| --- | --- | --- |
| 1 | Delhi | *India* |
| 2 | Sydney | _____ |
| 3 | Buenos Aires | _____ |
| 4 | Tokyo | _____ |
| 5 | New York | _____ |
| 6 | Rio de Janeiro | _____ |
| 7 | London | _____ |
| 8 | Berlin | _____ |
| 9 | Rome | _____ |
| 10 | Warsaw | _____ |

**b**  `1.8` Listen and check your answers. Repeat.

## Pronunciation

**5**  **a** Listen again. Count the syllables for each country.

*In – di – a = 3*

**b** Work in pairs. Say a city. Your partner says a country.

**A:** *Tokyo.*  **B:** *Japan.*

**c** Add more countries to the box in Ex. 4a.

### Lifelong learning

**A vocabulary notebook**

Write new words in a vocabulary notebook. Show the syllables and the stress.

**Countries**
Ar gen <u>ti</u> na
Ja <u>pan</u>

Sunny

Ana

Nicole

## Listening and reading

**6**  **a** [1.9] Look at the photos and listen. Complete the sentences below.

1  He's Sunny Deva. He's from India. He's in *the UK*.

2  She's Ana Goncalvez . She's from ____. She's in ____ .

3  She's Nicole Redman . She's from ____. She's in ____ .

**b**  Listen again and check your answers.

**c**  Work in pairs. Read the How to ... box. Greet your partner at airport arrivals.

<table>
<tr><td rowspan="5">HOW TO ...</td></tr>
</table>

| **greet someone at airport arrivals** |
| --- |
| A: *Mrs Cole?* |
| B: *Yes.* |
| A: *Hello, Mrs Cole. I'm Stephen Taylor. Welcome to the UK.* |
| B: *Thank you.* |

## Grammar | *he's/she's/it's*

**7**  Complete the Active grammar box with *'s*.

### Active grammar

| ➕ | He | *is* | |
| --- | --- | --- | --- |
| | He | *'s* | |
| | She | *is* | *from India.* |
| | She | __ | *from Argentina.* |
| | It | *is* | |
| | It | __ | |

*see Reference page 17*

**8**  **a** Complete the sentences with *he's*, *she's* or *it's*.

1  *He's* from Australia. (Russell Crowe)

2  _____ from the US. (Hillary Clinton)

3  _____ in Italy. (Venice)

4  _____ in London. (Gwyneth Paltrow)

5  _____ from Germany. (Angela Merkel)

6  _____ in Australia. (Melbourne)

7  _____ from the UK. (Anthony Hopkins)

8  _____ from Argentina. (the tango)

**b**  Work in pairs. Make true or false statements about cities.

A:  *Sydney is in Argentina.*

B:  *False! It's in Australia.*

**c**  Talk about people in your class.

*She's Olga. She's from St. Petersburg in Russia.*

## Speaking

**9**  Match the photos a–f below to the names in the box. Talk about the people.

| Penelope Cruz    Michael Schumacher |
| --- |
| Prince William    Thierry Henry |
| Condoleezza Rice    ~~Gisele Bündchen~~ |

*She's Gisele Bündchen. She's from Brazil.*

a    b    c

d    e    f

| Grammar | *Where are you from?* |
|---|---|
| Can do | introduce someone; start a conversation |

## Vocabulary | common phrases

**1**  **a**  Match the phrases in the box to the pictures 1–6.

> Sorry!   Nice to meet you.   No, thank you.   ~~Yes, please.~~   Pardon?
> Excuse me, ...

1  *Yes, please.*

**b**  🔊 **1.10**  Listen and check your answers.

**2**  🔊 **1.11**  Listen. Complete the conversations with a phrase from Ex. 1a.

1  *Pardon?*

2  _____

3  _____

Boris

## Listening

**3**  **a**  🔊 **1.12**  Listen. Put the sentences in the correct order.

A:  Hi, Boris.  `1`
L:  Nice to meet you, too.  ☐
B:  Hi, Andy. This is Luisa.  ☐
A:  Nice to meet you, Luisa.  ☐

**b**  Listen again. Check your answers.

**4**  **a**  Work in groups of three. Repeat the conversation in Ex. 3a.

**HOW TO ...**

> ### introduce people
> *This is (Paul).*
> *Nice to meet you.*
> *Nice to meet you, too.*

**b**  Read the How to ... box, then close your books. Introduce each other.

A:  *Hi, Britta.*
B:  *Hi, Pedro. This is Roxana.*

Andy

Luisa

**5** **a** [1.13] Listen. Complete the conversation between Luisa and Andy.

**Luisa:** Where are you from, Andy?

**Andy:** I (1) ___ from the US.

**Luisa:** Where (2) ____ you from in the US?

**Andy:** I'm from New York. Where are (3) _____ from?

**Luisa:** I'm (4) ____ Argentina.

**Andy:** Where are you from in Argentina?

**Luisa:** I'm from Rosario.

**b** True (T) or false (F)?

1 Andy is from Argentina.  ☐F☐
2 Andy is from New York.  ☐
3 Luisa is from New York.  ☐
4 Luisa is from Buenos Aires.  ☐
5 Luisa is from Rosario.  ☐

**6** **a** Work in pairs. Repeat the conversation.

**A:** *Where are you from, Andy?*

**B:** *I'm from New York.*

**b** Ask your partner.

**A:** *Where are you from, Eva?*

**B:** *I'm from ...*

## Grammar | questions with *be*

**7** Look at the Active grammar box. Match the questions to the answers.

> ### Active grammar
>
> ❓ Questions
>
> | 1 | Where are | you | from? |
> | 2 | Where are | you | from in the US? |
>
> ➕ Answers
>
> | a) | I | 'm | from Las Vegas. |
> | b) | I | 'm | from the US. |

*see Reference page 17*

**8** **a** Complete the conversation.

**A:** (1) *Where* are you from?

**B:** (2) _____ from Turkey.

**A:** (3) _____ are you from in Turkey?

**B:** I'm (4) _____ Istanbul.

**C:** Where are (5) _____ from?

**D:** I'm (6) _____ the UK.

**C:** Where (7) _____ you from in the UK?

**D:** I'm (8) _____ Bristol.

**b** Complete the questions and answers.

1 **A:** *Where are you from?*
  **B:** I'm from the UK.

2 **A:** _____ in India?
  **B:** I'm from Delhi.

3 **A:** Where are you from?
  **B:** _____ São Paolo in Brazil.

4 **A:** _____ Australia?
  **B:** I'm from Sydney.

## Pronunciation

**9** **a** [1.14] Listen. Mark the stress.

1 *Where* are you *from*?
2 Where are you from in Poland?
3 I'm from Warsaw.

**b** Listen again. Repeat.

## Speaking

**10** Work in groups of three, A, B and C.

**Student A:** introduce B and C.

**Student B:** ask where Student C is from.

**Student C:** ask where Student B is from.

**1**  **a** Match countries a–f to the countries in the table below.

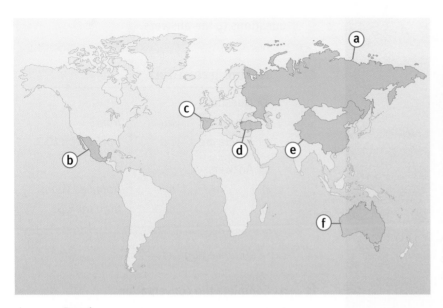

**a** *Russia*

**b** 1.15 Listen. Complete the dialling codes in the table below.

| Dial 00 + country code + telephone number | |
| --- | --- |
| COUNTRY | CODE |
| Australia | ____ |
| Brazil | 55 |
| China | ____ |
| Japan | 81 |
| Mexico | ____ |
| Russia | ____ |
| Spain | ____ |
| Turkey | ____ |
| the UK | 44 |
| the US | 1 |

**c** Read the How to ... box. Repeat the countries and country numbers.

> **HOW TO ...**
>
> ### say phone numbers
> 55 = double five
>
> o = oh 🇬🇧        o = zero 🇺🇸

**2**  **a** 1.16 Listen and complete the details below.

HOTEL: Hotel Lamden

WHERE: _____ , Italy.

PHONE NUMBER: _____ .

**b** Listen again. Put the sentences in the correct order.

[   ] **A:** Where is it?
[ 6 ] **C:** The number is: double o ...
[ 1 ] **A:** Directory enquiries.
[   ] **A:** Thank you.
[   ] **B:** The Lamden Hotel, please.
[   ] **B:** It's in Rome, in Italy.

**3**  Work in pairs. Take turns to practise the conversations in Ex. 2b with the information below.

1  **HOTEL:** Hotel Kelem
   **WHERE:** Istanbul, Turkey
   **PHONE NUMBER:** 00 902 129 6347

2  **HOTEL:** Hotel Marianne
   **WHERE:** Madrid, Spain
   **PHONE NUMBER:** 00 34 91 366 2119

3  **HOTEL:** Hotel Parkside
   **WHERE:** Shanghai, China
   **PHONE NUMBER:** 00 86 21 503 299

## Numbers 0–9

| 0 | zero |
|---|------|
| 1 | one |
| 2 | two |
| 3 | three |
| 4 | four |
| 5 | five |
| 6 | six |
| 7 | seven |
| 8 | eight |
| 9 | nine |

## Telephone numbers:

o = oh    o = zero

99 = *double nine*

020 8922 7255
= *oh–two–oh*
    *eight–nine–double two*
        *seven–two–double five*

## Letters a–z

a b c d e f g h i j k l m
n o p q r s t u v w x y z

These letters have the same vowel sound:

/eɪ/ (e**igh**t) = a h j k

/iː/ (thr**ee**) = b c d e g p t v

/e/ (t**e**n) = f l m n s x z

/aɪ/ (f**i**ve) = i y

/əʊ/ (zer**o**) = o

/uː/ (t**wo**) = q u w

/ɑː/ (**are**) = r

## Verb *to be* | affirmative

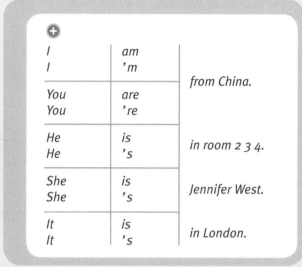

| | | |
|---|---|---|
| I | am | |
| I | 'm | from China. |
| You | are | |
| You | 're | |
| He | is | in room 2 3 4. |
| He | 's | |
| She | is | Jennifer West. |
| She | 's | |
| It | is | in London. |
| It | 's | |

Contractions = *I'm/You're/He's/She's/It's*
Contractions = informal English
**The full form** = *I am/You are/He is/She is/It is*
The full form = formal English

## Where are you from?

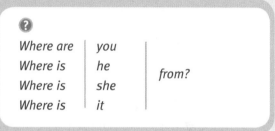

| | | |
|---|---|---|
| Where are | you | |
| Where is | he | from? |
| Where is | she | |
| Where is | it | |

*Where is ...? = Where's ...?*
*Where are = ~~Where're~~*

Add *in* + country
*Where are you from* **in Russia**? – Moscow
*Where is he from* **in the UK**? – London

### Key vocabulary

**Common phrases**
Good morning/afternoon/evening/night.
Sorry!
Excuse me, ...
Nice to meet you./Nice to meet you, too.
No, thank you./Thank you.
Yes, please.
Pardon?

**Countries**
Argentina   Australia   Brazil   China   France
Germany   Greece   India   Italy   Japan
Mexico   Poland   Russia   Spain   the UK
the US   Turkey

**1** Rewrite the sentences with contractions.

1 **A:** I am Maggie May.

**B:** You are in room 511.

**A:** *I'm Maggie May.*

**B:** _____ .

2 **A:** I am Ruby Tuesday.

**B:** You are in room 147.

**A:** _____ .

**B:** _____ .

3 **A:** I am Peggy Sue.

**B:** You are in room 312.

**A:** _____ .

**B:** _____ .

**2** Complete with *I'm* or *You're*.

1 **A:** Hello. Welcome to Hotel California.

**B:** Thank you. _____ Don Henley.

**A:** _____ in room 329, Mr Henley.

2 **A:** Hello.

**B:** Hello. I'm Ms Turner.

**A:** Welcome to Nutbush Hotel, Ms Turner.

_____ in room 808.

**B:** Thank you.

3 **A:** Hello. Welcome to the Kelly Hotel.

**B:** Thank you. _____ Trina Cassidy.

**A:** _____ in room 415, Ms Cassidy.

4 **A:** Hello.

**B:** Hello. _____ John Densmore.

**A:** Welcome to Hotel Morrison, Mr Densmore.

_____ in room 342.

**3** Where is he/she/it from?

1 Prince Charles: *He's from* the UK.

2 Madonna: _____ the US.

3 Champagne: _____ France.

4 Diego Maradona: _____ Argentina.

5 Sushi: _____ Japan.

6 Claudia Schiffer: _____ Germany.

7 Pele: _____ Brazil.

8 Sonia Gandhi: _____ India.

9 Kylie Minogue: _____ Australia.

10 Rock and roll: _____ the US.

**4** Complete the dialogues. Write one word in each gap.

1 **A:** Hi, Betina. (1) *This* is Cyrek.

**B:** Hello, Cyrek. Nice to meet you.

**C:** Nice to meet you, too.

**B:** (2) _____ are you from?

**C:** (3) _____ from Poland.

**B:** Where are you from (4) _____ Poland?

**C:** I'm from Krakow. Where (5) _____ you from?

**B:** I'm from Spain.

**C:** Where are you (6) _____ in Spain?

**B:** I'm from Salamanca.

2 **D:** Good morning, Edward.

**E:** Good morning, Daisy.

**D:** This (7) _____ Francesca.

**E:** Hello, Francesca. I'm Edward. Nice to meet you.

**F:** Nice to meet you, too.

**E:** Where (8) _____ you from?

**F:** I'm from Turin, in Italy. Where are (9) _____ from?

**E:** I'm from (10) _____ UK.

**F:** Where are you from (11) _____ the UK?

**E:** (12) _____ from Bristol.

**5** Write the phrases from the box below in the correct place.

> Good afternoon.   Thank you.   Pardon?
> Yes, please.   Nice to meet you, too.

1 **A:** Coffee?

**B:** _____ .

2 **A:** Nice to meet you.

**B:** _____ .

3 **A:** I'm from Izmir, in Turkey.

**B:** _____ .

**A:** I'm from Izmir, in Turkey.

4 **A:** Good afternoon.

**B:** _____ .

5 **A:** Welcome to Abbey Road Hotel.

**B:** _____ .

Karen

John

A

Lucy

Luke

# 2 My life

B

C

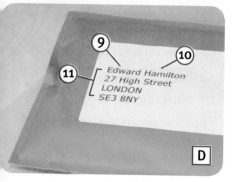

Edward Hamilton
27 High Street
LONDON
SE3 8NY

D

## Lead-in

**1**  **a** Look at photo A above. Complete the gaps 1–6 below with the words from the box.

> mother  husband  sister  daughter
> father  son  wife  brother

1  Karen – Luke = *mother – son*
2  John – Lucy = \_\_\_\_\_ – \_\_\_\_\_
3  Lucy – Luke = \_\_\_\_\_ – \_\_\_\_\_
4  John – Luke = \_\_\_\_\_ – \_\_\_\_\_
5  Karen – John = \_\_\_\_\_ – \_\_\_\_\_
6  Karen – Lucy = \_\_\_\_\_ – \_\_\_\_\_

**b** **2.1** Listen and check your answers. Repeat. Underline the main stress.

*mother*

**2**  **a** Match the objects 1–11 in the photos with the words in the box.

> phone  email address  address  ~~mobile phone~~  computer
> passport  first name  website  phone number  surname  photo

1  *mobile phone*

**b** **2.2** Listen and check your answers. Repeat. Underline the main stress.

*email address*

**3**  Work in pairs.

**Student A:** point to an object in Photos B–D.
**Student B:** say the word.

# 2.1 My family

| Grammar | Who ...?; my |
|---|---|
| Can do | give basic information about your family |

Tom, ____

Anna, ____

Marek, ____

Sofia, ____

James, ____

Sabrina, 37

Sarah, ____

Carl, ____

## Listening

**1** **a** Look at the photos of Sabrina and her family. How are the people related to Sabrina? Write a name next to each word below.

- **a** mother = *Sofia*
- **b** father = _____
- **c** brother = _____
- **d** sister = _____
- **e** son = _____
- **f** daughter = _____
- **g** husband = _____

**b** [2.3] Listen and check your answers.

**c** Listen again. Write the correct ages next to the names in the photos.

> 26  32  3  ~~37~~  1  57  60  40

## Vocabulary | numbers 10–99

**2** **a** [2.4] Listen and repeat.

**b** Close your books. Say numbers 1–20.

| 10 | 11 | 12 | 13 | 14 | 15 |
|---|---|---|---|---|---|
| ten | eleven | twelve | thirteen | fourteen | fifteen |
| | 16 | 17 | 18 | 19 | 20 |
| | sixteen | seventeen | eighteen | nineteen | twenty |

**3** **a** [2.5] Listen and repeat.

| 20 twenty | 21 twenty-one |
|---|---|
| 30 thirty | 33 thirty-three |
| 40 forty | 49 forty-nine |
| 50 fifty | 56 fifty-six |
| 60 sixty | 67 sixty-seven |
| 70 seventy | 74 seventy-four |
| 80 eighty | 88 eighty-eight |
| 90 ninety | 99 ninety-nine |

**b** Work in pairs. Write a number. Your partner says it.

A: *27*  B: '*twenty-seven*'

**c** Look at the How to ... box. How old are the people in the photos?

# Grammar | Who ...?; my

**4**   Complete the Active grammar box with *he* and *she*.

**Active grammar**

| ❓ *Who* | 's<br>(is) | *she?*<br>___?<br>*Sofia?* |
| --- | --- | --- |
| ➕ *Marek*<br>*He*<br>___ | 's<br>(is) | *my father.*<br>*my brother.*<br>*my sister.* |

*see Reference page 27*

**5**   Complete these dialogues.

A: Who's *he?*     B: He's _____ father.

A: _____ she?     B: _____ my mother.

A: Who's _____ ? B: _____ _____ brother.

A: _____ he?
B: It's OK. _____ _____ friend.

**6**   **a**   Complete these sentences for Sabrina.

1   Carl is *my brother.*
2   Anna is _____ .
3   Marek is _____ .
4   Sofia is _____ .
5   Sarah is _____ .
6   Tom is _____ .
7   James is _____ .

**b**   Write questions for Sabrina's answers.

1   *Who's Marek?*   He's my father.
2   _____ ?   He's my brother.
3   _____ ?   She's my mother.
4   _____ ?   She's my sister.
5   _____ ?   He's my son.
6   _____ ?   He's my husband.
7   _____ ?   She's my daughter.

## Pronunciation

**7**   **a**   [2.6]   Listen. Circle the correct number.

1   He's my brother. He's **a)** ⑬ **b)** 30.
2   Carol's my sister. She's **a)** 14 **b)** 40.
3   She's Helen. She's **a)** 18 **b)** 80.
4   My son's **a)** 15 **b)** 50.
5   He's my husband. He's **a)** 16 **b)** 60.
6   Roberto's **a)** 17 **b)** 70.

**b**   Listen again and repeat.

## Speaking

**8**   **a**   Write a list of five names from your family or friends.

**b**   Explain to your partner who the people on the list are.

A: *Who's Martin?*

B: *He's my brother. He's twenty-seven years old.*

---

**Lifelong learning**

**Talk about you!**

Use English in class as much as possible. Use English to talk about your family, your life, etc. It makes English more memorable.

*Sophie's my daughter. She's nineteen.*

## Listening

**1** **a** `2.7` **Listen and tick the correct addresses.**

1. **a** 59 Princes Street, Edinburgh ☑
   **b** 69 Princes Street, Edinburgh ☐
2. **a** 21 Globe Road, London ☐
   **b** 31 Globe Road, London ☐
3. **a** 18 Boulevard de Clichy, Paris ☐
   **b** 80 Boulevard de Clichy, Paris ☐
4. **a** 46 Lower Abbey Street, Dublin ☐
   **b** 26 Lower Abbey Street, Dublin ☐
5. **a** 17 Brook Street, Boston ☐
   **b** 70 Brook Street, Boston ☐

**b** Say the addresses in Ex. 1a.

**2** **a** `2.8` **The young man in the photo is Ben. Listen and complete the information a–f below.**

**a** Name: Ben G_bs_n.

**b** From: _____

**c** Age: _____ years old

**d** Address: _____ , Kings _____ , Angel, London.

**e** Phone number: _____

**f** Mobile phone number: _____

**b** Listen again and check your answers.

## Vocabulary | expressions

**3** **a** Match an expression (*great, good, OK, bad, awful*) to each person.

**b** `2.9` Listen to the auditions. What do the judges say about each singer? Complete column 1 below.

| | 1 Judges | 2 You |
|---|---|---|
| Ben | *He's awful.* | |
| Terri | | |
| Vittoria | | |
| Hans | | |
| Sanjay | | |

**c** What do you think of the singers? Complete column 2 above and compare with a partner.

**A:** *Ben's awful.*

**B:** *Yes, he's awful. Terri's OK.*

**A:** *Terri's great!*

**d** Talk about other singers you know.

**A:** *Mariah Carey's great.*

**B:** *Mariah Carey? She's OK.*

## Grammar | *What's your ...?*

**4**  **a** Complete the questions in the Active grammar box with one of these words.

> number  your  name  phone

### Active grammar

| ❓ What | 's (is) | your ____ ? |
| | | ____ address? |
| | | your ____ number? |
| | | your mobile phone ____ ? |

**b** Match the questions in the Active grammar box to the pictures below.

1 ? — Gloria Reed.

2 ? — My mobile number is 0719 482 388.

3 ? — 12 Kenton Road, Manchester.

4 It's 01232 499 8211. ?

*see Reference page 27*

**5**  **a** Write questions from the Active grammar box to these answers.

1  A: *What's your phone number?*
   B: It's 0441 85263.

2  A: _____
   B: 81 Plaxton Road, New Park.

3  A: _____
   B: My mobile number is 0170 8910104

4  A: _____
   B: Stephanie Brown.

**b** Work in pairs. Ask and answer the questions in the Active grammar box.

## Speaking

**6**  **a** `2.10` Listen and write the correct names and addresses.

1  Simon _____

2  82, _____ _____ , Rome

**b** Look at the How to ... box and complete the dialogue.

### HOW TO ... | ask for spelling

A: *What's your name?*

B: *Julian Carax.*

A: *How do you* _____ *that, please?*

B: *C – A – R – A –X.*

**7**  **a** Choose one person below. Find the information for that person on page 109 and complete the table for your person.

**b** Roleplay. Talk to other students and complete the table below for the other people.

| | Vittoria | Hans | Sanjay | Terri |
|---|---|---|---|---|
| Name | | | | |
| Age | | | | |
| From | | | | |
| Address | | | | |
| Phone number | | | | |
| Mobile phone number | | | | |

A: *Hello. What's your name?*

B: *I'm Hans Melo.*

A: *How do you spell that, please?*

## 2.3 Email friends

| Grammar | *a/an; his/her* |
| --- | --- |
| Can do | give information about other people; write a short personal profile |

## Reading and listening

1 **a** Look at the profiles. Where do the people come from?

> Canada   Japan   Germany

**a)** I'm Frieda Lang. I'm from Munich. I'm 52 years old. I'm a _____ .
frieda@teachernet.de

**b)** Hello. My name's Tom Mackintosh. I'm 34 years old. I'm an _____ . I'm from Toronto.
tom@mackintosh.com

**c)** My name's Junura Nakamura. I'm from Kyoto. I'm 18. I'm a _____ .
junura@jmail.jp

**b** **2.11** Listen and choose the information from the box about each person.

> accountant   teacher   student

2 **a** Look at the How to ... box. How do you say the email addresses in the profiles?

**HOW TO …**

**say email addresses**

john.smith@email.com

'john **dot** smith **at** email **dot** com'

**b** Exchange email addresses with a partner.

A: *What's your email address?*
B: *It's henrique99@vista.co.uk*
A: *How do you spell that?*
B: *Henrique: H – E – N ...*

3 Close your books and talk about the people in Ex. 1a.

*Frieda Lang is from Germany. She's ...*

# Vocabulary | jobs

**4**  **a**  Match the words in the box to the pictures 1–10.

> accountant  actor  engineer  teacher
> artist  student  manager  sales assistant
> police officer  doctor

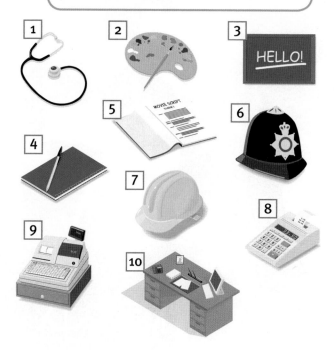

**b**  **2.12**  Listen and check your answers.

# Grammar 1 | a/an

**5**  Complete the Active grammar box with *a* or *an*.

> ### Active grammar
> | | |
> |---|---|
> | **a d**octor | **an a**ccountant |
> | ___ **police officer** | ___ **actor** |

*see Reference page 27*

**6**  **a**  **2.13**  Listen and complete.

1  He's _____ .       3  He's _____ .
2  She's an _____ .     4  She's _____ .

**b**  Write the jobs from Ex. 4a in the correct place in the table.

| a | an |
|---|---|
| manager | |

**c**  Work in pairs. What jobs do your friends and family do?

*My sister's a teacher.*

# Grammar 2 | his/her

**7**  Complete the Active grammar box with *his*, *he's*, *her* or *she's*.

> ### Active grammar
> **?**  What's <u>his</u> name?
> ____ name's Tom.
> What's ____ job?
> ____ an accountant.
>
> What's <u>her</u> name?
> ____ name's Maria.
> What's ____ job?
> ____ a student.

*see Reference page 27*

**8**  Complete the dialogues with *he, she, he's, she's, his* or *her*.

**A:** What's (1) *his* name?
**B:** (2) _____ name's Martin. (3) _____ my brother.
**A:** Where's (4) _____ from?
**B:** (5) _____ from the UK.
**A:** What's (6) _____ phone number?
**B:** It's 029 192 0329.

**A:** Who's (7) _____ ?
**B:** (8) _____ Lucy. (9) _____ my sister.
**A:** What's (10) _____ job?
**B:** (11) _____ an actor.
**A:** What's (12) _____ address?
**B:** It's 19 Wilson Road, Glasgow.

# Speaking

**9**  Work with a partner. Ask about his/her best friend.

**A:** *Who's your best friend?*
**B:** *Her name's Nina.*
**A:** *What's her job?*
**B:** *She's ...*

# Writing

**10 a**  Write a personal profile for emailfriends.net.

*My name's ...   I'm from ...*
*I'm ... years old and I'm a ... .*

**b**  Exchange information with your partner. Then tell the class about your partner.

*His name's Sebastian. He's from ...*

## My favourite singer is ...

1 **a** Match the words in the box to the pictures 1–8.

> singer   CD   city   actor   film   website
> book   restaurant

**b** Work in pairs. Choose a word from the box and talk about the picture.

A: *What's number 2?*

B: *It's a restaurant.*

2 **a** Think of three other examples for each word in Ex. 1a.

**Actor:** *Al Pacino, Salma Hayek ...*

**b** Test your partner.

A: *Who's Salma Hayek?*

B: *She's an actor.*

A: *What's Toronto?*

B: *It's a city.*

3 Write questions.

| What's<br>Who's | your favourite | restaurant?<br>website?<br>actor?<br>CD?<br>city?<br>singer?<br>film?<br>book? |
|---|---|---|

4 Work in pairs. Ask questions from Ex. 3. Use *great, good, OK, bad* or *awful* in your answers.

A: *Who's your favourite singer?*

B: *Dido. She's great.*

A: *Dido? She's ok.*

5 **a** Ask three classmates the questions from Ex. 3. Write the answers in the table below.

| | 1 _____ | 2 _____ | 3 _____ |
|---|---|---|---|
| city | | | |
| restaurant | | | |
| singer | | | |
| film | | | |
| book | | | |
| CD | | | |
| actor | | | |

*Number 1 is Ruth. Her favourite city is ...*

**b** Tell your partner about your three classmates.

## Questions

**Who** is for people.

*Who is he?*
*Who is Rachel?*
*Who's your best friend?*

**What** is for things.

*What's her surname?*
*What's his phone number?*
*What's your email address?*

*Who's ...?* and *What's ...?* = informal English

*Who is ...?* and *What is ...?* = formal written English

Mr Turner is my teacher.

Remember these questions with **How** ...?

*How do you spell that, please?*
*How old are you?*
*How old is he/she?*

## Possessive adjectives: *my, your, his, her, its*

*My, your, his, her* and its are possessive adjectives.
Possessive adjectives show ownership.

| Pronoun | Possessive adjective |
|---------|---------------------|
| *I am Robert.* | *My name is Robert.* |
| *You are 32.* | *Your sister is 21.* |
| *He is a singer.* | *Paul is his brother.* |
| *She is great.* | *Her CD is great.* |
| *It is in Europe.* | *Prague is its capital.* |

## Articles: *a/an*

Use *a* and *an* before single nouns.

*She's a teacher.*
*Her brother is an actor.*

*a* + consonant sound
*a car, a phone, a website*

*an* + vowel sound
*an email address, an actor, an engineer*

## Numbers 10–99

| 10 |
|----|
| ten |

| 11 | 12 | 13 | 14 | 15 |
|----|----|----|----|----|
| eleven | twelve | thirteen | fourteen | fifteen |
| 16 | 17 | 18 | 19 | 20 |
| sixteen | seventeen | eighteen | nineteen | twenty |

| 20 | twenty | 21 | twenty-one |
|----|--------|----|-----------|
| 30 | thirty | 37 | thirty-seven |
| 40 | forty | 44 | forty-four |
| 50 | fifty | 58 | fifty-eight |
| 60 | sixty | 65 | sixty-five |
| 70 | seventy | 76 | seventy-six |
| 80 | eighty | 82 | eighty-two |
| 90 | ninety | 99 | ninety-nine |

### Key vocabulary

**Family**
mother   father   sister   brother   wife
husband   daughter   son

**Personal details**
first name   surname   phone number
mobile phone number   address
email address

**Adjectives**
great   good   OK   bad   awful

**Jobs**
accountant   actor   artist   doctor   engineer
manager   police officer   sales assistant
teacher

**1** Look at the family tree. Complete the sentences.

1 **David:** _Julia's my_ daughter
2 **Karl:** _____ mother.
3 **Julia:** _____ brother.
4 **Adele:** _____ son.
5 **Julia:** _____ father.
6 **David:** _____ wife.
7 **Karl:** _____ sister.
8 **Adele:** _____ husband.

David          Adele

Julia                          Karl

**2** Write questions for each answer in Ex. 1.

1 _Who's Julia?_     5 _____ ?
2 _____ ?       6 _____ ?
3 _____ ?       7 _____ ?
4 _____ ?       8 _____ ?

**3** Rearrange the words to make questions.

1 address your What's
   _What's your address?_
2 phone What's number your
   _____ ?
3 name your What's
   _____ ?
4 are How you old
   _____ ?
5 you Where from are
   _____ ?
6 spell How please that, you do
   _____ ?

**4** Complete the conversation with questions from Ex. 3.

**A:** (1) _What's your name?_
**Gabriel:** Gabriel Willis.
**A:** (2) _____ ?
**Gabriel:** Willis: W – I – L – L – I – S.
**A:** (3) _____ ?
**Gabriel:** I'm 22.
**A:** (4) _____ ?
**Gabriel:** Cardiff in Wales.
**A:** (5) _____ ?
**Gabriel:** 70 Bridge Street, Fairwater, Cardiff.
**A:** (6) _____ ?
**Gabriel:** 00 48 58 3053 330.

**5** Write the questions.

| Mrs Letterman | Mr Garside |
| --- | --- |
| First name: Helen | First name: Oliver |
| Age: 33 | Age: 42 |
| Job: manager | Job: police officer |
| From: Australia | From: Ireland |

1 **A:** _What's her first name?_  **B:** Helen.
2 **A:** _____ ?  **B:** She's 33.
3 **A:** _____ ?  **B:** She's a manager.
4 **A:** _____ ?  **B:** She's from Australia.
5 **A:** _____ ?  **B:** Oliver.
6 **A:** _____ ?  **B:** He's 42.
7 **A:** _____ ?  **B:** He's a police officer.
8 **A:** _____ ?  **B:** He's from Ireland.

**6** Choose the correct word.

1 six + six = _eleven/twelve/thirteen_
2 She's a _doctor/actor/great._
3 What's your _passport/phone/address_?
4 He's an _teacher/accountant/student._
5 Who's your favourite _singer/restaurant/city_?
6 What's your _email/phone number/computer number_?

# 3 Travel

## Lead-in

**1** **a** Match a word in the box to a picture A–D.

> a castle   a cathedral   a palace   a museum

**b** Check the words below in a dictionary. Draw a simple picture for each word.

> a gallery   a department store   a market   a mountain   a lake

**c** **3.1** Listen to the words above and repeat. Mark the stress.

*a castle*

**2** **a** Complete these famous tourist attractions with the words above.

1  Dracula's *castle* in Romania
2  The Hermitage _____ in Russia
3  Buckingham _____ in the UK
4  Otavalo _____ in Ecuador
5  Macy's _____ in the US
6  Sugar Loaf _____ in Brazil
7  _____ Titicaca in Bolivia
8  The Uffizi _____ in Italy

**b** Make a list of other tourist attractions.

*The Prado Gallery in Madrid.*

**3** Discuss with a partner.

*What's your favourite tourist attraction in this country?/in this city?/ in the world?*

## 3.1 | We're in Istanbul

| Grammar | *we*'re/*they*'re; affirmative of *to be*; *our*/*their* |
| --- | --- |
| Can do | write a simple holiday email |

**Coach Holidays**

**West to East Tour**

Start
Birmingham

Day 1
Bruges

Day 2
Bonn

Day 3
Berlin

Day 4
Prague

Day 5
Vienna

Day 6
Bratislava

Day 7
Budapest

Day 8
Timisorara

Day 9
Bucharest

Day 10
Sofia

Day 11–12
Istanbul

## Vocabulary | adjectives

1   **a**   Look at the map. Match a city on the map to a photo below.

    **b**   Which adjective is correct?

Maiden's Tower in Turkey is *big*/*small*.

The Burgtheatre in Austria is *old*/*modern*.

Willy Brandt House in Germany is *old*/*modern*.

Charles Bridge in the Czech Republic is *beautiful*/*ugly*.

The House of the People in Romania is *big*/*small*.

Spaghetti Junction in the UK is *beautiful*/*ugly*.

2   Talk about three tourist attractions in your country.

    *The Guggenheim Museum in Bilbao is beautiful.*

## Reading

3   **a**   Rebecca and Steven are on the 'West to East' coach tour. Read the email. Who is in the photo in the email?

From: rebeccaclark55@gmail.com
To: tomandsusan.clark@yahoo.co.uk
Subject: We're in Istanbul!

Hi Mum and Dad

How are you? Steven and I are fine. **We're** in Istanbul in The Pera Palace Hotel. It's great! Istanbul is big.

Magda and Zarek are in the Pera Palace Hotel, too. They are **our** friends. **They're** from Poland.

The attachment is a photo of Magda and Zarek. They are in **their** car. It's a Mercedes. It's beautiful! Its colour is great.

Love Rebecca

    **b**   Write true (T) or false (F).

1   Steven and Rebecca are in Istanbul.   ☐ T
2   The Pera Palace Hotel is OK.   ☐
3   Istanbul is small.   ☐
4   Magda and Zarek are from Turkey.   ☐
5   The car is beautiful.   ☐

    **c**   <u>Underline</u> all the adjectives in the email.

# Grammar 1 | *to be* with *we* and *they*

**4** Look at the email on page 30 again. Complete the Active grammar box below.

### Active grammar

| ⊕ | I | 'm (am) | forty-one. |
|---|---|---|---|
| ⊕ | You | 're (are) | my friend. |
| ⊕ | He | | my father. |
| ⊕ | She | 's (is) | my mother. |
| ⊕ | It | | a gallery. |
| ⊕ | You | 're (are) | my friends. |
| ⊕ | We | ____ (__) | in Istanbul. |
| ⊕ | They | ____ (__) | from Turkey. |

*see Reference page 37*

**5** Complete the sentences. Use contractions.

1 They*'re* from Moscow.
2 You___ from France.
3 We___ in Buenos Aires.
4 It___ modern.
5 She___ my daughter.
6 I___ in the photo.
7 They___ in the gallery.
8 He___ great.

# Grammar 2 | *our* and *their*

**6** Complete the Active grammar box below.

### Active grammar

| I | She is **my** friend. |
|---|---|
| You | **Your** house is modern. |
| He | Rachel is **his** wife. |
| She | **Her** mother is great. |
| It | **Its** capital is Madrid. |
| You | **Your** photos are beautiful. |
| We | Andrea is _____ friend. |
| They | _____ daughter is in the car. |

*see Reference page 37*

**7** Complete the sentences with *our* or *their*.

Ben and Rebecca Morris     Zarek and Magda Adamski

1 **Magda:** *Their* surname is Morris.
2 **Zarek:** _____ suitcase is modern.
3 **Rebecca:** _____ car is beautiful.
4 **Magda:** _____ backpack is old.
5 **Zarek:** _____ friends and family are in Poland.
6 **Ben:** _____ friends and family are in the UK.

**8** Circle the correct word.

1 Are they *we're/*our* books?
2 *They're/Their* beautiful.
3 *We're/Our* in Berlin.
4 *We're/Our* students.
5 *They're/Their* photos are great.
6 *They're/Their* from Romania.
7 Where is *we're/our* car?
8 *They're/Their* in the photo.

# Pronunciation

**9 a** 3.2 Listen. Write the sentences. Use *they're* or *their*.

**b** Repeat the sentences.

# Writing

**10 a** Work in pairs. You and your partner are on holiday. Choose a destination from the map on page 30. Complete the details.

1 My partner is _____ . (name)
2 We are in _____ . (place) It is _____ . (adjective)
3 Our friends are _____ and _____ . (names)
4 Our hotel is _____ . (name) It is _____ . (adjective)

**b** Look at the Writing bank on page 126. Then write an email to a friend about your holiday.

| Grammar | plural nouns; negative of *to be* |
| Can do | say what's in your suitcase |

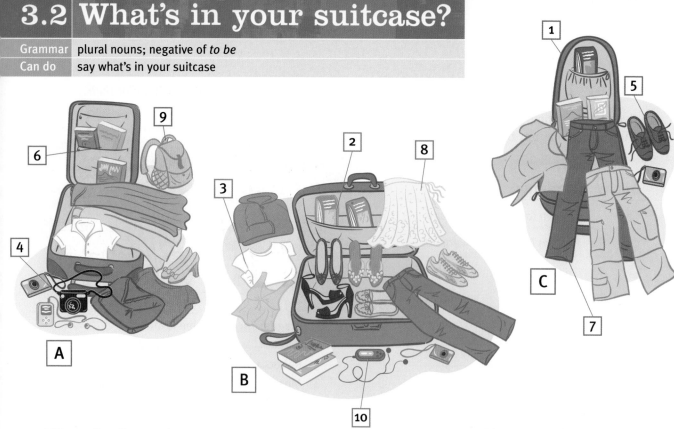

## Vocabulary | holiday things

**1** **a** Match a word in the box to a number in the pictures.

> camera   book   skirt   pair of shoes   suitcase   pair of trousers
> MP3 player   top   map   backpack

**b** **3.3** Listen and check your answers. Mark the stress and repeat.

*a suitcase*

## Listening

**2** **3.4** Listen. Match a conversation to a suitcase A–C.

## Grammar 1 | plural nouns

**3** **a** Listen again to conversation 3. Complete the Active grammar box.

> ### Active grammar
>
> | one book | _____ book**s** |
> | a top | _____ top**s** |
> | one pair of shoes | five pair**s** of _____ |

**b** Listen again. What is in each suitcase? Complete the lists below.

**Conversation 1:** a camera, two books
**Conversation 2:** a backpack
**Conversation 3:** a pair of trousers

**c** Listen and check your answers.

## Pronunciation

**4** **a** **3.5** Listen. How is the 's' pronounced: /s/, /z/ or /ɪz/?

a two suitcases
b five maps
c seven tops
d three cameras
e two pairs of shoes
f four books
g eight pairs of trousers
h six skirts

**b** Listen again and check your answers. Repeat.

> ## Lifelong learning
>
> **Record pronunciation**
>
> In your vocabulary notebooks, record important pronunciation.
>
> /əv/   /z/
>
> a **pair** of **shoes**

## Speaking

5   a   Work in pairs. Describe a suitcase from Ex. 2 Your partner guesses the suitcase.

A:   *What's in the suitcase?*

B:   *Two skirts, a pair of shoes, three books ...*

b   Work in pairs. Cover one of the suitcases. Remember what's in it.

c   What is in your suitcase when you go on holiday? Tell your partner.

## Listening

6   a   **3.6**   Listen. Answer the questions.

1   What is her name?

2   What is in her suitcase?

b   Listen again. Complete the phrases from the conversation.

**Jane:** ___ 'm not Miss Miles.

**Jane:** _____ isn't a camera.

**Jane:** _____ aren't books.

## Grammar 2 | the verb *to be* negative

7   Complete the grammar box with *aren't* or *isn't*.

**Active grammar**

| ⊖ | I | 'm not (am not) | Miss Miles. |
|---|---|---|---|
| ⊖ | You | _aren't_ (are not) | in room 324. twenty-one. |
| ⊖ ⊖ ⊖ | He She It | _____ (is not) | my brother. my sister. a camera. |
| ⊖ | We | _____ (are not) | from the US. students. |
| ⊖ | They | _____ (are not) | friends. in Istanbul. |

*see Reference page 37*

8   a   Choose the correct answer.

1   You *'m not/aren't* an actor.

2   I *'re not/'m not* from Brazil.

3   She *aren't/isn't* not my sister.

4   It *isn't/'m not* my camera.

5   You *aren't/isn't* in room 232.

6   It *'m not/isn't* my favourite city.

b   Complete the conversations with *'m not*, *aren't* or *isn't*.

A:   Hello Bob. This is my wife. Two tickets to New York, please.

B:   *I'm not* Bob, I'm Bill. You_____ eighteen years old, you're eight. And she_____ your wife, she's your sister.

A:   Is this your backpack, Mr Robson?

B:   I_____ Mr Robson, I'm Mr Clark. And it_____ my backpack, it's his backpack.

9   a   True (T) or false (F)?

| | You | Your partner | Your teacher |
|---|---|---|---|
| From this city | | | |
| A good singer | | | |
| 18–25 years old | | | |

b   Work in pairs. Write sentences using the information from Ex. 9a.

*We're from this city. Our teacher isn't from this city.*

## Speaking

10   Work in pairs. Continue the conversation in Ex. 6a between Mr Boyle and Mrs Miles.

| Mr Boyle | Mrs Miles |
|---|---|
| pair of trousers top MP3 player | skirt pair of trousers camera |

**Mr Boyle:**   *OK, an MP3 player.*

**Mrs Miles:**   *It isn't an MP3 player, it's a camera.*

## Vocabulary | days of the week

**1**  **a**  **3.7**  Listen and repeat the days of the week.

> Monday   Tuesday   Wednesday   Thursday
> Friday   Saturday   Sunday

**b**  Work in pairs. Say a day. Your partner says the next day.

**A:** *Thursday.*      **B:** *Friday.*

### The Whitechapel Art Gallery

The Whitechapel Art Gallery is small and beautiful. The photos and pictures are great.

It's <u>open</u> from Tuesday to Sunday.
It's <u>closed</u> on Mondays.
<u>Entrance</u> is free.

The Whitechapel Art Gallery
80–82 Whitechapel High Street
London, E1 7QX
020 7522 7888

info@whitechapel.org

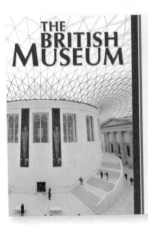

### THE BRITISH MUSEUM

The British Museum is the <u>top</u> tourist attraction in London. (5,000,000 visitors every year!) It's near Oxford Street. It's open from Monday to Sunday. It's big and it's <u>free</u>!

The British Museum
Great Russell Street
London WC1B 3DG
020 7323 8299

visitorinformation@thebritishmuseum.ac.uk

### HAMPTON COURT PALACE

| Hampton Court Palace East Molesey Surrey KT8 9AU 0870 752 7777 | Hampton Court is a beautiful palace. It's <u>near</u> London, on the River Thames. It's open from Monday to Sunday. Entrance is £12.00. info@hrp.org.uk |
| --- | --- |

## Reading

**2**  **a**  Work in pairs. Say the addresses, phone numbers and email addresses in the text.

**b**  Look at the <u>underlined</u> words in the text. Check them in a dictionary.

**c**  Read the texts. Choose the correct word in the sentences below.

1  The British Museum *is/isn't* closed on Sundays.
2  The Whitechapel Art Gallery *is/isn't* big.
3  Hampton Court Palace *is/isn't* open on Sundays.
4  The British Museum *is/isn't* in London.
5  The Whitechapel Art Gallery *is/isn't* open on Mondays.
6  Hampton Court Palace *is/isn't* in London.

## Listening

**3**  **a**  **3.8**  Listen. Match a conversation 1–3 to a tourist attraction in the text.

**b**  Read the How to ... box then listen again and complete the phrases below with *here*, *there* and *Here's*.

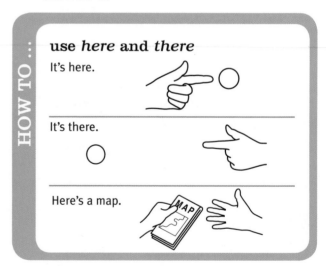

**HOW TO ...**

**use *here* and *there***

It's here.

It's there.

Here's a map.

**Conversation 1**

1  Is [beep] near <u>here</u>?
2  It's about 12km from _____ .
3  _____ a map. We are _____ and it is _____ .

**Conversation 2**

4  Good. Is it near _____ ?
5  Yes, it is. _____ a map. We are _____ and it is _____ .

## Grammar | Yes/No questions with *to be*

**4 a** Compare the ⊕ and ❓ forms below:

⊕ *The British Museum **is** in London.*

❓ ***Is** the British Museum in London?*

**b** Look at tapescript 3.8 on page 145.
<u>Underline</u> all the example of questions with *be*.

**c** Complete the Active grammar box with *Is,
Are* or *Am*.

### Active grammar

| ❓ | *Am* | *I* | *your friend?* | *Yes, you are.*<br>*No, you aren't.* |
|----|------|------|----------------|---------------------------------------|
| ❓ | ___ | *you* | *from Italy?* | *Yes, I am.*<br>*No, I'm not.* |
| ❓ | ___ | *he*<br><br>*she* | *your brother?*<br><br>*your sister?* | *Yes, he/she is.*<br>*No, he/she isn't.* |
| ❓ | ___ | *we* | *near the lake?* | *Yes, we are.*<br>*No, we aren't.* |
| ❓ | ___ | *they* | *in London?* | *Yes, they are.*<br>*No, they aren't.* |

*see Reference page 37*

**5 a** Complete the questions and answers.

1 Are you from China?
Yes, I _____ .

2 _____ it a cathedral?
No, it _____ .

3 _____ she your sister?
Yes, she _____ .

4 _____ we near Hampton Court?
Yes, we _____ .

5 Are _____ students?
No, they _____ .

6 _____ the museum closed today?
Yes, it _____ .

7 _____ they from the UK?
No, they _____ .

8 _____ you in room 324?
Yes, I _____ .

**b** Rearrange the words to make a question. Then
write a short answer.

1 open is today it
A: *Is it open today?* B: *Yes, it is.*

2 you Italy are from
A: _____ ? B: No, _____ .

3 the UK is from she
A: _____ ? B: Yes, _____ .

4 a museum it is
A: _____ ? B: No, _____ .

5 is open the shop
A: _____ ? B: Yes, _____ .

6 you an actor are
A: _____ ? B: No, _____ .

## Reading and speaking

**6** Work in pairs.

**Student A:** read the text below about Harrods
and answer your partner's questions. Ask for
information about the Louvre.

**Harrods**

Harrods is a department store in London. It's open from Monday to Saturday but it isn't open on Sunday. Harrods is big and old. It's a beautiful department store and entrance is free.

**LOUVRE**

**What?** _____
**Where?** _____
**Open Monday–
Sunday?** _____
**Small?** _____
**Old?** _____
**Beautiful?** _____
**Entrance free?** _____

**Student B:** look at page 109. Read the text about
the Louvre and answer your partner's questions.
Ask for information about Harrods.

# 3 | Communication

## See you on Friday

**2** **3·9** Listen and read the conversation below. Answer the questions.

1 Where is Sara?
2 Is she in Casablanca?
3 Is Marakesh beautiful?
4 Is Marakesh hot?
5 Is the hotel nice?
6 Is the food nice?

**Louis:** Hello.
**Sara:** Hi, Louis. It's Sara.
**Louis:** Hi, Sara. How are you and Paul?
**Sara:** We're fine, thanks. And you?
**Louis:** Fine, thanks. Where are you?
**Sara:** We're in Morocco.
**Louis:** Are you in Casablanca?
**Sara:** No, we aren't. We're in Marakesh.
**Louis:** Is it beautiful?
**Sara:** Yes, it is. It's very beautiful.
**Louis:** Is it hot?
**Sara:** Yes, it is. It's very hot.
**Louis:** Is your hotel nice?
**Sara:** No, it isn't. It's very small and very old.
**Louis:** Oh dear! Is the food nice?
**Sara:** Yes, it's very nice. Are Mum and Dad OK?
**Louis:** Yes, they are. They're fine.
**Sara:** OK, see you on Friday.
**Louis:** See you on Friday. Bye.
**Sara:** Bye.

**1** **a** Look at the words in the box. Check the meaning of new words in a dictionary.

> skirt  small  suitcase  book  food  old
> bad  beautiful  ugly  hot  cold  backpack
> good  nice  camera  modern  big  map
> awful  great  new  fine

**b** Put the words in the correct column.

| Nouns | Adjectives |
|-------|------------|
| skirt | small |
|  |  |

**c** Which words follow *very*: nouns or adjectives?

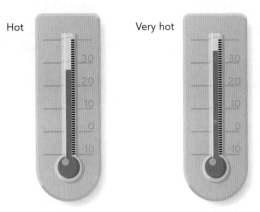

Hot          Very hot

**3** **a** Work in pairs. Read and repeat the conversation.

**b** Change partners. Look at the words below. Remember the conversation.

| Louis | Sara |
|-------|------|
| Hello. | It's ... |
| How ...? | Fine ... you? |
| Where ...? | Morocco |
| Casablanca? | Marakesh |
| beautiful? | Yes |
| hot? | Yes |
| hotel nice? | No |
| food nice? | Yes. Mum and Dad? |
| fine | Friday |
| Friday. Bye | Bye |

**4** **a** Write a new conversation. Use new people, new places and other adjectives.

**Esther:** *Hello.*
**Flavia:** *Hi, Esther. It's Flavia.*

**b** Practise your conversation with a partner.

## The verb *to be*

**+**

| I | 'm (am) | |
|---|---|---|
| You | 're (are) | |
| He She It | 's (is) | in Istanbul. from Turkey. |
| We | 're (are) | |
| They | 're (are) | |

**−**

| I | 'm not (am not) | Miss Miles. |
|---|---|---|
| You | aren't (are not) | in room 324. twenty-one. |
| He She It | isn't (is not) | my brother. my sister. a camera. |
| We | aren't (are not) | from the US. students. |
| They | aren't (are not) | friends. in Istanbul. |

**?**  Short answers

| Am | I | your friend? | Yes, you are. No, you aren't. |
|---|---|---|---|
| Are | you | from Italy? | Yes, I am. No, I'm not. |
| Is | he | your brother? | Yes, he/she/it is. No, he/she/it isn't. |
| | she | your sister? | |
| | it | open? | |
| Are | we | near the lake? | Yes, we are. No, we aren't. |
| Are | they | in London? | Yes, they are. No, they aren't. |

*He's/She's/It's not* and
*We're/You're/They're not* are also possible.

*They're not at home.*

## Possessive adjectives

| Pronoun | Possessive adjective |
|---|---|
| *I'm from New York.* | *My wife is from Rome.* |
| *You're in Istanbul.* | *Your son is in London.* |
| *He's Mr Hanson.* | *His manager is Mr Reid.* |
| *She's my sister.* | *Her daughter is three.* |
| *It's not a big hotel.* | *Its rooms are small.* |
| *We're on holiday.* | *Our hotel is very nice.* |
| *They're in Italy* | *Their children are at home.* |

## Days of the week

**weekdays:** Monday, Tuesday, Wednesday, Thursday, Friday

**the weekend:** Saturday, Sunday

Use *on* + days of the week  *Her birthday is on Monday.*

Use *at* + *the weekend*  *His party is at the weekend.*

## Adjectives

old  modern  big  small  beautiful  ugly
great  good  OK  bad  awful  open  closed
near  free  hot  cold  new  fine  nice

Noun + verb *to be* + adjective
*It's modern.*    *They're great.*

Noun + verb *to be* (+*a/an*) + adjective + noun
*She's a good teacher.*    *It's a big market.*

**Key vocabulary**

**Tourist attractions**
a castle  a cathedral  a palace  a museum
a gallery  a department store  a market
a mountain  a lake

**Holiday things**
backpack  book  camera  map
MP3 player  pair of shoes
pair of trousers  top  skirt  suitcase

# 3 Review and practice

**1** Complete the sentences in the plural.

1 Jon is my friend.
   Sally and Paul _are my friends_, too.
2 Jason's from Manchester.
   Teresa and Jackie _____ , too.
3 His favourite car is a BMW.
   _____ is a BMW, too.
4 I'm in my room in The Radford Hotel.
   We _____ in the Radford Hotel, too.
5 She's an accountant.
   They _____ accountants, too.
6 This is my favourite film.
   This is _____ film, too.

**2** Complete the sentences with _we're, our, they're_ or _their_.

|  | Michelle and I | Alan and Di |
|---|---|---|
| From? | Scotland | Ireland |
| Job? | doctors | teachers |
| House? | in Glasgow | in Dublin |
| Where now? | on holiday in Brazil | on holiday in France |

Alan and Di are (1) _our_ friends. (2) _____ from Ireland and (3) _____ teachers. Michelle and I are from Scotland. (4) _____ doctors. (5) _____ house is in Glasgow. (6) _____ house is in Dublin. Right now (7) _____ on holiday in Ireland. (8) _____ on holiday in Scotland.

**3** Complete the negative sentences with a word from the box.

> aren't   not   isn't   'm   You   I   She

1 I_'m_ not Miss Carter. I'm Ms Carter.
2 It_____ open today. It's open tomorrow.
3 You _____ a good singer.
4 _____isn't from the UK.
5 You _____ twenty-one. You're twenty-three.
6 _____'m not from Germany.
7 You_____ my friend.
8 She _____ my sister. She's my mum.
9 _____ aren't in room 324. You're in room 325.
10 I'm _____ Peter. I'm Tom.

**4** Rearrange the words to make questions.

1 near gallery the we Are
   _Are we near the gallery?_
2 museum Is open the
   _____ ?
3 Italy they from Are
   _____ ?
4 she your Is friend
   _____ ?
5 here the near lake Is
   _____ ?
6 department stores Are today open the
   _____ ?
7 we Are York Hotel in the
   _____ ?

**5** Write short answers for each question in Ex. 4.

1 (✓) _Yes, we are._         5 (✓) _____ .
2 (✗) _No, it isn't._         6 (✗) _____ .
3 (✓) _____ .             7 (✓) _____ .
4 (✗) _____ .

**6** Complete the dialogues with the pairs of words in the box.

> Wednesday/Thursday   museum/gallery
> ~~MP3 player/suitcase~~   cathedral/palace
> big/small

1 Where's your _MP3 player?_
   It's in my _suitcase_.
2 Is his house _____ ?
   No, it isn't. It's _____ .
3 Is it _____ today?
   No, it isn't. It's _____ .
4 Is Tate Modern a _____ ?
   No, it isn't. It's a _____ .
5 Is Hampton Court a _____ ?
   No, it isn't. It's a _____ .

A

# 4 In town

B

C

D

## Lead-in

1 **a** Match the words in the box to letters A–D in the photos and E–M in the small pictures.

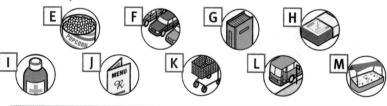

E  F  G  H

I  J  K  L  M

> chemist   supermarket   ~~café~~   bookshop   train station
> bus stop   bank   cinema   newsagent   car park   restaurant
> cashpoint   market

A *café*

**b** 4.1 Listen and check your answers. Mark the stress.

A *c̲afé*

**c** Work in pairs. Cover the words. Look at the pictures. Say the places.

2 Work in pairs. Ask *What's your favourite ...?*

A: *What's your favourite supermarket?*
B: *Quickbuy is my favourite.*

## Vocabulary | food and drink

**1   a** Look at the photos below. Match the pictures 1–6 with the words in the box below.

milk

sugar

1    2    3    4    5    6

a black filter coffee    a white coffee
a cappuccino    an iced coffee    an espresso
an instant coffee

**b** 〔4.2〕 Listen and check your answers. Match a coffee to these countries: Spain, Italy, the UK, the US, Greece.

**c** What coffee is popular in your country?

**2   a** Complete these sentences for you with one of the coffees (don't use *a/an*).

1   _____ is my favourite.

2   _____ is very nice.

3   _____ is awful.

**b** Work in pairs. Read your sentences to your partner.

*Espresso is my favourite.*

**3   a** Label the food and drink 1–6 in the pictures A–C with a phrase from the box below.

~~an orange juice~~    a mineral water
a sandwich    a piece of cake    a salad
a cup of tea

**b** 〔4.3〕 Listen. Match a picture A–C to a conversation 1–3.

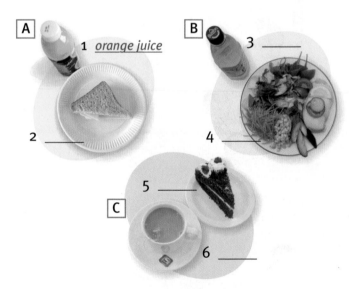

A
1   *orange juice*
2   _____

B
3   _____
4   _____

C
5   _____
6   _____

**4   a** Listen to the three conversations again. Complete the phrases below with the words in the box.

chocolate    large    ~~chicken~~    cheese    small

1   a *chicken* salad
2   a _____ mineral water
3   a _____ sandwich
4   a _____ orange juice
5   a piece of _____ cake

**b** Check your answers in tapescript 4.3 on page 146. Repeat the conversations in pairs.

## Grammar | *Can I have ...?*

**5** Look at the Active grammar box. Match a phrase on the left to a phrase on the right.

### Active grammar

| Can I have a | orange juices, please? |
| Can I have an | cheese sandwich, please? |
| Can I have two | iced coffee, please? |

Certainly/Sure. Anything else?

No, thank you./Yes, please. Can I have ... ?

*see Reference page 47*

**6 a** Complete the conversations with the words/phrases in the Active grammar box.

A: Hello. Can I help you?

B: Yes. (1) _____ iced coffee, please?

A: Certainly. Anything (2) _____ ?

B: Yes, please. (3) _____ small chicken salad, too?

A: Sure.

C: (4) _____ large cappuccino, please?

A: Certainly. (5) _____ else?

C: No, (6) _____ .

**b** Read the conversations in pairs.

## Pronunciation

**7** 〔4.4〕 Listen and repeat.

Can I /kæ – naɪ/

Can I have a /kæ – naɪ – hæ – və/

Can I have a small coffee /kæ – naɪ – hæ – və – smɔːl – kɒ – fiː/

## Vocabulary | *prices*

**8 a** Complete the chart.

| 49p | | | forty-*nine* | pence |
|---|---|---|---|---|
| 80c | | | eighty | cents |
| £1.50 | One | (pound) | _____ | |
| €1.99 | One | (euro) | ninety-nine | |
| $2.20 | Two | (dollars) | _____ | |
| €5.90 | Five | (euros) | _____ | |

**b** 〔4.5〕 Listen. Circle the correct prices in each conversation.

1  a  £1.00    b  £1.10    c  £1.20

2  a  2.98    b  3.89    c  3.98

3  a  $1.19    b  $1.90    c  $1.99

4  a  €4.34    b  €3.34    c  €4.43

5  a  £3.13    b  £3.19    c  £3.39

**c** Work in pairs. Say a price. Your partner writes the price.

## Speaking

**9 a** Read the How to ... box. Close your books. Write a conversation in a coffee shop.

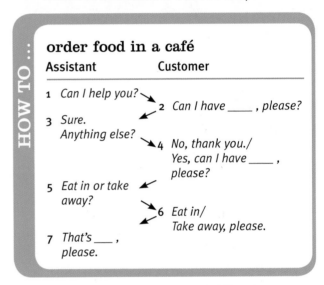

**HOW TO ...**

### order food in a café

| Assistant | Customer |
|---|---|

1 Can I help you?

2 Can I have ____ , please?

3 Sure. Anything else?

4 No, thank you./ Yes, can I have ____ , please?

5 Eat in or take away?

6 Eat in/ Take away, please.

7 That's ___ , please.

**b** Read your conversation to the class.

**10** Work in pairs. Look at the menu.

**Student A:** you are an assistant in a coffee shop.

**Student B:** you are a customer. Order food and drink.

| Coffee | small | medium | large |
|---|---|---|---|
| Espresso | 60c | – | 90c |
| Black coffee | 75c | €1.00 | €1.25 |
| White coffee | 80c | €1.05 | €1.30 |
| Cappuccino | 90c | €1.15 | €1.40 |
| Iced coffee | – | €1.50 | €2.05 |
| **Drink** | | | |
| Mineral water | 79c | 99c | €1.19 |
| Orange juice | €1.09 | €1.45 | €1.99 |
| **Food** | | | |
| Green salad | | €1.99 | |
| Chicken salad | | €2.89 | |
| Cheese salad | | €2.65 | |
| Chicken sandwich | | €2.05 | |
| Cheese sandwich | | €1.95 | |

## Reading

**1**  **a** Work in pairs. Make a list of famous markets in your country/city.

**b** Read the text. Match a question in the box to the information 1–6.

> Is it free?   Where is the market?
> When is it open?   Is it big?   What is it?
> What is on sale in the market?

### Portobello Market

**1.** _____
It's in Notting Hill. Notting Hill is in west London.

**2.** _____
It's an antiques market.

**3.** _____
Yes, it is. It's very big. It's two kilometers from end to end. It's a market for Londoners and tourists.

**4.** _____
It's not open on weekdays. It's only open on Sundays.

**5.** _____
Yes, it is.

**6.** _____
Modern things, old things, beautiful things, ugly things … Antiques, old clothes and food are popular.

**c** Mark the sentences true (T) or false (F).

1 Portobello Market is in Notting Hill.  ☐ *T*
2 It's not small.  ☐
3 It's open on Fridays.  ☐
4 Food is on sale in the market.  ☐

**2**  **a** Choose a market or shop in your country. Answer the questions from Ex. 1b. Write notes.

**b** Work in pairs. Talk about your market or shop.

A: *Where is it?*     B: *It's in Tokyo.*

## Vocabulary | clothes and colours

**3**  **a** **4.6** Listen. Match a colour 1–9 to the clothes a–i.

*a green T-shirt*

| | | | |
| --- | --- | --- | --- |
| 1 | ~~green~~ | a) | pair of shoes |
| 2 | white | b) | skirt |
| 3 | orange | c) | coat |
| 4 | red | d) | pair of trousers |
| 5 | yellow | e) | shirt |
| 6 | black | f) | dress |
| 7 | blue | g) | bag |
| 8 | brown | h) | hat |
| 9 | pink | h) | ~~T-shirt~~ |

**b** Match a phrase above to a picture below.

**c** Work in pairs. What clothes and colours are in your classroom?

# Listening and speaking

**4** Look at the How to ... box. Point to the things in the picture below. Talk about the prices.

> **HOW TO ...**
>
> ### talk about prices
>
> **A:** *How much is it?*  **B:** *It's four pounds fifty.*
>
> **A:** *How much are they?*  **B:** *They're six pounds each.*

**5** **a** `4.7` Listen. How much is/are **a)** the blue hat, **b)** the beautiful dresses, **c)** the yellow skirt, **d)** the white shirts, **e)** the orange shirts?

**b** Listen again. Complete the questions. Check your answers in tapescript 4.7 on page 146.

1 How much is _____ blue hat?

2 How much are _____ beautiful dresses?

3 How much is _____ yellow skirt?

4 How much are _____ white shirts?

that/those

this/these

# Grammar | *this, that, these, those*

**6** Complete the Active grammar box with *that, these* or *those*.

> ### Active grammar
>
>
>
> *this* hat
>
> _____ bag
>
> _____ bracelets
>
> _____ jumpers

*see Reference page 47*

**7** Look at the picture in Ex. 5. Complete the questions with *this, that, these* or *those*.

1 How much are *those* white shirts?

2 How much are _____ orange shirts?

3 How much are _____ dresses?

4 How much are _____ bags?

5 How much is _____ blue hat?

6 How much is _____ black hat?

# Speaking

**8** Work in pairs.

**Student A:** look at the picture in Ex. 5. Write prices for the clothes and bags in the picture.

**Student B:** ask for the prices of the clothes and bags in the picture in Ex. 5.

# Writing

**9** Write a paragraph about your favourite shop or market from Ex. 2a. Use the text about Portobello market to help you. You can start like this:

*My favourite shop/market is ... It's in ...*

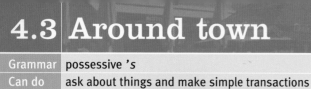

# 4.3 Around town

| | |
|---|---|
| Grammar | possessive *'s* |
| Can do | ask about things and make simple transactions |

Shula

Mike

Stefan

## Vocabulary | irregular plurals

1  **a**  Look at the photos a–d. Where is each photo?

**Photo a =** *a supermarket*

**b**  Match a description below to each photo.

1  a man, a woman and a child
2  a man, a woman and her baby in a shop
3  a man and two women
4  people in a shop

2  **a**  Complete the chart of irregular plurals below.

| singular | plural |
|---|---|
| one person | two *people* |
| one _____ | two men |
| one woman | two _____ |
| one _____ | two children |
| one _____ | two babies |

**b**  Look at the photos on page 109. What is in each photo?

1  photo A – *two men*
2  photo B – _____
3  photo C – _____
4  photo D – _____
5  photo E – _____
6  photo F – _____

## Reading and listening

3  **a**  **4.8**  Listen. Match each conversation to a photo.

Conversation 1 – photo ___
Conversation 2 – photo ___
Conversation 3 – photo ___
Conversation 4 – photo ___

**b**  Listen again. Complete the gaps in the conversations.

1  **A:** Can I have three (1) *tickets* to Bristol, please. Two adults and one child?
   **B:** Single or return?
   **A:** Return, please.
   **B:** That's forty-two thirty, please. Thank you. (2) _____ you are.

2  **A:** Can I help you?
   **B:** Yes, please. Can I have a packet of aspirin, please?
   **A:** Twenty-four or (3) _____ ?
   **B:** Twenty-four, please.
   **A:** That's one forty-nine, (4) _____ . Thank you.

3  **A:** Can I (5) _____ two tickets for *ChickenMan Returns*, please.
   **B:** That's fifteen pounds ninety, please.
   **A:** (6) _____ I pay by credit card?
   **B:** Sure. Sign here, please. Thank you. Here you are.
   **A:** Thanks.

Jack

4 A: Thirty-one pounds and seven pence, please.

B: Here (7) _____ are.

A: Thank you. Enter your PIN (8) _____ , please. Thank you.

4 **a** Work in pairs. Repeat the conversations.

**b** Repeat the conversations but change the details.

A: *Can I have two tickets to London, please.*

B: *Single or return?*

5 **a** Cover the conversations in Ex. 3b. Complete the phrases in the How to ... box.

**HOW TO ...**

### survive in town

| Train station | Can I have three tickets _to_ Bristol, please? Single or _____ ? |
|---|---|
| Shop/ Cinema | Can I have a _____ of aspirin, please? _____ one forty-nine, please. Can I _pay_ by credit card? Sign _____ , please. Here _____ are. Enter _____ PIN number, please. |

**b** Work in pairs. Close your books. Write a new conversation in a shop or train station.

**c** Act out your conversation to the class.

## Grammar | possessive '*s*

6 **a** Match the things below to people in the photos.

1 *Jack*  2 _____  3 _____

4 _____  5 _____

**b** Complete sentences 3, 4 and 5 in the Active grammar box.

### Active grammar

Use '*s* to show possession.

1 They're Jack's cinema tickets.

2 She's Shula's baby.

3 She's _____ daughter.

4 It's _____ packet of aspirin.

5 It's_____ train ticket.

*see Reference page 47*

7 Rewrite the sentences with the name + '*s*.

1 It's his passport. (Kevin)
   *It's Kevin's passport.*

2 They're her shoes. (Rosie)
   _____ .

3 This is his email address. (Takumi)
   _____ .

4 What is her address? (Adele)
   _____ .

5 Are you her brother? (Teresa)
   _____ .

6 That is his suitcase. (Janek)
   _____ .

## Speaking

8 **a** Each student gives something to the teacher (e.g. a bag, a pencil). Check that you know the names for each thing.

**b** Guess who each thing belongs to.

A: *Is that Anna's bag?*

B: *No, it isn't. It's Helen's bag.*

# 4 Communication

**1** **a** Match a sentence 1–4 to a picture A–D below.

1 The car park is on West Street.
2 The supermarket is opposite the bookshop.
3 The chemist is next to the market.
4 The bus stop is near the bank.

**b** 4.9 Listen and complete the map with places in the box.

gallery   train station   supermarket

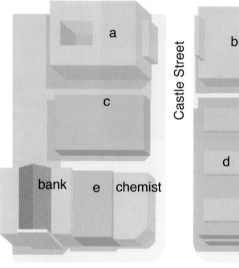
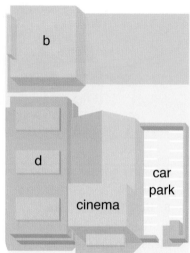
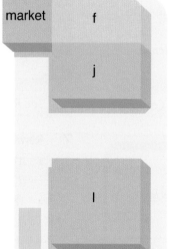

A
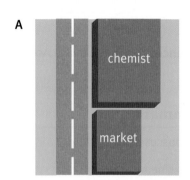

B
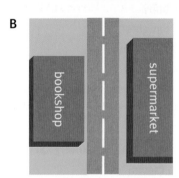

C
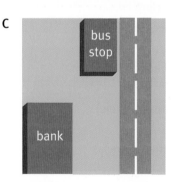

D
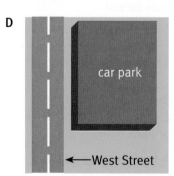

← West Street

**2** **a** Look at the How to ... box. Ask questions about the map.

**HOW TO ...**

**ask where something is**

A: *Excuse me, where's the ...?*
B: *It's ...*                    *I'm sorry. I don't know.*
A: *Thank you.*                  *OK. Never mind. Thank you.*
B: *You're welcome.*

**b** Work in pairs. Ask questions about your map. Your partner gives you the information.

**Student A:** look at page 112.
**Student B:** look at page 110.

## Can I have ...?

| Can I have | a cappuccino,<br>a piece of cake,<br>an espresso,<br>an orange juice,<br>a return ticket to Paris,<br>two mineral waters, | please? |
| --- | --- | --- |
| Certainly./Sure. | | |

Use *Can I have ...?* to ask for things in shops/cafés/train stations, etc.

## this/that/these/those

this

these

that

those

|  | near | far |
| --- | --- | --- |
| Singular | *this* | *that* |
| Plural | *these* | *those* |

*How much are those shirts?*

*Are these books free?*

*That hat is great!*

*This jumper is beautiful.*

## Possessive 's

Use *'s* to show possession.

*That is Herbie's passport.*

*Mary is Dylan's daughter.*

*Those are Jody's tickets.*

*Claire and Emma are Damien's daughters.*

Be careful not to confuse possessive *'s* (as in *Jody's tickets*) with contraction *It's = It is*.

## Irregular noun plurals

Regular plurals = noun + *s*

*ticket* → *tickets*

Some nouns are irregular in the plural.

*child* → *children*    *woman* → *women*

*man* → *men*         *person* → *people*

Other irregular plurals:

Words ending in *-s*, *-sh*, *-ch* = add *-es* /ɪz/

*sandwich – sandwiches    address – addresses*

Words ending in *-y* → *-ies*

*baby – babies*

Words ending in *-ife* → change *f* to *v*

*wife – wives*

## Prices

To ask and answer about prices, use:

*How much is/are ...?*     *It's/They're ...*

*How much is that computer?*     *It's €799.*

*How much are those books?*     *They're €8.*

When you say prices, it is normal to leave out the currency.

*€1.99*     *one ninety-nine*

*£3.50*     *three fifty*

*$12.20*     *twelve twenty*

When the price is less than one euro/pound/dollar, it is normal to say the currency.

*80c*     *eighty cents*

*39p*     *thirty-nine pence (or thirty-nine p)*

---

### Key vocabulary

**Places**

bank   bookshop   bus stop   café   car park
cashpoint   chemist   cinema   market
newsagent   restaurant   supermarket
train station

**Coffee and other drinks**

a large cappuccino   a small black coffee
a medium iced coffee   a cup of tea
an orange juice   a mineral water

**Food**

a cheese sandwich   a piece of chocolate cake
a chicken salad

**Colours**

black   white   red   blue   green   yellow
orange   brown   pink

**Clothes**

coat   dress   hat   pair of shoes   shirt
pair of trousers   skirt   T-shirt

**1** Complete the sentences with *Can I have + a, an* or *two*.

1 *Can I have an* espresso, please?
2 _____ cappuccino, please?
3 _____ chicken salad, please?
4 _____ iced coffees, please?
5 _____ mineral water, please?
6 _____ pieces of cake, please?

**2** Put these lines in the correct order to make a conversation.

[ ] That's €4.55, please.
[ ] Yes. Can I have a chicken sandwich and an espresso, please.
[ ] Take away.
[ ] No, thank you.
[ 1 ] Good morning. Can I help you?
[ ] Eat in or take away?
[ ] Certainly. Anything else?

**3** Underline the correct word in each sentence.

1 A: What's *this/that/these/those* near your bed?
   B: It's my new top.
2 A: How much are *this/that/these/those* shirts here?
   B: They're €12.99 each.
3 A: Here you are.
   B: What's *this/that/these/those*?
   A: It's a present. Happy birthday!
4 A: What are *this/that/these/those* sandwiches on that table?
   B: They're chicken.
5 A: Where's my car?
   B: Is *this/that/these/those* your car in the car park?
   A: No, it isn't. My car is blue.
6 A: Who are *this/that/these/those* people in that café?
   B: They're my friends.

**4** Rewrite the sentences with possessive 's.

1 He is Jamie. This is his suitcase.
   *This is Jamie's suitcase.*
2 She's Dorota. That's her baby.
   That's _____ .
3 He's Placido. They're his daughters.
   They're _____ .
4 That's Jay. That is his restaurant.
   That's _____ .
5 He's Michael. They're his friends.
   They're _____ .
6 She's Lillian. He's her brother.
   He's _____ .
7 This is Pat. They are her children.
   They're _____ .
8 He's my Dad. That's his café.
   That's _____ .

**5** Add four more possessive *'s* to this email.

From: jay@totalmail.co.uk
To: pat@englishmail.co.uk
Subject: my wife*'s* parents!

Hi Pat

How are you? What's your news?
Our house is very busy. Ann's mother – Hilda – is here. She's in Paul bedroom. Paul is in Tom bedroom with Tom. They aren't happy. Bob – Hilda husband – isn't here. He's at home with Hilda dog!

See you soon,
Jay

**6** Rearrange the letters to make a word.

1 What's your favourite *tsrtuaenar*? *restaurant*
2 Can I have a *opacucnic*, please? c_____
3 How much is that pair of *rotressu*? t_____
4 Are those *olppee* your friends? p_____
5 Excuse me, where is the *artni antsiot*?
   t_____ s_____
6 How much is a bottle of *limenar rawet*?
   m_____ w_____
7 That *genoar* skirt is nice. o_____
8 Marge's *dhlcnrie* are in the café. c_____
9 Can I have an *cedi efofce*, please?
   i_____ c_____
10 Is that Sharon's *clbak gba*? b_____ b_____

Darwin

A

Alice Springs

Brisbane

Perth

Adelaide

N
W    E
S

# 5 | Places

B

C

D

## Lead-in

**1**   **a** Match the places 1–5 with the words in the box.

> south    north    west    east    centre

1   Darwin =      4   Adelaide =
2   Perth =      5   Alice Springs =
3   Brisbane =

**b**   **5.1**   Listen and check your answers. Repeat the sentences.

**2**   Talk about your country. What cities are in the north, south, east, west and centre of the country?

*Malaga is in the north of Spain.*

**3**   **a**   Which photos B–D match these words?

city _____      countryside _____      coast _____

**b**   Match the words in the box to the places above.

> buildings    trees    a river    a beach    a road    the sea

**c**   **5.2**   Listen and check your answers.

**4**   **a**   Add more words for each place. Ask your teacher or use a dictionary.

**b**   Work in pairs. Talk about the photos.

**A:** *What's in photo B?*    **B:** *A hill, a river and ...*

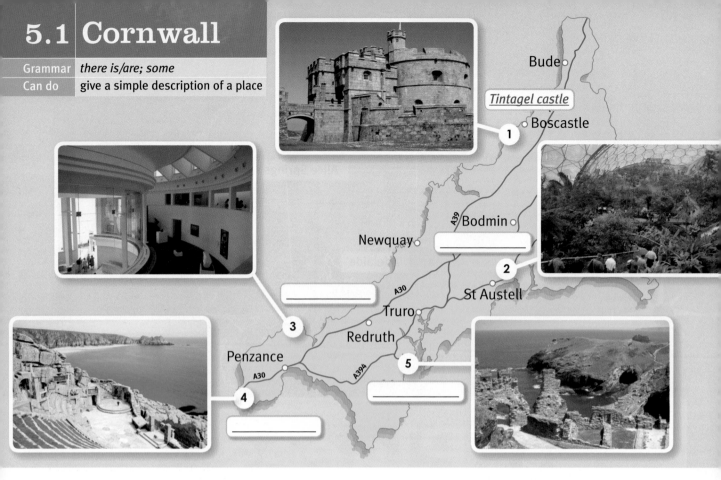

# Reading

**1** **a** Work in pairs. What is your favourite place for a holiday? Tell your partner.

*My favourite place for a holiday is the south of France.*

**b** Read the text. Label the map with the underlined places in the text.

My favourite place for a holiday is Cornwall. Cornwall is in the south-west of England. The coast and the countryside are very beautiful and the beaches are great.

There are two famous castles in Cornwall. Tintagel Castle is in the north of Cornwall and Pendennis Castle is in the south.

There's a great art gallery in the west of Cornwall. It's called Tate St Ives.

There is a new tourist attraction in south-east Cornwall. It's called The Eden Project. It's near Bodmin. There are plants from all over the world.

There's a beautiful outdoor theatre in the west of Cornwall. It's called the Minack Theatre.

**2** **a** Answer the questions.

1  Where is Cornwall?
2  Where are the famous castles?
3  What is Tate St Ives?
4  What is The Eden Project?
5  Where is the Minack Theatre?

**b** **5.3** Close your books and listen. When you hear the 'beep', say the next word.

My favourite place for a holiday is Cornwall. Cornwall is in the south-west of (beep)

**Students:** ... *England.*

# Speaking

**3** **a** Look at the list. What is important for a good holiday? Choose three things.

> great beaches    beautiful countryside
> good food    great tourist attractions
> good theatres and museums
> good shops    beautiful buildings

**b** Read the How to ... box.

| HOW TO ... | **give an opinion** |
| | I think ... |
| | *I think beautiful beaches are important (for a good holiday).* |

**c** Work in pairs. What is important for a good holiday?

# Grammar | *there is/are*

**4** **a** Look at the text again. Circle all the examples of *there's, there is* and *there are*.

**b** Complete the Active grammar box with *is* or *are*.

---

**Active grammar**

| There | 's | a great gallery. |
|-------|------|------------------|
| There | (____) | a theatre. |
| There | _____ | two famous castles. four great hotels. |

---

*see Reference page 57*

**5** **a** Complete the sentences with *There's* or *There are*.

1  *There's* a famous castle in Edinburgh.
2  _____ a beautiful beach in Barcelona.
3  _____ good restaurants in São Paolo.
4  _____ beautiful beaches in Greece.
5  _____ nice hotels in New York.
6  _____ a spice market in Istanbul.
7  _____ good museums in London.
8  _____ a famous mountain near Tokyo.

**b** Look at the map of Los Angeles. Talk about the tourist attractions.

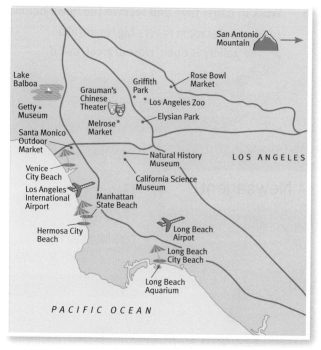

*There are two airports in Los Angeles. Los Angeles International Airport is in the west. Long Beach Airport is ...*

# Vocabulary | *some, a lot of*

**6** **a** Match the sentences to the pictures.

**a** There are *some* people in the theatre.
**b** There are *a lot of* people in the theatre.
**c** There's one person in the theatre.

1          2          3

**b** [5.4] Listen and check your answers. Repeat.

**7** **a** Look at the chart. Complete the sentences.

| Newchester | |
|------------|--------------------------|
| Cinemas | •••••••• |
| Galleries | ••••••• |
| Lakes | • |
| Shops | ••••••••••••••••••• |
| Restaurants | •••••••••••••••••••• |
| Rivers | • |

1  *There are some* galleries in Newchester.
2  _____ restaurants in Newchester.
3  _____ river in Newchester.
4  _____ lake in Newchester.
5  _____ shops in Newchester.
6  _____ cinemas in Newchester.

**b** Add the following adjectives to each sentence in Ex. 7a in the correct place.

---
nice   good   beautiful   big   great   modern
---

1  *There are some nice galleries in Newchester.*

# Writing

**8** Make notes about your favourite place for a holiday. Tell your partner.

*There are a lot of good restaurants in the centre of town.*

**9** **a** Look at the Writing bank on page 127.

**b** Write a description of your favourite place for a holiday.

| Grammar | *Is/Are there ...; there isn't/aren't; some, any* |
|---|---|
| Can do | ask for and understand basic information about a new town |

## Vocabulary | prepositions of place

1　**a** Match the prepositions in the box to the pictures a–h.

> under　opposite　in　on　in front of
> near　next to　behind

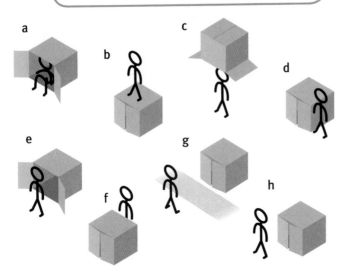

**b** Look at the map of the town square below. Complete the sentences.

1　The newsagent is _____ the hotel.
2　The café is _____ the train station.
3　The chemist is _____ the Italian restaurant.
4　The cinema is *behind* the town square.
5　The department store is _____ the chemist.

**c** 5.5 Listen and check your answers. Cover the sentences and talk about the town square.

## Listening

2　**a** 5.6 Listen to people in the Royal Hotel asking for directions. Complete a–e in the map below.

**b** Listen again and look at the map. Are these sentences true (T) or false (F)? Correct the false sentences.

1　There are two cafés near the hotel. [T]
2　There is a restaurant next to the train station. ☐
3　There aren't any banks near the hotel. ☐
4　The bank is open today. ☐
5　The cathedral and the museum are tourist attractions. ☐
6　There's a gallery in the square. ☐

3　**a** Read the How to ... box.

**HOW TO ...** receive good and bad news

Good news:
*Good!*　　*Great!*

Bad news:
*Never mind!*　　*Oh no!*

**b** Work in pairs. Give and receive the news below.

1　Your hotel room is very big/small/nice.
2　The gallery is open/closed/great/awful.

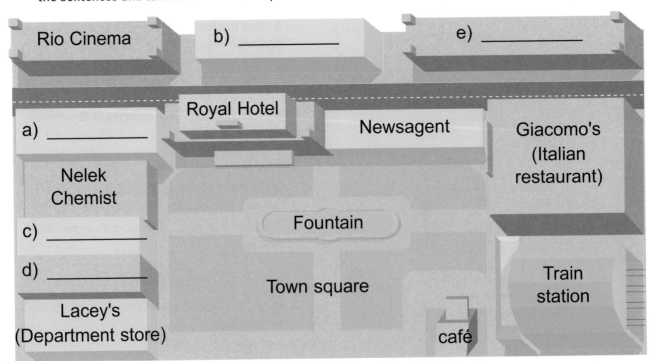

Rio Cinema

b) _____

e) _____

Royal Hotel

Newsagent

Giacomo's
(Italian
restaurant)

a) _____

Nelek
Chemist

c) _____

Fountain

d) _____

Town square

Train
station

Lacey's
(Department store)

café

## Grammar | *There isn't/aren't any; Is/Are there any …?*

**4** Complete the Active grammar box with *is, isn't, are* or *aren't*.

**Active grammar**

| | | |
|---|---|---|
| ➖ There | isn't<br>(is not ) | a bus stop near here. |
| ➖ There | _____<br>(are not) | any galleries near here. |
| ❓ _____ | there | a bank near here? |
| Yes there is. | | No, there _____ . |
| ❓ Are | there any hotels near here? | |
| Yes, there _____ . | | No, there _____ . |

any: use *any* for plurals in negatives and questions with *there is/are*

*see Reference page 57*

**5** Look at the map on page 52 again. Complete the sentences with *There isn't/aren't*.

1 *There aren't* any bus stops in the square.
2 _____ a supermarket in the square.
3 _____ car parks in the square.
4 _____ a market in the square.
5 _____ a cinema in the square.
6 _____ any galleries in the square.

**6 a** Write questions for your partner about his/her home town.

1 good cinemas
2 big museum
3 nice department stores
4 palace
5 modern supermarkets
6 popular galleries

*Are there any good cinemas in your home town?*

**b** Work in pairs. Ask and answer the questions in Ex. 6a.

A: *Are there any good cinemas in your home town?*
B: *Yes, there are. There are a lot of good cinemas.*

## Vocabulary | nationalities

**7 a** Write a country for each word in *italics*.

1 a *French* restaurant    4 an *Indian* restaurant
2 an *Italian* restaurant    5 a *Chinese* restaurant
3 an *English* restaurant

**b** Match the types of restaurants 1–5 to the restaurant names below.

Chez Pierre

WONG LI

King Henry's

The Taj Mahal

LA SPIGA

**c** 5.7 Listen and check your answers.

**8 a** Add more countries and nationalities to the chart below. Use your dictionary.

| Country | Nationality |
|---|---|
| England<br>Scotland | English<br>_____ |
| _____<br>Wales | Irish<br>_____ |

**b** Work in pairs. Discuss the questions. Use nationalities in your answers.

What is your favourite kind of food/restaurant/music?

*My favourite kind of food is Italian.*

## Speaking

**9** Work in pairs.
**Student A:** You are a hotel receptionist. Look at page 111.
**Student B:** You are a hotel guest. Look at page 114. Ask questions with *Is there a … near here?* or *Are there any … near here?* Complete the chart.

B: *Are there any cafés near here?*
A: *Yes, there are. There's a café next to the newsagent's and there's a café …*

# 5.3 Can she cook?

| Grammar | *can/can't* |
|---------|-------------|
| Can do | talk about general abilities |

## Harefield College

**Welcome to Harefield College.** We are Harefield's top language school. Our Language Plus! courses are very popular with students from all over the world.

**Language Plus! Courses: A1 English**

| | | | |
|---|---|---|---|
| **Course 171:** | A1 English 09:00 – 11:00 | + |  |
| **Course 172:** | A1 English 14:00 – 17:00 | + |  |
| **Course 173:** | A1 English 19:00 – 21:00 | + |  |
| **Course 174:** | A1 English 09:00 – 12:00 | + |  |
| **Course 175:** | A1 English 18:00 – 20:00 | + |  |
| **Course 176:** | A1 English 14:00 – 16:00 | + |  |
| **Course 177:** | A1 English 10:00 – 12:00 | + |  |
| **Course 178:** | A1 English 13:00 – 15:00 | + |  |

## Vocabulary | abilities

1  **a** Look at the brochure above. Match a symbol to a word/phrase in the box.

> cook   play golf   drive   play the piano   swim
> use a computer   sing   dance

**b** Work in pairs. Point to a symbol. Your partner says the word/phrase.

## Listening

2  **a** ⓹·⑧ Listen to Patricia and James. Complete the information about Vanda.

Name: *Vanda*

From: Augsburg in _____.

Relationship to James: _____

English level: _____

**b** ⓹·⑨ Listen to part 2 of the conversation. Write *Yes* or *No* next to each activity for Vanda.

1  drive        *Yes*
2  swim       _____
3  play golf    _____
4  cook       _____
5  use a computer _____
6  dance     _____
7  sing       _____
8  play the piano _____

**c** Listen again. Check your answers. Which courses are good for Vanda?

**d** Which courses are good for you?

3  Read the How to ... box. Greet your partner.

> **HOW TO ...**
>
> ### greet a friend
>
> **A:** *How are you?*
>
> **B:** *Fine/OK/Not bad, thanks. And you?*
>
> **A:** *Fine/OK/Not bad, thanks.*

## Grammar | *can/can't*

**4** Complete the Active grammar box with *can* or *can't*.

<table>
<tr><td colspan="3">Active grammar</td></tr>
<tr><td>➕ : I/you/</td><td><u>can</u></td><td>swim.</td></tr>
<tr><td>➖ : he/she/<br>: we/they</td><td>_____</td><td>play golf.</td></tr>
<tr><td>❓ : _____</td><td>I/you/he/she/<br>we/they</td><td>cook?<br>dance?</td></tr>
</table>

Yes, I/you/he/she/we/they can.
No, I/you/he/she/we/they can't.

*see Reference page 57*

**5** **a** Write the sentences.

1 (They / ✗ / dance)     *They can't dance.*
2 (you / swim?)            _____ ?
3 (He / ✓ / speak Italian)  _____ .
4 (she / drive?)            _____ ?
5 (you / play golf?)        _____ ?
6 (I / ✗ / play the piano)  _____ .
7 (We / ✓ / cook)          _____ .
8 (they / use a computer?)  _____ ?

**b** Ask your partner questions with the words from Ex. 1a.

A: *Can you drive?*
B: *Yes, I can.*

## Pronunciation

**6** **a** 5.10 Listen. Tick the word you hear.

| | can | can't | | can | can't |
|---|---|---|---|---|---|
| 1 | ☐ | ☐ | 4 | ☐ | ☐ |
| 2 | ☐ | ☐ | 5 | ☐ | ☐ |
| 3 | ☐ | ☐ | 6 | ☐ | ☐ |

**b** Listen again. Write the sentences.

**c** Talk about the languages **a)** you **b)** your friends/family can speak.

*I can speak (some/good) German and French. I can't speak Italian or Spanish. My brother can speak Spanish.*

## Vocabulary | telling the time

**7** 5.11 Listen and repeat the times.

a **10:00**    d **08:00**
b **15:00**    e **13:00**
c **19:00**    f **20:00**

**8** **a** Say a time from the brochure in Ex. 1a. Your partner tells you the course.

A: *From two o' clock in the afternoon to four o' clock in the afternoon.*
B: *Course 176.*

**b** What time are your English lessons?

## Speaking

**9** Look at the job adverts. Talk to your classmates. Find one person for each job.

**ENTERTAINER FOR CRUISE SHIP NEEDED**
Skills required:

A: *Can you dance?*
B: *Yes, I can.*
A: *Can you play the piano?*
B: *Yes, I can. But I can't sing.*
A: *Oh no!*

**PERSONAL TRAINER NEEDED**
Skills required:

**CHEF NEEDED**
Skills required:

Grazie
Ciao!
Prego

# 5 | Communication

## A Bed and Breakfast

1  **a** What is a Bed and Breakfast (*B&B*)?

   **b** Work in pairs. Match the words in the box to the letters a–f in the picture.

   > blanket   shower   towels   fridge   kettle   television

   **c** `5.12` Listen to the conversation. Check your answers.

   **d** Close your books. What can you remember about the bedroom?

   *There are some towels on the bed.*

2  Listen to the conversation again. What time is
   a) breakfast b) checkout?

3  **a** `5.13` Look at the clock. Listen and repeat.

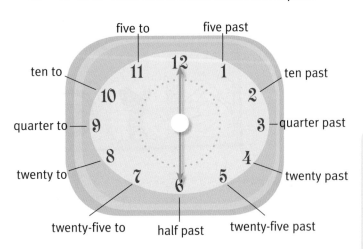

five to   five past
ten to   ten past
quarter to   quarter past
twenty to   twenty past
twenty-five to   half past   twenty-five past

   **b** Work in pairs. Say the times.

   | | | | | | |
   |---|---|---|---|---|---|
   | **a** | 03.30 | **e** 19:10 | **i** | 09:35 | **m** 10:10 |
   | **b** | 17:15 | **f** 19:45 | **j** | 08:15 | **n** 21:40 |
   | **c** | 20:45 | **g** 06:20 | **k** | 14:25 | **o** 12:15 |
   | **d** | 11:30 | **h** 13:05 | **l** | 04:55 | |

4  **a** You are the owner of a *B&B* with one room. Complete the details about your *B&B* room below. Write yes (Y) or no (N).

   | Room | (Y) | (N) | Where? |
   |---|---|---|---|
   | Double bed? | | | |
   | En-suite? | | | |
   | Television? | | | |
   | Extra blanket? | | | |
   | Towels? | | | |
   | Kettle? | | | |
   | Fridge? | | | |
   | (other?) | | | |

   **b** Work in pairs. Welcome your partner to your *B&B*. Show your partner the room. Tell him/her the times for breakfast and checkout.

## Lifelong learning

**Remember words together**

You can write and remember some new words in phrases. Phrases are often more useful than single words.

a <u>double</u> <u>bed</u>     an <u>en-suite</u> <u>bath</u>room
an <u>extra</u> <u>blanket</u>

## There is/are

| | | | |
|---|---|---|---|
| ⊕ | There's / There is | a/an | museum near here. gallery near here. |
| ⊖ | There isn't | | |
| ⊕ | There are | two some a lot of | cafés near here. galleries in town. museums in town. |
| ⊖ | There aren't | any | |
| ❓ | Is there | a/an | supermarket near here? |

Yes, there is.    No, there isn't

| | | | |
|---|---|---|---|
| ❓ | Are there | any | tourist attractions near here? |

Yes, there are.    No, there aren't.

Use *there is/isn't/are/aren't* to say that something exists or doesn't exist in a place.

## some/a lot of/any

Use *some* and *a lot of* in affirmative sentences with *There are* + plural nouns.
*There are some cafés near the bank.*

*A lot of* = a large number.
*There are a lot of people in the bank.*

Use *any* in negative sentences and questions with plurals.
*There aren't any hotels in this town.*

*Are there any markets in this town?*

## can/can't

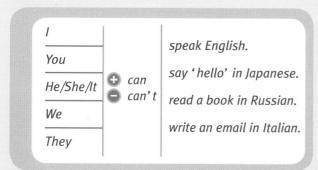

| | | | |
|---|---|---|---|
| I You He/She/It We They | ⊕ can ⊖ can't | | speak English. say 'hello' in Japanese. read a book in Russian. write an email in Italian. |

Use *can* and *can't* before he verb to show ability

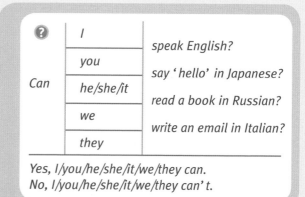

| | | |
|---|---|---|
| Can | I you he/she/it we they | speak English? say 'hello' in Japanese? read a book in Russian? write an email in Italian? |

Yes, I/you/he/she/it/we/they can.
No, I/you/he/she/it/we/they can't.

## Prepositions of place

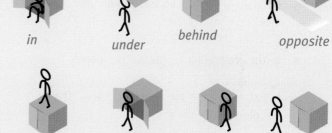

in          under          behind          opposite

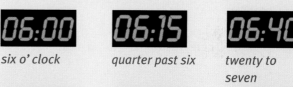

on          in front of          next to          near

## Telling the time

| 06:00 | 06:15 | 06:40 |
|---|---|---|
| six o' clock | quarter past six | twenty to seven |
| 06:10 | 06:30 | 06:45 |
| ten past six | half past six | quarter to seven |

### Key vocabulary

**Nationalities**
American   Argentine/Argentinian
Australian   Brazilian   British
Chinese   French   German   Greek   Indian
Italian   Japanese   Mexican   Polish
Russian   Spanish   Turkish

**Abilities**
cook   dance   drive   play golf
play the piano   sing   swim   use a computer

# 5 Review and practice

**1** Underline the correct word or words.

My office is in the centre of town. There (1) *is/are* a nice café near the office and there (2) *is/are* two good restaurants, too. There are (3) *a/some* beautiful buildings in the north of the city and there are (4) *a/a lot* of tourist attractions in the south of the city. There (5) *is/are* a great museum in the west of the city and there are (6) *one/some* nice hotels in the east.

**2** Put the words in the correct order.

1 any your Are theatres town? in there
*Are there any theatres in your town?*

2 here. isn't nice There restaurant a near
_____ .

3 hotel There is house. near my a nice
_____ .

4 a in Barcelona? there Is beach
_____ ?

5 a of the in lot cinema. are There people
_____ .

6 aren't here. any galleries There near
_____ .

7 museums Are this near hotel? there any
_____ ?

8 next There café. is to a chemist this
_____ .

**3** Write questions and answers with *there*.

1 A: *Is there an Italian restaurant near here?*
(Italian restaurant/near here)
B: *Yes, there is.* (Yes)

2 A: *Are there a lot of people in your hotel?* (a lot of people/in your hotel)
B: *No, there aren't.* (No)

3 A: _____ ? (car park/in front of the hotel)
B: _____ . (No)

4 A: _____ ? (good galleries/near your hotel)
B: _____ . (Yes)

5 A: _____ ? (Indian restaurant/on this street)
· B: _____ . (No)

6 A: _____ ? (beautiful people/in your office)
B: _____ . (Yes)

**4** Correct the mistakes.

1 I can't to use a computer.
*I can't use a computer.*

2 They can plays the piano.
_____ .

3 Can she cooks Italian food?
_____ .

4 A: Can you drive? B: No, I can.
_____ .

5 We sing can but we dance can't.
_____ .

6 drive you Can?
_____ .

7 He's only 6 years old but he cans play golf.
_____ .

8 A: Can your dog swim? B: Yes, he can't.
_____ .

**5** Complete the sentences with the words in the box.

> any some French blanket under
> o'clock use play ~~past~~ quarter

1 A: What's the time?
B: It's ten *past* nine.

2 There's a really good _____ restaurant on the High Street.

3 A: Where's my mobile phone?
B: It's on the table _____ that book.

4 Are there _____ people in the cinema?

5 Can you _____ a computer?

6 Breakfast is from eight _____ to half past ten.

7 There are _____ people in the garden. Who are they?

8 He can't _____ golf but she can.

9 A: What's the time?
B: It's _____ to four.

10 Is there an extra _____ in the room?

# 6 | People

## Lead-in

**1** **a** Look at the adjectives in the box. Check the meaning in a dictionary.

> thin  good-looking  tall  fat  short  not intelligent
> happy  ugly  young  rich  old  poor  sad  intelligent

**b** **6.1** Listen and repeat.

**c** Test your partner. Say a word. Your partner says the opposite.

**A:** *Short.*  **B:** *Tall.*

**2** **a** Put the sentences in the box in the correct place.

> He's not very rich.  He's rich.  He's very rich.  He's quite rich.

➕➕➕ _____  ➕➕ _____  ➕ *He's quite rich.*  ➖ _____

**b** Talk about the people in the photos. Use the adjectives with *very, quite* or *not very*.

**3** Talk about famous people with your partner.

**A:** *Jude Law is very good-looking.*

**B:** *Yes, he is.*

| Grammar | Present Simple (1) *I/you; object pronouns; me/you/him/her/it/us/them* |
|---|---|
| Can do | say what you like/don't like |

## Listening

1    **a**   The woman in the picture is called Cynthia. Write five questions for her.

*Where are you from?*

**b**   **6.2**   Listen. Can you answer any of your questions?

**c**   Listen again. What does Cynthia like? Draw 😊 or 😞 next to each word/phrase below.

1   Dublin
2   Irish music
3   Brazilian music
4   half past nine in the morning
5   football
6   AC Milan football team
7   American food
8   Indian food
9   German cars
10   Italian fashion

## Grammar 1 | Present Simple (1): *I like*

2    **a**   Complete the Active grammar box with *do* or *don't*. Look at tapescript 6.2 on page 147 to help you.

**Active grammar**

| ⊕ : | I | like | German cars. |
|---|---|---|---|
| ⊖ : | I | **don't** like | Irish music. |
| ❓ : | _____ you | like | football? |
| Yes, I _____ . | | No, I _____ . | |

*see Reference page 67*

**b**   Complete more sentences for Cynthia.

1   (😊 Rio) *I like Rio*.
2   (😞 chicken) *I don't like chicken*.
3   (😊 London) _____ .
4   (😊 yellow and green) _____ .
5   (😞 Mondays) _____ .
6   (😊 Spanish films) _____ .
7   (😞 Manchester United) _____ .
8   (😞 six o'clock in the morning) _____ .

**c**   Write questions for each of the sentences above.

1   *Do you like Rio?*

## Pronunciation

3    **a**   **6.3**   Listen. Write the questions.

1   *Do you like Italian food?*

**b**   Listen again. Repeat.

# Speaking

**4** **a** Write one thing/person you like and one thing/person you don't like for each category below.

- food
- music
- famous people
- time of day
- football teams
- colours
- cars
- places

*food: like = Italian food   don't like = salad*

**b** Tell your partner.

*I like Italian food. I don't like salad.*

**c** Ask your partner questions with your things/people from Ex. 4a.

*Do you like Italian food?*

## Grammar 2 | *me, you, him, her, it, us, them*

**5** **a** Match a sentence a–f to a picture 1–6.

a   I don't like *her*.
b   ~~Do you like *me*?~~
c   I like *them*.
d   I don't like *him*.
e   I like *you*.
f   I like *it*.

1

*Do you like me?*

2 _____

3 _____

4 _____

_____   _____

**b** 〔6.4〕 Listen and check.

**c** Complete the chart with the words in *italics* from Ex. 5a.

| SUBJECT PRONOUN | OBJECT PRONOUN |
|---|---|
| I | _____ |
| you | _____ |
| he | _____ |
| she | _____ |
| it | _____ |
| we | *us* |
| they | _____ |

**6** **a** Work in pairs.

**Student A:** look at the list below.

**Student B:** look at the list on page 112.

1   George Bush
2   Angelina Jolie
3   beautiful beaches
4   department stores
5   instant coffee
6   Bill and Hillary Clinton
7   golf

Read your list to your partner. Your partner says *I like/don't like* + object pronoun.

**A:** *Tony Blair.*

**B:** *I don't like him.*

**b** Read the How to ... box.

**c** Say more people and things to your partner. Your partner says *I like/don't like* + object pronoun.

## Speaking

**7** **a** Write eight new questions. Use:

*Do you like ...?*

*Who's/What's your favourite ...?*

**b** Do a 60-second interview with your partner. Use your questions from Ex. 7a.

# 6.2 Making friends

| Grammar | Present Simple (2) we/they; Wh- questions |
|---|---|
| Can do | start and continue a conversation with someone you don't know |

Anthony

Catherine

## Vocabulary | jobs and activities

1 **a** Match the pictures a–f to the jobs in the box.

architect   sales rep.   designer   reporter
chef   builder

a

b

c

d

e

f

a = *designer*

**b** Write a verb from the box below in each gap.

sell   write   build   cook   design (x2)

1   What do architects do?
    They *design* buildings, for example houses and shops.
2   What do sales reps do?
    They _____ things, for example computers and books.
3   What do designers do?
    They _____ things, for example clothes and shoes.
4   What do reporters do?
    They _____ articles, for example newspaper articles.
5   What do chefs do?
    They _____ food, for example Chinese food and Italian food.
6   What do builders do?
    They _____ buildings, for example houses and shops.

**c** 6.5 Listen and check.

2 **a** Add another example for each answer above.
*Architects design restaurants, too.*

**b** Ask a question from Ex. 1b. Your partner gives the answer.

## Listening

3 **a** 6.6 Listen. Match jobs from Ex. 1a to the people in the photo.

**b** Listen again. Mark the sentences true (T) or false (F).

**Sharon and Pat**
1   They live in Ireland.
2   They are on business.
3   They design shops and office buildings.

**Catherine and Anthony**
4   They are on holiday.
5   They live in Canada.
6   They are sales reps.

## Grammar 1 | Present Simple (2) we/they

4 **a** Complete the Active grammar box with *do* or *don't*.

**Active grammar**

| ➕ | We/They | design | houses. |
| ➖ | We/They | ____ live | in Canada. |
| ❓ | Do | we/they | sell | computers? |

Yes, we/they ____ . / No, we/they ____ .

see Reference page 67

**b** Are the sentences below true for you? Write yes (Y) or no (N) next to the sentences.

1   I like American films.   4   I live near this school.
2   I like Italian food.       5   I like football.
3   I like British music.     6   I live in London.

**c** Work in pairs. Make sentences about you and your partner.

*We don't like American films.*

Sharon

Pat

## Grammar 2 | *Wh-* questions

**5** Complete the Active grammar box with *Who, What* or *Where.*

### Active grammar

| *What* | do | you | do? |
|--------|----|----|----|
| _____ | do | you | work/live? |
| _____ | do | you | sell/design/write? |
| _____ | do | you | work for? |

*see Reference page 67*

**6** Write questions from the Active grammar box for each answer below.

1 **A:** *What do you do?* **B:** I'm a sales rep.
2 **A:** *What do you write?* **B:** I write articles.
3 **A:** _____ ? **B:** I work in Paris.
4 **A:** _____ ? **B:** I work for GT Designs.
5 **A:** _____ ? **B:** I design cars.
6 **A:** _____ ? **B:** I'm a chef.
7 **A:** _____ ? **B:** I live in Zurich.
8 **A:** _____ ? **B:** I sell books.

**7** Work in pairs. Read the How to ... box. Ask your partner questions from the Active grammar box.

**HOW TO ...**

### show interest
**A:** *What do you do?*
**B:** *I'm a builder/designer/sales rep., etc.*
**A:** *Oh really?/Great! What do you build/ design/sell, etc.?*

## Reading

**8** **a** Read the magazine article. Complete the details.

| Name: Martin _____ | Name: Clarissa _____ |
|----------------------|------------------------|
| Job: _____ | Job: _____ |
| Age: _____ | Age: _____ |

## We're best friends!

**Clarissa Hanson and Martin Dolan are best friends.** Read our interview with them.

**How old are you?**
Clarissa: He's 23 and I'm ... over sixty.

**What do you do?**
Martin: I'm an accountant and she's an actor. We're best friends.

**How are you the same?**
Clarissa: We're the same in a lot of ways. We like good conversation, good food, good films. We're not rich but we're not poor.
Martin: We're quite intelligent. We like galleries, museums, that kind of thing.

**How are you different?**
Martin: I'm young and Clarissa is ...
Clarissa: ... I'm young-at-heart!

**b** Read the article again. Write Clarissa (C), Martin (M) or not Clarissa/Martin (N) next to each adjective below.

1 rich *N*   3 intelligent   5 young-at-heart
2 young   4 poor

## Speaking

**9** Work in groups of four as two pairs.
**Students A and B:** read your details on page 110.
**Students C and D:** read your details on page 112.
You are in a restaurant. Have a conversation with the other pair. Ask questions like this:
*Where are you from? What do you do?*

# 6.3 Daily routines

| | |
|---|---|
| Grammar | Present Simple (3) *he/she/it* |
| Can do | talk about the routines of people you know |

Roberta

Adam

## Vocabulary | verbs of routine

**1 a** Read the sentences. Write the correct <u>underlined</u> verb phrase under each picture.

1 I <u>start work</u> at half past seven in the morning.
2 I don't <u>have a shower</u> every day.
3 I <u>eat salad</u> every day.
4 I <u>get up</u> at eleven o'clock.
5 I don't <u>watch TV</u>.
6 I <u>eat fast food</u> for breakfast.
7 I <u>finish work</u> at nine o'clock.
8 I don't <u>go to bed</u> early.

**a**

*get up*

**b**

_____

**c**

_____

**d**

_____

**e**

_____

**f**

_____

**g**

_____

**h**

_____

**b** Change the sentences in Ex. 1a to make them true for you. Tell your partner.

1 *I get up at half past seven every day.*

## Reading

**2 a** Work in pairs. Look at the photos above. Guess who says the sentences in Ex. 1a.
*I think Adam says sentence 1.*

**b** Read the text. Check your answers.

Emma

Elaine is my best friend. She's a yoga teacher. She's poor but she's happy. She eats salad every day. She doesn't eat fast food and she doesn't watch TV.

Frank is my brother and he's a biker. He's quite short and very intelligent. He eats fast food for breakfast every day. He doesn't have a shower every day.

Roberta is my aunt. She's a sales rep. She starts work at half past seven in the morning and she finishes work at nine o'clock in the evening. She's not a happy person.

Adam is a musician. He gets up at eleven o'clock in the morning and he goes to bed at two o'clock in the morning. He's not very intelligent – but it's OK – he's good-looking and he's my husband. I love him!

**c** Answer the questions with *Yes, he/she does* or *No, he/she doesn't*.

1 Does Frank have a shower every day?
   *No, he doesn't.*
2 Does Adam get up at eight o'clock?
3 Does Elaine eat fast food?
4 Does Roberta start work at half past seven?
5 Does Frank eat fast food for breakfast?
6 Does Elaine watch TV?

Frank

Elaine

## Grammar | Present Simple (3) he/she/it

**3** Look at the text again and complete the Active grammar box.

### Active grammar

| ⊕ He/She/It | start_<br>finish_ | work at half past seven.<br>work at nine o' clock |
|---|---|---|
| ⊖ He/She/It | ____ eat<br>____ like | fast food.<br>salad. |

| ❓ Does | he<br>she | get up<br>have | at nine?<br>breakfast early? |
|---|---|---|---|

Yes, he/she/it does.   No, he/she/it doesn't.

| ⊕ He/She/It | has | a shower every day. |
|---|---|---|

*see Reference page 67*

**4 a** Complete the text with a verb in the correct form.

have   start   get   like   ~~work~~   finish   watch   eat

My best friend is Yasmin. She's a chef in a Spanish restaurant. She (1) *works* in the evening so she (2) _____ up around ten or eleven o'clock in the morning. She (3) _____ breakfast and lunch together – it's called 'brunch'. She (4) _____ TV in the afternoon and she (5) _____ work around four o'clock. She (6) _____ dinner at work. She (7) _____ work around midnight. She (8) _____ her job but we don't meet – she's always at work!

**b** Complete the sentences below with the correct form of the words in **bold**.

1  He *doesn't like* this music. **not like**
2  _____ they _____ here? **work**
3  What _____ he _____ ? **do**
4  Sarah _____ _____ a lot of emails. **not write**
5  What time _____ Mo _____ work? **finish**
6  _____ you _____ work early? **start**
7  Paul and Jo _____ _____ to bed early. **not go**
8  What _____ she _____ ? **write**

## Speaking

**5 a** Complete each sentence below with the name of a friend/family member.

1  _____ is my best friend.
2  _____ is very intelligent.
3  _____ is very good-looking.
4  I love _____ .

**b** Make notes about each person above.

* What does he/she do? (e.g. he's a teacher)
* What adjectives describe him/her (e.g. she's young, happy)
* What are his/her routines? (e.g. he gets up at eight o'clock)

**c** Tell your partner about these people.

A: *Who's Erik?*
B: *He's my father. He's very intelligent. He's a sales rep. He's quite short. He gets up at ...*

## Listening

**6 a** [6.7] Listen to Adam's song. Write all the verbs you hear.

**b** Listen again and check.

**c** Work in pairs. Do you like the song? Write more lines for the song.

## Writing

**7 a** Look at the Writing bank on page 128.

**b** Write a letter to a friend. Tell him/her about your life now.

# 6 | Communication

**1** **a** Look at the words in the box. Tick (✓) the words you know.

> book DVD MP3 player tie bag flowers suitcase travel iron
> saucepans wallet CD cookery book candles pen

**b** Match nine words in the box to the pictures on the website.

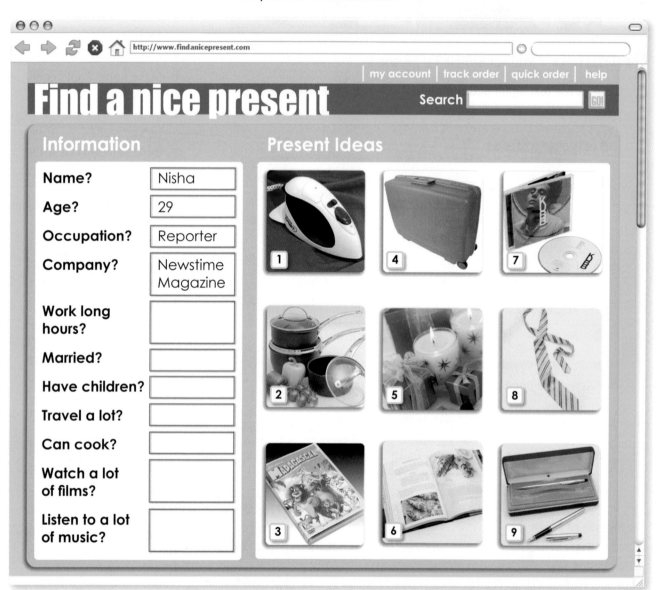

**2** **6.8** Listen to part 1 of the conversation. What is the problem?

**3** **a** Look at the website above. Check the new words in a dictionary.

**b** **6.9** Listen to part 2 of the conversation. Complete the website for Josef's friend, Nisha. Write yes (Y) or no (N).

**c** Look at the findanicepresent chart on page 113. What are the three presents for Nisha?

**4** **a** Work in pairs. Add two questions and four presents to the chart.

**b** Find a new partner.

**Student A:** close your book. Think of a friend.

**Student B:** look at the findanicepresent chart on page 113. Ask questions from your chart. Find a good present for Student A's friend.

## Lifelong learning

**Review, review and review again**

It's very important to revise. Before every lesson, look at grammar and vocabulary from your last lessons.

## The Present Simple

| ➕ | | |
|---|---|---|
| I | live | |
| You | work | |
| He | lives | in Munich. |
| She | works | near my brother. |
| It | | next to a cinema. |
| We | live | |
| They | work | |

With *he, she* and *it,* add *-s* to the verb.

| ➖ | | | |
|---|---|---|---|
| I | don't | like | |
| You | | eat | |
| He | doesn't | like | chicken. |
| She | | eat | coffee. |
| It | | | salad. |
| We | don't | like | |
| They | | eat | |

| ❓ | | | |
|---|---|---|---|
| Do | I | design | |
| | you | write | |
| Does | he | design | books? |
| | she | write | magazines? |
| | it | | |
| Do | we | design | |
| | they | write | |

Yes, I/you/we/they do.
Yes, he/she/it does.

No, I/you/we/they don't.
No, he/she/it doesn't.

What do you design?
Where do you live?
Who do you like?

For verbs ending in *-ch, -sh, -ss* and *-o*, add *-es* to the verb with *he, she* and *it: He/She/It watches*

*Have* is irregular: *He/She/It has*

| | | |
|---|---|---|
| I | have | breakfast. |
| You | go to | work. |
| We | finish | work early. |
| They | watch | TV. |
| He | has | breakfast. |
| She | goes to | work. |
| It | finishes | work early. |
| | watches | TV. |

## Object pronouns

Object pronouns are the object of a verb. They come after the verb.

| SUBJECT PRONOUNS | OBJECT PRONOUNS |
|---|---|
| I/you/he/she/it/we/they | me/you/him/her/it/us/them |

Do you like *me*?   I like *you*.   We like *him*.
He likes *her*.   She likes *it*.   They like *us*.
I like *them*.

### Key vocabulary

**Adjectives**
tall   short   ugly   rich   not intelligent
poor   happy   sad   fat   thin   young
old   good-looking   intelligent

**Jobs and activities**
architects design buildings
builders build building
designers design things
chefs cook food
reporters write articles
sales reps sell things

**Verbs of routine**
get up   go to bed   have breakfast
have a shower   start work   finish work
watch TV   eat salad

Use *not very* to make negative descriptions more polite:
*She's not very intelligent.*
*They're not very rich.*

**1** Complete the conversation with *I like, I don't like* or *Do you like.*

**A:** (1) *Do you like* American music?

**B:** No, I don't. But (2) _____ British music.

**A:** Really? (3) _____ Coldplay?

**B:** They're OK but they're not my favourite. (4) _____ Radiohead and Gorrillaz.

**A:** (5) _____ Radiohead, but (6) _____ Oasis and U2.

**B:** Yes, U2 are great but they aren't British. They're Irish.

**A:** I know. (7) _____ Irish music – U2, Gemma Hayes, etc. (8) _____ Bruce Springsteen?

**B:** Yes, I do. He's great.

**A:** He's American – so you like American music!

**2** Complete each sentence or question with an object pronoun: *me, you, him, her, it, us* or *them.*

1 She's really nice. Do you like *her*?

2 I don't like this programme. Do you like _____ ?

3 Bill and Jenny aren't my friends. I don't like _____ .

4 I really like him but I don't think he likes _____ .

5 You are great! I think he likes _____ .

6 He's my friend. I like _____ .

7 We like them but do they like _____ ?

**3** Complete each question with *What, Where* or *Who.*

1 **A:** *Where* do you live?
   **B:** In the centre of Glasgow.

2 **A:** _____ do you work for?
   **B:** A small software company.

3 **A:** _____ do you do?
   **B:** I'm a sales rep.

4 **A:** _____ do you sell?
   **B:** I sell computer software.

5 **A:** _____ do you work?
   **B:** In Edinburgh.

6 **A:** _____ do you design?
   **B:** I design clothes.

**4** Put the verb in brackets into the correct form.

Hi Victor,

How are you? I'm fine but my new flatmate is a problem. His name is Oscar. He's a designer. He (1) *designs* (design/✓) shoes. He (2) _____ (get up/✓) at 11 o'clock every day. He (3) _____ (have a shower/✗). He (4) _____ (eat/✗) breakfast but he (5) _____ (watch/✓) TV for two or three hours. Then he (6) _____ (start/ ✓) work at about two o'clock in the afternoon. He (7) _____ (work/✗) in an office – he (8) _____ (work/✓) from home. He (9) _____ (finish/✓) work at about six o'clock. That's just four hours! He (10) _____ (go/✓) to bed at three o'clock in the morning.

What can I do?

Love, Julia

**5** Write complete sentences.

1 I/not like/French food.
   *I don't like French food.*

2 She/get up/at 8 o'clock
   _____ .

3 They/start work/early?
   _____ .

4 Thomas/not eat/salad.
   _____ .

5 Clara/watch TV/every day?
   _____ .

6 Paul and I/write/articles for *Newsmag.*
   _____ .

7 Where/Lorraine/live?
   _____ .

8 Jo and Ian/not go to bed/late.
   _____ .

**6** Match a verb 1–8 to a word or phrase a–h.

| | | | |
|---|---|---|---|
| 1 | cook | a | a shower |
| 2 | watch | b | in an office |
| 3 | finish | c | TV |
| 4 | have | d | work at 10 o'clock |
| 5 | design | e | to bed late |
| 6 | go | f | Indian food |
| 7 | work | g | in a small house |
| 8 | live | h | shoes |

# 7 | Work

B

C

D

## Lead-in

1   **a**  What can you see in the photos?

**b**  Match a word in the box to one of the photos/pictures A–H.

> office   factory   shop   hospital   university   school   restaurant
> call centre

 E

 F

 G

 H

2   **a**  Match a person 1–8 below to a place A–H above.

1   a waiter                         5   a sales assistant
2   a PA (personal assistant)        6   a lecturer
3   a factory worker                 7   a call centre worker
4   a nurse                          8   a teacher

**b**  **7.1**  Listen and check.

**c**  **7.2**  Listen. Who is he/she? Where does he/she work?

1   She's a *sales assistant*. She works *in a shop*.
2   She's a _____ . She works _____ .
3   He's a _____ . He works _____ .
4   He's a _____ . He works _____ .
5   She's a _____ . She works _____ .
6   He's a _____ . He works _____ .
7   He's a _____ . He works _____ .
8   She's a _____ . She works _____ .

## Listening and vocabulary

**1**   **a**  Look at the pictures above. Who are the people? Where are they?

**b**  **7.3**  Listen. Answer the questions.

1   What is the man's name?

2   What is the woman's name?

3   What is the boy's name?

**c**  Listen again. Write a conversation number next to each phrase below.

| Phrase | Conversation |
|---|---|
| a   Please sit down. | 2 |
| b   Hold the line, please. | ___ |
| c   Be quiet. | ___ |
| d   Turn off your mobile phone. | ___ |
| e   Listen to the conversation. | ___ |
| f   Look at page 32. | ___ |
| g   Come in. | ___ |

**d**  Match a phrase a–g above to a picture 1–7 below.

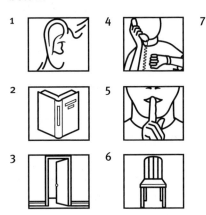

## Grammar | imperatives

**2**   Write a verb from Ex. 1c in the Active grammar box.

---

### Active grammar

**＋**   Be quiet.
　　 _____ at page 45.

**－**   Don't _____ in.
　　 Don't _____ down.

Use *please* to make an imperative polite. **Please** be quiet. **Please** don't look at my emails.

---

*see Reference page 77*

**3**   Put a word/phrase from each box into the correct gap.

> Turn off   ~~Don't be~~   Speak   Use

**Our English class**

(1) *Don't be* late.

(2) _____ English in class.

(3) _____ your mobile phone.

(4) _____ a good dictionary.

> don't get up   eat   don't eat   don't watch

Hi David

Please (5) _____ late and (6) _____ TV all day. And please (7) _____ a sandwich or salad for lunch. (8) _____ chocolate!

Thanks!

Mum

**4** `7.4` Work in pairs. Listen. Match an announcement/imperative to a place a–e below.

a hospital  b shop  c airport  d restaurant
e school

**5** Write imperatives for **a)** How to learn English and **b)** How to succeed at work.

Learn English

1 *Speak English every day.*

## Speaking

**6 a** Read the How to … box.

HOW TO …

> **make a business phone call**
> B: *Hello. Parkside School.*
> A: ***Can I speak to** Mrs Fisher, please?*
> B: **Hold the line, please.**
> C: *Hello. Alice Fisher.*
> A: *Hello, Mrs Fisher.* **My name's** *Jake Parker./* **It's** *Jake.*
>
> Use *My name's* for people you don't know.
> Use *It's* for people you know.

**b** Work in groups of three. Practise phone calls. Use the names below.

1 Company = JK Designs
   A = Paul Walker    B = PA
   C = John Keen

2 Company = Bodgit Builders
   A = Angelo Romano    B = PA
   C = Sally Wood

3 Company = Renzo Rogers Architects
   A = Helen Davis    B = PA
   C = Eduardo Medina

---

### Lifelong learning

**Try your English in the real world**

Sometimes it's a good idea to try your English in the real world. For example, phone a hotel in the UK and ask for prices.

What other examples can you think of?

---

## Reading

**7** Read the text. Answer the questions.

1 What time does Tim start work?
2 What does Tim do between 8 a.m. and 9 a.m.?
3 Where does Tim have lunch?
4 What does Tim do between 3.30 p.m. and 6 p.m.?
5 What time does Tim finish work?
6 When does Tim have a long holiday?

### Tim Clarke – a teacher in the UK

I get up at quarter to seven in the morning. I have a shower, I have breakfast and I go to school. I start work at eight o'clock. I look at students' books and prepare lessons. I teach from nine o'clock to half past twelve. I have lunch in my classroom – a sandwich or a salad.

In the afternoon I teach from half past one to half past three. After school, I teach football or I work in my classroom. I go home at six o'clock and I have dinner. After dinner, I look at students' books and prepare lessons. I finish work at half past nine in the evening. Teachers work a lot but we have a long holiday in July* and August.

* for help with months look at Ex. 8a

## Vocabulary | months

**8 a** `7.5` Read the months and listen. Mark the stress.

| January | February | March | April |
| May | June | July | August |
| September | October | November | December |

**b** Listen again and repeat.

**c** Look at the calendar pictures of the UK on page 111. Guess the month.

**d** Work in pairs. Complete the sentences with months. Explain your reasons.

1 My favourite month is …
2 I don't like …

*My favourite month is June. It's not cold and it's not very hot.*

## Vocabulary | work phrases

**1**　**a**　What jobs can you remember? Write a list.

**b**　Look at these work phrases. Match each phrase to a picture 1–10.

> have meetings　work outdoors
> travel abroad　work from home
> call customers　give presentations
> take work home　help people
> answer the phone　write reports

**c**　Think of one job for each work phrase.

*work from home – artist*

## Listening

**2**　**a**　**7.6** Listen to the *What's your job?* game. Tick yes (Y) or no (N) in the table below.

| WHAT'S YOUR JOB? | Yes | No |
| --- | --- | --- |
| work from home | —— | ✓ |
| have meetings | —— | —— |
| give presentations | —— | —— |
| call customers | —— | —— |
| write reports | —— | —— |
| take work home | —— | —— |
| travel abroad | —— | —— |
| answer the phone | —— | —— |
| work outdoors | —— | —— |
| help people | —— | —— |

**b**　Listen again. Complete the conversation below with the words and phrases in the box.

> always　usually　often　sometimes
> not often　not usually　never

H:　OK, John. Are you ready?

J:　Yes, I'm *always* ready! I love this game.

H:　Good. Let's start. Do you work from home?

J:　No, I _____ work from home.

H:　Do you have meetings?

J:　Yes, but *not*_____ .

H:　Do you give presentations?

J:　Yes, I _____ give presentations.

H:　Do you call customers?

J:　No, _____ . I don't have customers.

H:　Do you write reports?

J:　Yes, I do. I _____ write three or four reports a week.

H:　Do you take work home?

J:　No, *not*_____ .

H:　Do you travel abroad?

J:　No, I _____ travel abroad.

H:　Do you answer the phone?

J:　Yes, I quite _____ answer the phone.

H:　Do you work outside?

J:　Yes, very _____ .

H:　Do you help people?

J:　Yes, I _____ help people.

H:　Are you a teacher?

J:　No, I'm not.

H:　Oh!! What is he?

## Grammar | adverbs of frequency

**3** Look at the conversation in Ex. 2b again. Complete the Active grammar box.

> **Active grammar**
>
> 100% ↖ always
>   usually
>    often
>     sometimes
>      not often/not usually
> 0% ↘ never
>
> 1) verb *to be* + **adverb of frequency**
>    I'_ _____ ready! I love this game.
> 2) **adverb of frequency** + verb
>    I _____ _____ three or four reports a week.
>    I *don't usually* take work home.

*see Reference page 77*

**4** **a** Correct the mistakes.

1 I work never from home.
  *I never work from home.*
2 She often doesn't travel abroad.
3 I take usually work home.
4 Always we call customers.
5 We write sometimes reports in the evening.
6 Never he works outdoors.
7 I don't give often presentations.
8 Always they call their customers.

**b** Write sentences about your daily routines. Use a phrase from the box and an adverb of frequency.

> get up   go to bed   start work   finish work
> watch TV   have a shower
> have (something for) breakfast/lunch/dinner

*I usually get up at seven o' clock.*

## Pronunciation

**5** **a** **7·7** Listen. Write the sentences.

**b** Listen again. Repeat the sentences.

## Speaking

**6** Work in pairs.
Student A: choose a job.
Student B: ask questions. Guess Student A's job.

## Writing

**7** **a** Read the notes 1–3 below. Match each one to a picture a–c.

**1**
Hi Uma
Can you answer my phone this afternoon? I have a meeting at two o'clock. Thanks,
Guy

**2**
Warren
I'm at home today. Can you call me? I have some questions for you.
Many thanks,
Piotr

**3**
Hello Livvy
Can you come to my office at 3 o'clock?
Thanks,
Ivan

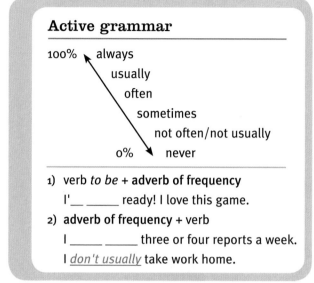

a   b   c

**b** Read the How to ... box. Then look at the list below and write a request note to Benita.

> **HOW TO …**
>
> **write a request note**
> Start:   Hello/Hi, Jay.
> Request: Can you + request?
> Finish:  Thanks,/Many thanks, + your name.

> **To do**
>
> ~~call Mrs. Santiago~~
> ~~write report on visit to China~~
> email to Benita — come to my office at 7 o'clock tomorrow morning?

# 7.3 Would you like a coffee?

Grammar *would like*

Can do welcome a visitor to your place of work

June
mon tues wed thur fri sat sun
1 2 3 4 5
6 7 8 9 10 11 12
13 14 15 16 17 18 19
20 21 22 23 24 25 26
27 28 29 30


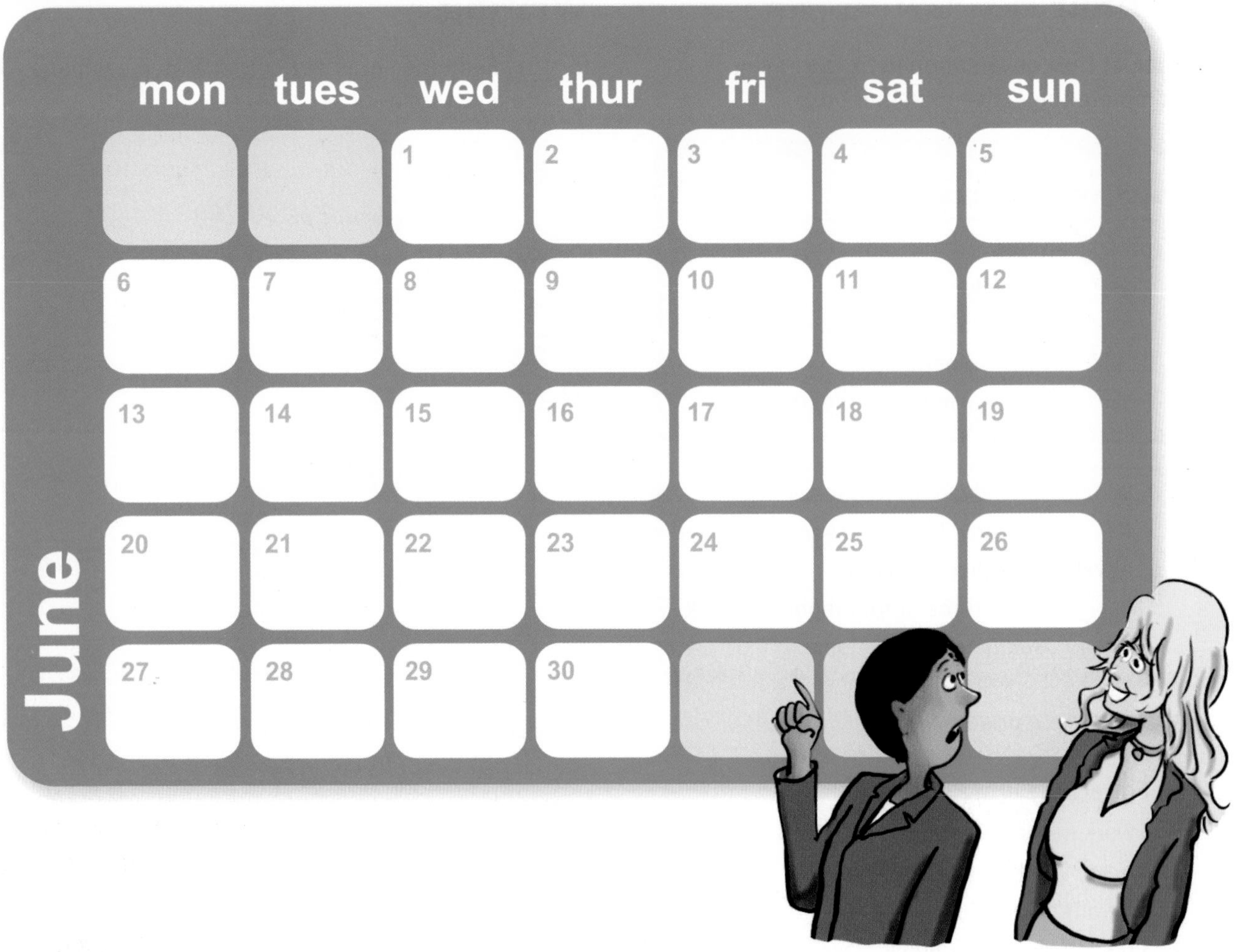

## Listening

**1** **a** Work in pairs. Remember the months of the year.

**b** 7.8 Listen and write on the calendar:
1) today
2) Mr. Wu's visit
3) Mrs King's visit
4) Miss Brown's visit
5) Mr Rogers' visit

**2** Michelle welcomes Mr Rogers and his colleague to the office. Work in groups of three. Act out the conversation..

**Michelle:** *Hello, Mr Rogers. My name's ...*

## Vocabulary | ordinal numbers

**3** **a** 7.9 Look at the calendar again. Listen and repeat the ordinal numbers.

**b** Work in pairs. Look at the ordinal numbers chart on page 77. Say the ordinal numbers.

**4** Read the How to ... box.

HOW TO ...

### write and say dates

Write *-th* after the number (but remember 1st, 2nd and 3rd!).

| Write | Say |
|---|---|
| 1st September | the first of September |
| 2nd July | the second of July |
| 3rd April | the third of April |
| 15th January | the fifteenth of January |

*see Reference page 77*

**5** **a** Write a date in numbers. Your partner says the date.

*20/09*

*the twentieth of September*

**b** Ask and answer.

A: *When is your birthday?*

B: *It's on ...*

## Grammar | *would like*

**6** **a** `7.10` Read and listen to the conversation. Complete the gaps.

**Michelle:** Please, come in. Sit down. What would you like (1) *to* drink? Tea? Coffee?

**Mr Rogers:** I'd like a coffee, please.

**Ms Khan:** I'd (2) _____ a cup of tea, please.

**Michelle:** Would you like milk and sugar?

**Mr Rogers:** No, thank you.

**Ms Khan:** Milk, no sugar, please.

**Michelle:** (3) _____ you like a biscuit?

**Mr Rogers:** Yes, please.

**Ms Khan:** No, (4) _____ you.

**b** Listen again and check.

**c** Read the conversation aloud in groups of three.

**7** Complete the Active grammar box with *would* or *'d*.

### Active grammar

*would like* + noun

**?** : What would you like (to drink/to eat)?
_____ you like a coffee/a biscuit?
Yes, please.        No, thank you.

| **+** : I _____ like ('d = would) | a cup of tea. an orange juice. |
|---|---|

*Would you like ...?* and *I'd like ...* are polite.
*Do you want ...?* and *I want ...* are informal.

*see Reference page 77*

**8** Complete the conversations with phrases from the Active grammar box.

1 **A:** *What would you like* to drink?
  **B:** _____ a coffee, please.
2 **A:** _____ a cup of tea?
  **B:** _____ (Yes)
3 **A:** _____ to eat?
  **B:** _____ a sandwich, please.
4 **A:** _____ biscuit?
  **B:** _____ (No)
5 **A:** _____ a coffee?
  **B:** _____ (No)
6 **A:** _____ to drink?
  **B:** _._____ an orange juice, please.

## Listening and vocabulary

**9** **a** Match the words below to the pictures.

> soup   fruit   vegetables   main courses
> desserts   starters   salad   drinks   snacks

**b** `7.11` Listen to Michelle, Mr Rogers and Ms Khan. Complete a–d on the map of the staff canteen.

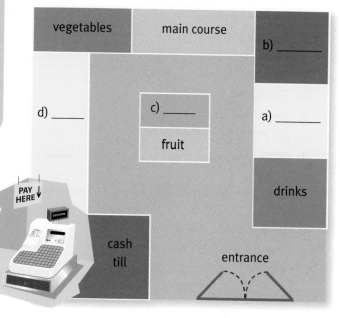

## Speaking

**10** Work in pairs.

**Student A:** you are a visitor.

**Student B:** welcome Student A to your office. Offer drinks/snacks.

**A:** *Hello Mrs Capriati. My name is Uri Osman.*

**B:** *Nice to meet you, Mr Osman.*

**A:** *Please, come in.*

## Take the lift to the third floor

|  | |
|---|---|
| **5th Floor** | PAs |
| **4th Floor** | Managers |
| **3rd Floor** | Sales reps |
| **2nd Floor** | Accountants |
| **1st Floor** | Canteen |
| **Ground Floor** | Reception |

### 3rd Floor

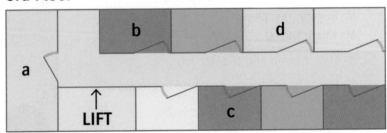

1   Work in pairs. Talk about the different floors of the building.

A: *What floor are the sales reps on?*

B: *They're on the third floor.*

2   **a**   Who says the phrases below, the receptionist (r) or the visitor (v)?

1   I'm here to see …

2   How do you spell that?

3   What's your name, please?

4   Take the lift to the third floor.

5   Thank you.

6   You're welcome.

7   Do you have an appointment?

**b**   **7.12**   Listen and check your answers. What do *left* and *right* mean?

3   Listen again. Match the places 1–4 below to the letters a–d on the floor plan.

1   Patrick Swinton's office

2   Martina Hafner's office

3   toilet

4   Lorda Romero's office

4   **a**   Work in pairs.

**Student A:** you are the receptionist. Think of the name of someone who works in the building. Write it on the floor plan. Tell your partner the name.

**Student B:** you are a visitor. Listen to the name Student A tells you. You have a meeting with this person. Act out the conversation.

A: *Good morning.*

B: *Good morning. I have a meeting with …*

**b**   Find a new partner and repeat.

## Imperatives

### Affirmative imperatives

| | |
|---|---|
| | *sit down.* |
| | *hold the line.* |
| | *be quiet.* |
| (Please) | *turn off your mobile phone.* |
| | *listen to the conversation.* |
| | *look at page 32.* |
| | *come in.* |

### Negative imperatives

| | |
|---|---|
| | *don't sit down.* |
| (Please) | *don't turn off your mobile phone.* |
| | *don't look at page 32.* |
| | *don't come in.* |

Use *Please* to make the imperative more polite.

## Adverbs of frequency

100% always
usually
often
sometimes
not often/not usually
0% never

Adverbs of frequency come **after** the verb *to be*.

*She's <u>always</u> late.*

*They're <u>never</u> happy.*

*I'm <u>sometimes</u> at work at half past six.*

Adverbs of frequency come **before** other verbs.

*I <u>never</u> answer the phone.*

*He <u>doesn't often</u> give presentations.*

*We <u>don't usually</u> eat desserts.*

You can also use *every + day/week*

*I see him every day.*

*We go to London every year.*

## Would you like ...? I'd like ...

Use *would like* to offer food/drink to guests.

*What would you like?*

*What would you like to drink?*

*Would you like a coffee? Yes, please./No, thank you.*

Use *I'd like ...* to say what you want.

*I'd like a cup of tea, please.*

*I'd like a starter, please.*

## Ordinal numbers

| Add -*th* to make ordinal numbers. Green=irregular | | |
|---|---|---|
| 1st first | 11 eleventh | 21 twenty-first |
| 2nd second | 12 twelfth | 22 twenty-second |
| 3rd third | 13 thirteenth | 23 twenty-third |
| 4th fourth | 14 fourteenth | 24 twenty-fourth |
| 5th fifth | 15 fifteenth | 25 twenty-fifth |
| 6th sixth | 16 sixteenth | 26 twenty-sixth |
| 7th seventh | 17 seventeenth | 27 twenty-seventh |
| 8th eighth | 8 eighteenth | 28 twenty-eighth |
| 9th ninth | 19 nineteenth | 29 twenty-ninth |
| 10th tenth | 20 twentieth | 30 thirtieth |

## Dates

### Writing dates

*My holiday is from 21st August to 5th September.*

### Saying dates

*'My holiday is from the twenty-first of August to ...'*

**Note:** Americans put the month before the day when they write and say dates.

**Written:** *the meeting is on July 12th*

**Spoken:** *the meeting is on July the 12th*

---

**Key vocabulary**

**Work places**
office   factory   shop   hospital   university
school   restaurant   call centre

**Months**
January   February   March   April   May   June
July   August   September   October
November   December

**Work phrases**
work from home   have meetings
give presentations   work outdoors
call customers   write reports   take work home
travel abroad   answer the phone

**Food**
snacks   drinks   starters   soup   vegetables
main courses   salad   desserts   fruit

**1 Put the words into the correct order to make imperatives.**

1 down Please sit
   _Please sit down._

2 your phone mobile Turn off
   _____ .

3 late don't Please be
   _____ .

4 the Hold please line,
   _____ .

5 at look 50 page Please
   _____ .

6 up late get Don't
   _____ .

**2 Underline the correct word.**

1 I *never/always/often* travel abroad – I don't like it.

2 They don't *sometimes/often/never* give presentations.

3 I *sometimes/never/usually* get up late. I get up at 6 o'clock every day.

4 He *never/doesn't usually/often* takes work home. He's a manager and he has a lot of work.

5 Rebecca is a cook. She *always/doesn't often/usually* cook Chinese food. She doesn't like it.

6 Tom and Kevin are good sales reps. They *always/never/sometimes* listen to their customers.

**3 Put the word in bold in the correct place.**

1 Francis works from home. **always**
   _Francis always works from home._

2 I have meetings on Mondays.
   **often** _____

3 She doesn't watch TV in the evening. **usually**
   _____

4 He is late for work. **never**
   _____

5 She sings in the shower. **sometimes**
   _____

6 You aren't at home in the evenings. **usually**
   _____

7 Sales reps don't work from home. **often**
   _____

8 Her boyfriends are rich. **always**

**4 Match a question 1–5 to a reply a–e.**

1 What would you like to eat?
2 What would you like to drink?
3 Would you like a coffee?
4 Would you like some biscuits?
5 Would you like milk and sugar?

a I'd like a mineral water, please.
b No, thank you. I don't like them.
c I'd like a chicken salad, please.
d Milk, no sugar, please.
e Yes, please.

**5 Add one word to each line of the dialogue.**

1 **A:** Hello, Mr Burns. Come in. Please sit. ⋏ *down*
2 **B:** Thank you, Mr Simpson. This Mr Smith.
3 **A:** Hello, Mr Smith. Nice meet you.
4 **C:** Nice to meet, too.
5 **A:** Would you like coffee?
6 **B:** Yes, please. Black, sugar, please.
7 **C:** No, thank.
8 **A:** What would you to eat?
9 **B:** I'd like a piece chocolate cake, please.
10 **C:** I'd some fruit, please.

**6 Complete each phrase or list with another word.**

1 March, April, _May_
2 starter, main course, _____
3 take work _____
4 a sales _____
5 June, July, _____
6 answer the _____
7 a call centre _____
8 September, October, _____
9 work from _____
10 a factory _____
11 fifth, sixth, _____
12 nineteenth, twentieth, _____

A

# 8 Leisure

B

C

D

## Lead-in

1  **a** Match an activity in the box to a picture below.

> go cycling   eat out   play chess   play tennis   go sightseeing
> go for a walk   read a book   play football   ~~go to the theatre~~
> do exercise   go swimming   watch TV

1  *go to the theatre*   5 _____   9 _____

2 _____   6 _____   10 _____

3 _____   7 _____   11 _____

4 _____   8 _____   12 _____

**b** 8.1 Listen and check. Repeat.

**c** Which activities can you see in the photos?

2  Work in pairs. Say an activity from Ex. 1a without the verb. Your partner says the verb.

**A:** *swimming*   **B:** *go swimming*

3  **a** How often do you do these leisure activities? Tell your partner.

*I usually watch TV in the evening.   I never go to the theatre.*

**b** Find a new partner. Tell him/her about your old partner.

*He always goes swimming on Saturdays.*

79

## Speaking

1  **a**  Look at the hotels below. Say the phone numbers and email addresses.

**b**  What can you see in the photos?

**c**  Read the How to ... box. What leisure activities can you do at each hotel?

HOW TO ...

### talk about things to do
Use *You can ...* or *We can ...* to talk about things to do in a place (e.g. hotel/city/country).

*You can play golf at the Langstone Hotel.*

*We can go sightseeing in Paris.*

2  Do you know any good hotels? What can you do there?

*I like The Palace Hotel in Vienna. You can swim. You can play tennis.*

## Listening

3  **a**  `8.2`  Listen. What is Gary and Annie's problem?

**b**  `8.3`  Listen. Complete the sentences.

1  Gary wants to go to the _____ Hotel.

2  Annie wants to go to the _____ Hotel.

3  They both want to go to the _____ Hotel.

**c**  Listen again. Make a list of the leisure activities that you hear.

*play golf*

## New Metro Hotel

Tel: 0991 722 3781

newmetrohotel@metromail.com

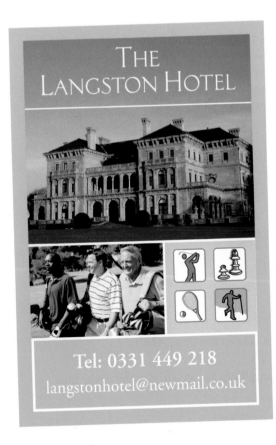

### THE LANGSTON HOTEL

Tel: 0331 449 218

langstonhotel@newmail.co.uk

### Blue Sea Hotel

TEL: 0649 559 221

blueseahotel@netmail.co.uk

## Grammar | *like + -ing; want + infinitive*

**4** Complete the Active grammar box with *want* or *like*. Check tapescript 8.3 on page 149 for help.

---

### Active grammar

➕ I _____ to go sightseeing.
➖ I don't _want_ to play golf.

➕ I _____ playing golf.
➖ I don't _____ going sightseeing.

---

*see Reference page 87*

**5** **a** Choose the correct form of the verb to complete the sentences.

1 I like (going out)/to go out with friends.
2 Gary doesn't like (watching)/to watch TV.
3 Do you want *playing/to play* tennis?
4 We like *going/to go* sightseeing.
5 She doesn't want e*ating out/to eat out*.
6 Do they like *playing/to play* chess?
7 I don't like *swimming/to go swimming*.
8 Martin wants *reading/to read* now.

**b** Complete the conversations. Put the verb in brackets into the correct form.

A: Can you swim?
B: Yes, I can, but I don't like (1) *swimming* (swim). I like football.
A: Football? Can you play football?
B: No, but I like (2) _____ (watch) it on TV.

C: Do you want (3) _____ (play) golf?
D: No, thanks. I don't like (4) _____ (play) golf. I like (5) _____ (go) for a walk.

E: Where do you want (6) _____ (go)?
F: To the beach. I want (7) _____ (go) swimming. Where's your bicycle?
E: It's at home. But I don't want (8) _____ (go) swimming. I don't like (9) _____ (go) swimming. I want (10) _____ (go) for a walk.

**6** Work in pairs. Look at the leisure activities on page 79. Answer these questions.

1 What do you like doing?
2 What don't you like doing?
3 What do you want to do this evening?
4 What do you want to do this Saturday and Sunday?

## Vocabulary | adjectives

**7** **a** Match a word in the box to a situation below.

> boring ~~exciting~~ difficult interesting fun easy

1 This is really *exciting*.    2 This is very _____ .

3 This is _____ .    4 This is _____ .

5 This is very _____ .    6 This is really _____ .

**b** What do you think of the leisure activities on page 79? Tell your partner.

*I think playing chess is difficult.*

## Speaking

**8** Choose a hotel from Ex. 1 for next weekend. Find other students to go with you.

A: *I want to go to the New Metro Hotel. I like going sightseeing. It's exciting.*
B: *I don't like going sightseeing. It's boring. I want to go to the Blue Sea Hotel …*

## Writing

**9** **a** Look at the Writing bank on page 129.

**b** Write an email to one of the hotels in Ex. 1. Ask for more information.

*How much is a double room?*

*Is a double room available for Saturday 29th and Sunday 30th next month?*

## Vocabulary | rooms and furniture

**1 a** Look at the house. Where do you:

| **a** cook | **b** watch TV | **c** have a shower |
|---|---|---|
| **d** go to bed | **e** park your car | **f** play football |

*You cook in the kitchen.*

**b** Match the words below to the letters a–p in the picture.

> washing machine   basin   coffee table   sofa   bicycle   bed
> fridge   bath   armchair   lamp   cooker   wardrobe   toilet
> sink   car   mirror

**c** 8.4 Listen and check. Repeat.

**2 a** Make lists.

1 What can you find in a hotel room?
2 You buy a new house. What seven things do you buy first?

**b** Compare with your partner.

**c** Work in pairs. What things in your house do you like? What things don't you like?

*I like my bath. It's big.*

*I don't like my television. It's old.*

## Listening

**3 a** 8.5 Listen. Which things from Ex. 1b do you hear?

**b** Listen again. Answer the questions.

1 When is Paul's sister's wedding?
2 What does Paul's sister like doing?
3 What things from Ex. 1b has she got?
4 What things from Ex. 1b hasn't she got?

**c** Look at Jo's suggestion for a wedding present on page 112. Do you think it's a good idea?

**d** What is a good wedding present in your country?

## Grammar | *have got/has got*

**4**   **a**   Look at tapescript 8.5 on page 149. <u>Underline</u> examples of *have got* and *has got*.

   **b**   Complete the Active grammar box with *have* or *has*.

> ### Active grammar
>
> | ⊕ I | | |
> |---|---|---|
> | ⊖ You We They | _____ got ('ve got) haven't got | a bicycle. a sofa. a garden. a garage. |
> | ⊕ He ⊖ She It | _____ got ('s got) hasn't got | |
> | ❓ *Have* | I/you/we/they got | a bicycle? an armchair? |
> | ❓ _____ | he/she/it got | |
>
> Yes, I/you/we/they _____ . Yes, he/she/it _____ .
> No, I/you/we/they ___n't. No, he/she/it ___n't.

*see Reference page 87*

**5**   **a**   Ask your partner questions with the words in Ex. 1b.

   **A:** *Have you got an armchair?*

   **B:** *Yes, I have. I've got two armchairs in my living room and I've got one armchair in my bedroom.*

   **b**   Complete the texts with *'ve*, *'s*, *haven't* or *hasn't*.

I live with my wife in a small house. We (1) **_'ve_** got a bedroom, a living room, a kitchen and a bathroom. We (2) _____ got a small garden – it's beautiful. But we (3) _____ got a garage.
My wife (4) _____ got a car. She drives to work every day. I (5) _____ got a car. I can't drive. But I (6) _____ got a bicycle.

I live in my sister's house. She (7) _____ got four bedrooms and two living rooms. She (8) _____ got a TV in her bedroom. She watches TV in bed. But she (9) _____ got a TV in the living room. She (10) _____ got a sofa and a big armchair in the living room.
She (11) _____ got a big cooker in the kitchen – it's great. We like cooking. She (12) _____ got a microwave oven. She doesn't like them.

## Pronunciation

**6**   **a**   [8.6] Listen and check your answers.

   **b**   How do you pronounce *I've*, *we've* and *she's*?

   **c**   Read the texts in Ex. 5b aloud.

## Speaking

**7**   Find a new partner. Talk about your house, flat or bedroom.

   *My family has got a house. It's quite big. I've got a small bedroom. I've got a TV and a computer in my bedroom but I haven't got ...*

## Reading

**8**   Do the *Technology* quiz on page 113. Ask your partner the questions and write his/her answers in your notebook.

   **A:** *Have you got a camera-phone?*

   **B:** *No, I haven't, but I want one.*

**9**   **a**   What is your score and what is your partner's score?

   **A** = 2 points   **B** = 1 point   **C** = 0 points

   **b**   Read your profile below.

> **0–6 points:** you don't like new technology, you like old things. Your photographs are on paper, not on your computer. You've haven't got any DVDs or MP3s (but you've got some CDs). You use a map – you don't use a GPS device. Your television is quite old.

> **7–12 points:** you like new technology and you sometimes buy new things. You've got some DVDs and you've got some MP3s. You sometimes read about new technology in newspapers and magazines. You take a digital camera on holiday.

> **13–18 points:** you really like new technology. You've got a digital camera and you've got a lot of photos and MP3s on your computer. You've got a modern mobile phone. You often read about new technology in newspapers and magazines. You take a digital camera, an MP3 player and a camcorder on holiday.

   **c**   Work in pairs. Is your profile true for you and your partner?

   **d**   Write a true profile for you.

| Grammar | question words |
|---|---|
| Can do | suggest a restaurant; book a restaurant; order food in a restaurant |

El Bulli

The Fat Duck

The Fat Duck
heston blumenthal

French Laundry

## Reading

1  Work in pairs. Discuss.

1  Do you eat out a lot?

2  What is your favourite restaurant?

2  a  Work in groups of three. Read about the top three restaurants in the world.

**Student A:** Read about *The Fat Duck* on page 111.
**Student B:** Read about *El Bulli* on page 113.
**Student C:** Read about *French Laundry* on page 110.

b  Tell your partners about your restaurant.

c  Discuss. Which restaurant in the article do you want to go to?

## Listening

3  a  **8.7**  Listen to Mark and Alda. Which restaurant do they want to go to?

a  *Sinatra's*   b  *Wasabi*   c  *Carlitto's*

b  Listen again. Put the questions in the order you hear them.

| | |
|---|---|
| Where's that? | ☐ |
| What food do they serve at *Wasabi*? | ☐ |
| How about dinner next Friday? | ☐ 1 |
| How big is it? | ☐ |
| What about *Carlitto's*? | ☐ |
| Which restaurant do you want to go to? | ☐ |

4  a  Read the How to ... box.

**HOW TO ...**

### make suggestions

*What about dinnner next week?*

*How about Luciano's Restaurant?*
_____
*Good idea!/Yes/OK.*

*No. I don't like that restaurant.*

b  Work in pairs. Suggest a local restaurant to go to this evening.

## Grammar | question words

5  Match the questions in the Active grammar box to the answers below.

### Active grammar

| Where | 1 Where is *Carlitto's*? |
|---|---|
| Who | 2 Who is Gordon? |
| What | 3 What does she do? |
| What + noun | 4 What food does he like? |
| Which + noun | 5 Which restaurant do you like – the new one or the old one? |
| How + adjective | 6 How tall is he? |

a) He likes Spanish food.   b) It's near my house.
c) She's a chef.   d) He's one metre ninety.
e) I like *Taste of India*.   f) He's my friend.

*see Reference page 87*

6  Complete the sentences with a question word from the Active grammar box.

1  *How* rich is she?

2  _____ café do you want to go to?

3  _____ fruit do you like?

4  _____ do you live?

5  _____ is the waiter?

6  _____ 's your name?

7  _____ good-looking is he?

8  _____ sofa do you like – this one or that one?

7  Ask your partner questions.

A: *How tall are you?*

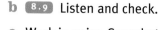

# Listening

**8** **a** [8.8] Listen. Alda books a table at Carlitto's restaurant. What time is her booking?

**b** Listen again. Complete the How to ... box.

## book a table at a restaurant

| | |
|---|---|
| Customer: | I'd ___ to book a table for Friday lunch/Saturday evening. |
| Waiter: | ___ many people? |
| Waiter: | ___ time? |
| Waiter: | ___ name, please? |

**c** Work in pairs.

**Student A:** phone *Carlitto's* restaurant. Book a table for Saturday evening.

**Student B:** you work at *Carlitto's* restaurant. Answer the phone.

## Vocabulary | food

**9** **a** Match the underlined words in the menu to the pictures.

*Menu*
— CARLITTO'S —

**STARTERS**

<u>Seafood</u> cocktail
<u>Fish</u> soup
Green salad

**MAIN COURSES**

Roast <u>beef</u> *
Roast <u>chicken</u>*
<u>Lamb</u> chops *
Vegetable <u>pasta</u>
* with <u>potatoes</u> or <u>rice</u>

**DESSERTS**

Ice cream
<u>Chocolate</u> cake
<u>Cheese</u> and biscuits

1
2
3
4
5
6
7

8
9
10

**b** [8.9] Listen and check.

**c** Work in pairs. Say what food you like/don't like from the menu.

**d** Choose your favourite starter, main course and dessert from the menu. Tell the class.

*My favourite starter is fish soup, I like lamb chops for the main course and ice cream for dessert.*

**10** **a** [8.10] Listen. What do Mark and Alda choose from the menu?

**b** Work in groups of three. Look at tapescript 8.10 on page 150. Read the conversation aloud but change the food.

**Waiter:** *Are you ready to order?*

**Mark:** *Yes. I'd like a green salad, please.*

# Speaking

**11** Work in groups of three.

**Student A:** you are the waiter at *Salt and Pepper* restaurant.

**Students B and C:** you are customers at *Salt and Pepper* restaurant. Look at the menu on page 114. Enter the restaurant and order your meal.

**A:** *Good evening. Do you have a reservation?*

**B:** *Yes, we do. My name is ...*

**1 a** Work in pairs. Look at the people and their flats. What have they got in their flats?

*14a: He's got a lot of books in his flat.*

**b** What does each person like doing? Tell your partner.

*16c: He likes playing golf.*

**2** Work in pairs.

**Student A:** look at page 111. Complete four of the addresses below. Don't show your partner.

**Student B:** look at page 114. Complete four of the addresses below. Don't show your partner.

**3** Ask your partner questions to complete the other four addresses.

**Student A:** *Has Mr J. Coe got a lot of books in his flat?*

**Student B:** *No, he hasn't. Has Mrs A. Walker got ...*

**IMPORTANT!**

- Ask Yes/No questions. *Has X got ...? Does X like ...?*
- Ask one question. Then your partner asks one question. Then you ask another question, and so on.

Mr O. Pamuk
*16c Brooklyn Road*

Mrs A. Walker
_____

Mr G. Dyer
_____

Miss T. Morrison
_____

Mr J. Heller
_____

Miss Z. Smith
*16b Brooklyn Road*

Mr J. Coe
_____

Mr M. Haddon
_____

Mrs M. Atwood
_____

Mrs A. Levy
_____

## like + -ing; want + infinitive

When a verb follows *like*, it is usually in the gerund form (*-ing*).

*I like eating out.*

When a verb follows *want*, it is always in the infinitive form (*to* + verb).

*I want to eat out.*

## Have got

*Have got* means *have*.

*I've got a sports car.*

*I have a sports car.*

*Have got* is very common in British English. It is not common in American English.

| | | | |
|---|---|---|---|
| ⊕ ⊖ | *I*<br>*You*<br>*We*<br>*They* | *have got ('ve got)*<br>*haven't got* | *a CD player.*<br>*a television.*<br>*a brother.*<br>*two sisters.* |
| ⊕ ⊖ | *He*<br>*She*<br>*It* | *has got ('s got)*<br>*hasn't got* | |
| ? | *Have* | *I/you/we/they* | *got* | *any cousins?* |
| ? | *Has* | *he/she/it* | | *a cat?* |

*Yes, I/you/we/they have.*
*Yes, he/she/it has.*
*No, I/you/we/they haven't.*
*No, he/she/it hasn't.*

## Question words

- Use *where* for places.

*Where are you from?*

*Where do you live?*

- Use *who* for people.

*Who are you?*

*Who do you play tennis with?*

You can also use *who* to ask about the company someone works for.

*Who do you work for?*

- Use *what* for things.

*What's your name?*

*What do you do?*

You can put a noun directly after *what*.

*What time do you get up?*

*What music do you like?*

- Use *which* for things. When there is a choice.

*Which dictionary have you got?*

*Which John Lennon song is your favourite?*

- Use *how* + adjective for amounts.

*How tall is he?*

*How old are you?*

- Note these questions:

*How much is it?* (price)

*How many cars have you got?* (quantity)

*How often do you go out?* (frequency)

## Making suggestions

Use *What about ...?* or *How about ...?* + noun to make suggestions.

*What about the new restaurant on Clerk Street?*

*How about a holiday in Cornwall this summer?*

You can also use *What about ...?* or *How about ...?* + *-ing*.

*What about going for a walk this afternoon?*

*How about eating out tonight?*

---

### Key vocabulary

**Leisure activities**

go cycling   go sightseeing   go swimming
go for a walk   do exercise   eat out
play tennis   read a book   play football
watch TV   play chess   go to the theatre

**Adjectives**

boring   exciting   difficult   easy   fun
interesting

**Rooms and furniture**

**living room:** coffee table   sofa   armchair
lamp

**bedroom:** bed   wardrobe   window

**kitchen:** cooker   sink   washing machine
fridge

**bathroom:** bath   toilet   basin

**garage:** car   bicycle

**Food**

seafood   fish   beef   lamb   pasta   rice
potatoes   chocolate   cheese   chicken

**1** Complete the conversation with the word in brackets.

**A:** Do you want (1) _to go_ (go) to a film this afternoon?

**B:** There's a good film on TV. Do you want (2) _____ (watch) TV?

**A:** No! I don't like (3) _____ (watch) TV in the afternoon.

**B:** OK. Well, I like (4) _____ (swim) and it's hot today. Do you want (5) _____ (go) swimming

**A:** I can't swim and I don't want (6) _____ (do) exercise. I want (7) _____ (go) sightseeing and then eat out this evening.

**B:** Good idea. I want (8) _____ (take) some photos with my new camera.

**2** Complete the email with the correct form of *have got*.

Hi Benita,

Thanks for your email. Please come to my house when you visit London. (1) _I've got_ (I/✓) three bedrooms so you can stay in one of them.
(2) _____ (it/✓) a big bed and an armchair.
(3) _____ (it/✗) a television but
(4) _____ (it/✓) an en-suite bathroom.
Can you drive? (5) _____ (I/✗) a car but
(6) _____ (my friends/✓) one
(7) _____ (you) a bicycle?
(8) _____ (My husband/✓) one and you can use it.

See you next week!

Love, Amy

**3** Write questions and answers using *have got* and the words in brackets.

1 **A:** _Has your sister got a washing machine?_ (your sister/washing machine)
  **B:** _Yes, she has._ (Yes)
2 **A:** _____ ? (you/car)
  **B:** _____ . (No)
3 **A:** _____ ? (your parents/TV)
  **B:** _____ . (No)
4 **A:** _____ ? (James/bath)
  **B:** _____ . (Yes)
5 **A:** _____ ? (they/new email address)
  **B:** _____ . (No)
6 **A:** _____ ? (she/good dictionary)
  **B:** _____ . (Yes)

**4** Correct the mistakes.

1 Which restaurant are you like?
2 Which do you do? Are you an accountant?
3 Where you do live?
4 How intelligent she is?
5 Which time is it?
6 Who do work for you?
7 There are two armchairs. What armchair do you like?
8 Where your brother is?

**5** Write a question for each answer.

1 _What do you do?_
  I'm a teacher.
2 _____ ?
  She's one metre fifty-five.
3 _____ ?
  I like Italian food and Chinese food.
4 _____ ?
  I like this coffee table. That coffee table is small.
5 _____ ?
  I live in Lisbon in Portugal.
6 _____ ?
  She's my friend.

**6** Complete the questions and sentences with a word or phrase from the box.

reads   fun   fridge   potatoes   ~~eat out~~
chocolate   garden   How   playing chess
boring

1 Do you want to _eat out_ tonight?
2 Do you like _____ with your friends?
3 She _____ a book every week.
4 I don't like this game. It's _____ .
5 I like holidays. They're always _____ .
6 Is there any food in the _____ ?
7 Do you play football in your _____ ?
8 _____ about that new restaurant on Carlin Street?
9 Do you want rice or _____ with your lamb chops?
10 Can I have a piece of _____ cake, please?

Sydney Harbour Bridge: Millennium Celebrations

# 9 The past

Wall Street Crash B

Fall of the Berlin Wall C

Mandela: New President of South Africa D

## Lead in

1   Look at the photos A–D. Match each one to a year below.

1989   1994   2000   1929

2   **a**   **9.1**   Look at the years in the box. Listen and repeat.

> 1963   1946   1981   1977   1957   1912   2002   1990

**b**   Match a year in the box to a headline a–h below.

a   Sputnik in Space
b   Charles and Di Royal Wedding
c   First iPod in Shops
d   Titanic Disaster
e   Nelson Mandela Free
f   Martin Luther King: 'I have a dream'
g   Juan Peron: President of Argentina
h   Elvis Presley is Dead

**c**   Work in pairs. Tell your partner what you think.

A:   *I think 'Sputnik in Space' is 1957.*
B:   *I think it's 1963.*

**d**   **9.2**   Listen and check.

3   Write headlines from your life. Your partner guesses the year.

**David:** David's First Day at University.
**Paola:** Is that 1995?
**David:** No, it's 1999.

Bruce Lee

| Grammar | past of *to be* affirmative |
| Can do | make simple statements about people from history |

Diana, Princess of Wales

Princess Grace

Elvis Presley

## Reading

1    **a**   Look at the <u>underlined</u> words in the texts.
Check their meanings in a dictionary.

     **b**   Read the texts. Match a text to a photo.

> **1**   He was a singer and an actor. He was born on 8th January, 1935, in Mississippi. His parents were very poor. He was a factory-worker, then a driver. His first song was *That's All Right*. He was 'The King of Rock and Roll'.
> Famous quote: 'When I was a child, ladies and gentlemen, I was a <u>dreamer</u>.'

> **2**   She was an actor and a princess. She was born on 12th November, 1929, in Philadelphia. Her parents were very rich. She was a <u>model</u> and then an actor. Her first film was *Fourteen Hours* in 1951. Her husband was Prince Rainier III of Monaco.
> Famous quote: (about flowers) 'I talk to them and they talk to me.'

> **3**   He was an actor and <u>fighter</u>. He was born on 27th November, 1940, in San Francisco. His parents were from Hong Kong. They weren't rich. His father was a singer. His last film was *Enter the Dragon*. He was short and thin but he was very strong and very fast.
> Famous quote: 'Don't think. Feel.'

> **4**   She was a princess and a fashion icon. She was born on 1st July, 1961, in Sandringham. Her parents were rich. She wasn't a good student at school but she was a good <u>pianist</u>. Her wedding was in St Pauls' Cathedral in London. Her husband was Prince Charles. Their life together was not happy.
> Famous quote: 'There were three of us in this marriage.'

**c**   Complete the sentences with names from the photos.

1   *Diana* and *Grace* were princesses.
2   _____ , _____ and _____ were born in the US.
3   _____ , _____ and _____ were actors.
4   _____ and _____ were poor as children.
5   _____ and _____ were the wives/husbands of famous people.

**d**   Close your books. Work in pairs. What can you remember about the people in the texts?

*Bruce Lee was born in San Francisco. His parents were ...*

## Grammar | past of *to be*: affirmative

**2** **a** Complete the Active grammar box with *was* or *were*.

### Active grammar

| I | *was* | an actor. |
|---|---|---|
| You | *were* | a singer. |
| He<br>She<br>It | _____<br>_____<br>_____ | happy.<br>born in 1982.<br>great. |
| We<br>They | *were*<br>_____ | singers.<br>rich. |

**b** `9.3` Listen and check.

*see Reference page 97*

**3** **a** Complete the sentences with *was* or *were*.

1 Coco Chanel *was* a fashion designer.
2 My husband and I _____ call centre workers from 2001 to 2004.
3 Colonel Tom Parker _____ Elvis Presley's manager.
4 Jackie Chan and Oprah Winfrey _____ born in 1954.
5 Prince William and I _____ born in 1982.
6 We _____ good football players in 1990. I can't play football now.
7 I _____ a good pianist at school.

**b** Who is your favourite 20th-century icon? Tell your partner about the person.

**4** **a** Read the How to ... box.

<table>
<tr><td rowspan="5" style="writing-mode: vertical-rl">HOW TO ...</td></tr>
<tr><td>talk about childhood</td></tr>
<tr><td>When I was a child, I was a good singer.</td></tr>
<tr><td>When they were young, they were very poor.</td></tr>
</table>

**b** Write two true sentences and one false sentence about you and your family.

**c** Read your sentences to your partner. Your partner guesses true or false.

A: *When my father was young, he was an actor.*
B: *False.*
A: *No, it's true!*

## Listening and vocabulary

**5** **a** `9.4` Listen to the radio game show. Guess the person.

**b** Look at page 110. Check your answer.

**c** Listen again. Write true (T) or false (F).

1 He was born in 1950.
2 His parents were Julia and Alfred.
3 He was famous for his music.
4 He was from London.
5 He was married to Yoko Ono in his twenties.

**6** **a** Read the texts below. Check any new words in your dictionary. Then complete the texts with a preposition from the box.

> on   for   with   ~~in~~   to   of   to   at

She was born (1) *in* 1929 in New York. She was **good** (2) ____ horse-riding and painting. She was **married** (3) ____ John F. Kennedy, the **President** (4) ____ the US, and then to Aristotle Onassis, a Greek businessman.

Billie Holiday was **born** (5) ____ the 7th of April, 1915, in Philadelphia. She was **famous** (6) ____ her music. She was **friends** (7) ____ the jazz musician Lester Young. Her second husband was **similar** (8) ____ her first husband. They were bad men and Billie Holiday was unhappy.

**b** Say a word in **bold** from the texts. Your partner says the preposition.

A: *similar*       B: *similar to*

**7** **a** Think of a famous person from history. Write sentences about him/her.

**b** Read your sentences to your partner. Your partner guesses the person.

# 9.2 My first, my last ...

| Grammar | past of *to be*: negatives and questions |
|---------|-------------------------------------------|
| Can do  | give a short description of a past experience |

## Speaking

1 Talk about the games. Use the phrases below.

*I know how to play ...*

*I don't know how to play ...*

*It's difficult/easy/boring/ exciting/fun/ interesting.*

## Listening

2 **a** `9.5` Listen to Cristof, Isabella and Jasmine playing a game called *My first, my last*. In the game you can't answer questions with *yes* or *no*. What does Isabella talk about?

**b** Listen again. Circle the correct words for Cristof and Jasmine below.

### CRISTOF'S FIRST TEACHER

1 Her name was *Miss/Mrs Lloyd.*
2 She was about *fifty/sixty* years old.
3 She was a *good/bad* teacher.
4 Her favourite student was *Francoise/Cristof.*

### JASMINE'S LAST HOLIDAY

1 Jasmine's last holiday was *two/three* years ago.
2 It was on a *Greek/Spanish* island.
3 Jasmine was with her *parents/a friend.*
4 There were *castles/beautiful beaches* on the island.

## Grammar | past of *to be*: negatives and questions

3 Look at the dialogue from Ex 2 and complete the Active Grammar box with *was*, *wasn't*, or *were*.

Jasmine: <u>Was</u> she a good teacher?
Cristof:  She <u>was</u> a good teacher but I <u>wasn't</u> a good student.
Isabella: <u>Were</u> you her favourite student?

### Active grammar

| ➖ | | |
|---|---|---|
| I _____ (was not) | a good student. |
| You *weren't* | happy at school. |
| He/She/It _____ | my teacher. |
| We *weren't* | a good school. |
| They *weren't* | in my class. |

| ❓ | | |
|---|---|---|
| *Was* I | a good student? |
| _____ you | happy at school? |
| _____ he/she/it | my teacher? |
| *Were* we | a good school? |
| *Were* they | in my class? |

What was her name?
Where were your books?
Who was your favourite teacher?
When was your lesson?

*see Reference page 97*

**4  a** Complete the sentences with *was*, *wasn't*, *were* or *weren't*.

1  I *was* very quiet at school. (✓)

2  My first car _____ very big but it was fun. (✗)

3  Who _____ your friends at school?

4  What _____ your favourite subject at school?

5  My first computer games _____ easy but they were exciting. (✗)

6  You _____ my English teacher at school. (✗)

7  _____ you late this morning?

8  Where _____ your last house?

**b** Work in pairs. Ask and answer the questions in *My first teacher,* Ex. 2b.

## Pronunciation

**5  a** 〔9.6〕 Listen. Mark the stress.

1  I was a good student.

2  I wasn't very intelligent.

3  Was she a good teacher?

4  Who was your best friend?

**b** How is *was/wasn't* pronounced in each sentence?

**6  a** 〔9.7〕 Listen. Write the sentences. Mark the stress.

**b** How is *were/weren't* pronounced in each sentence?

**7** Work in pairs. Ask and answer the questions in *My last holiday,* Ex. 2b.

## Vocabulary | *yesterday, last, ago*

**8  a** Look at tapescript 9.5 on page 150. <u>Underline</u> the examples of *ago* and *last*.

**b** Complete the time expressions with *ago* or *last*.

1  today

2  yesterday

3  _____ night

4  yesterday morning/afternoon/evening

5  two days _____

6  _____ week

7  _____ month

8  six months _____

9  _____ year

10  ten years _____

## Speaking

**9  a** When were these past experiences? Tell your partner.

- Your first day at school
- Your last meal in a restaurant
- Your last film at the cinema
- Your last flight
- Your first job
- Your first email

*My first day at school was twenty-two years ago.*

**b** Ask your partner questions with *Where were you ...?* and a time expression.

A:  *Where were you yesterday afternoon?*

B:  *I was at home.*

**10  a** Work in groups of three. Remember the rules for *My first, my last.*

**b** Play *My first, my last* on page 115.

## Writing

**11** Write a paragraph about your first teacher or your last holiday. You can start like this:

*My first teacher was ... She/He was ...*

*My last holiday was (six months) ago ... It was ...*

## Vocabulary | housework

**1 a** Match a phrase in the box to a picture below.

> do the laundry
> vacuum the house
> cook dinner
> clean the bathroom
> wash the dishes
> iron a shirt

**b** ⟨9.8⟩ Listen and check. Mark the stress.

**2 a** Who does these things in your house? Tell your partner.

*My wife does the laundry.*

*I iron my shirts.*

**b** What housework do you like doing? What housework don't you like doing?

*I don't like cooking dinner.*

## Reading

**3 a** Look at the text. <u>Underline</u> phrases from Ex. 1a.

# Who does the housework now?

In the 1950s, life was simple. Women were housewives and men were factory workers, managers, sales reps, sales assistants, etc. But in the 21st century, life is different. Now, there are over 21,000 househusbands in the UK. They don't have a job, they stay at home and look after the children. Are they crazy? We talk to one househusband, Jeff Timberland.

**Do you like your job as a househusband?**
**Jeff:** Yes, I do. Plus, childcare is £125 for one week, for one child. It's very expensive*.

**What does your wife do?**
**Jeff:** She's an architect.

**Do you like doing housework?**
**Jeff:** I don't like ironing my shirts – it's very boring. And I don't like washing the dishes. But I like vacuuming the house and cooking dinner.

**Really?**
**Jeff:** Yes, really.

**What was your job before?**
**Jeff:** I was a sales rep. I was a good sales rep. and I was happy. But my children are my job now.

**Do you want to get another job?**
**Jeff:** Yes, but not now. Billy and Harry are very young. They want their dad, not a stranger.

\* expensive = costs a lot of money

**b** Read the text again. Answer the questions below.

1 How many househusbands are there in the UK now?
2 Does Jeff like his job as a househusband?
3 What is Jeff's wife's job?
4 What housework does Jeff like doing?
5 What was Jeff's job before?
6 Does Jeff want to get a new job now?

**c** Work in small groups. Discuss.

1 Are there a lot of househusbands in your country?
2 Who usually looks after young children in your country?
3 Jeff says, 'They want their dad, not a stranger'. Do you agree?

## Listening

**4** **a** `9.9` Listen to four events in Jeff's week. Match each conversation 1–4 to a picture a–d.

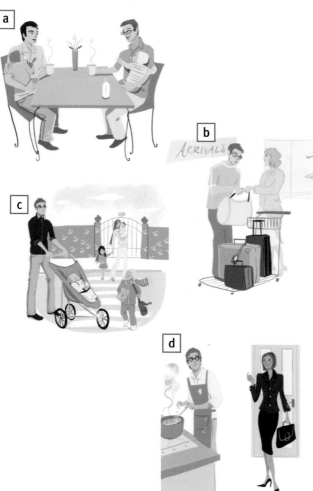

**b** Listen again. Who are the people in the pictures? Write the questions you hear beginning with *How ...?*

**5** **a** Read the How to ... box.

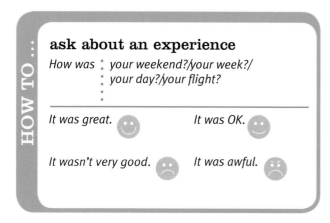

**HOW TO ...**

### ask about an experience

How was : your weekend?/your week?/
       : your day?/your flight?

It was great. 😊      It was OK. 🙂

It wasn't very good. 🙁      It was awful. ☹️

**b** Work in small groups. Ask questions with *How was ...?*

A: *How was your weekend?*

B: *It was fine, thanks. I was at home on Sunday ...*

## Grammar | Can/Could you ...?; Can/Could I ...?

**6** **a** Look at tapescript 9.9 on page 150. Complete these sentences.

**Aunt Sally:** Could you *carry* my suitcases?

**Billy:** Can I _____ chocolate for dinner?

**Karen:** Can I _____ on the TV?

**Friend:** Could you _____ the milk?

**b** Complete the Active grammar box with *I* or *you*.

### Active grammar

| Can Could | _____ | use your telephone? have a coffee? |
|---|---|---|
| Yes, ____ can. | | No, ____ can't. |
| Can Could | _____ | carry my bags? iron my shirt? |
| Yes, of course. | Sorry, *I* can't. | |

*see Reference page 97*

**7** Ask your partner questions.

- use your pen
- spell your name
- use your mobile phone
- give me your email address
- give me €1
- open the window
- look at your book

A: *Could I use your pen?*   B: *Yes, of course.*

## Speaking

**8** **a** Tick (✓) the things below you have got. Cross (✗) the things you haven't got.

a good dictionary     a camera
a washing machine     a car
an MP3 player     a computer

**b** Match a thing above to a phrase below.

listen to music     *MP3 player*
take a photo of me and my friends
drive me to the train station
read my emails at your house
do my laundry
help me with these new English words

**c** Find six people to help you with the requests in Ex. 8b. Use *Can I/you* or *Could I/you.*

A: *Can I read my emails at your house?*

B: *Sorry, you can't. I haven't got a computer.*

A: *Could you take a photo of me?*

B: *Yes, of course. I've got a digital camera.*

# 9 | Communication

## School days

**1 a** Match a subject in the box to a picture 1–6.

maths   languages   science   music   art   sport

 1
 2
3

4
5 $2(3x-11)=8$ $y=?$

6   Hello  Bonjour
      Hola  Guten Tag

**b** 〔9.10〕 Listen and repeat.

**c** Complete the sentences with a subject above.

1 When I was at school, I was good at ...
2 When I was at school, I was bad at ...

**2 a** 〔9.11〕 Listen and complete the chart for Louise.

### My school days

School name: *William Morris High School*

Where: _____

Years: _____

Good/bad school: _____

Good/bad student: _____

Good at: _____

Bad at: _____

Favourite lessons: _____

Best friend: _____

**b** Listen again. Check your answers.

---

### Lifelong learning

**Listening skills**

When you listen in English, don't try to understand every word. It's very stressful and it's usually not possible. Listen for important (stressed) words and try to guess when you don't understand.

**3 a** Complete the chart in Ex. 2a for you.

**b** Make sentences. Tell your partner.

A: *I was very good at maths.*
B: *Really? I wasn't. I was good at music.*

**4** Work in groups. Close your books and talk about your school days.

## The past of *to be*

| + | | |
|---|---|---|
| I | was | |
| You | were | a teacher. |
| He | | born in 1963. |
| She | was | very good. |
| It | | |
| We | were | teachers. |
| They | were | born in 1963. |

| – | | |
|---|---|---|
| I | wasn't (was not) | |
| You | weren't (were not) | a teacher. born in 1963. very good. |
| He | | |
| She | wasn't (was not) | |
| It | | |
| We | weren't (were not) | teachers. born in 1963. |
| They | weren't (were not) | |

| ? | | |
|---|---|---|
| Was | I | |
| Were | you | a teacher? |
| | he | born in 1963? |
| Was | she | very good? |
| | it | |
| Were | we | teachers? |
| Were | they | born in 1963? |

**?**
Who was your manager?
What were their jobs?
Where was your school?
Which shop was your favourite?
When was the interview?
How old were you in 1990?

## Asking permission

| Can I | call you this evening, please? |
|---|---|
| Could I | speak to Mrs Walsh, please? |
| | use your computer, please? |
| | ask a question, please? |
| | go home early, please? |

Yes, you can./Sure.
No, you can't./I'm sorry. You can't.

Use *Can I* and *Could I* to ask permission. *Can I* and *Could I* have the same meaning. *Could I* is a bit more polite/formal.

## Making requests

| Can you | call me this evening, please? |
|---|---|
| Could you | answer the phone, please? |

Yes, of course./Sure.
No, I can't./I can't, I'm afraid.

Use *Can you* and *Could you* to make a request. *Can you* and *Could you* have the same meaning but *Could you* is a bit more polite/formal.

## Time expressions

**Yesterday**
yesterday    yesterday evening    yesterday afternoon
yesterday morning

**Last**
last night    last week    last month    last year

**Ago**
five months ago    eight years ago    two days ago
a week ago

---

**Key vocabulary**

**Adjectives and prepositions**
born in (Paris)    born on (3rd October)
good at (tennis / dancing)    bad at (football)
married to (Prince Charles)
the President of (Russia)
similar to (my brother)    famous for (his books)
friends with (the king)

**Housework**
do the laundry    vacuum the house
cook dinner    clean the bathroom
wash the dishes    iron a shirt

**1** Complete the text with *was* or *were* and guess the famous person.

Who am I?

I am a singer with a very famous band. I (1) <u>was</u> born on 26th July, 1943, in the UK. My father and my grandfather (2) _____ teachers. My mother (3) _____ from Australia. I (4) _____ a student at the London School of Economics – but only for two years. Jerry Hall and Bianca Moreno de Macias (5) _____ my wives. *Paint it Black* and *Satisfaction* (6) _____ two of my band's famous songs.

**2** Write sentences with *wasn't/was* or *weren't/were*, as in the examples.

1  (Sally/late/early)
   *Sally wasn't late. She was early.*

2  (My parents/at home/in a restaurant)
   *My parents weren't at home. They were in a restaurant.*

3  (I/at the theatre/at the cinema)
   _____ .

4  (Ian/born in 1981/born in 1979)
   _____ .

5  (It/a good film/very boring)
   _____ .

6  (We/rich/quite poor)
   _____ .

7  (You/my best friend/a good friend)
   _____ .

8  (Kerry and Mark/in Bogota/in Cali)
   _____ .

**3** Complete the dialogue with *was, wasn't, were* or *weren't*.

A:  (1) <u>Were</u> you at work last week?
B:  No, I (2) _____ .
A:  (3) _____ you on holiday?
B:  Yes, I (4) _____ . I (5) _____ on holiday with Emily. We (6) _____ at her parent's house in the south of France.
A:  (7) _____ it nice?
B:  It (8) _____ beautiful! Her parents (9) _____ there so we (10) _____ alone.

**4** Rearrange the words to make questions. Then match them to an answer a–e.

1  born?  When  you  were
   <u>When were you born?</u> = c

2  was  Who  manager?  your
   _____ = __

3  school?  your  Where  was
   _____ = __

4  first  What  your  job?  was
   _____ = __

5  weekend?  your  was  How
   _____ = __

a  I was a call-centre worker.
b  It was great, thanks.
c  In 1966.
d  Her name was Ms Dickson.
e  It was on Peak Street, opposite the hospital.

**5** Choose the correct word in each sentence.

1  Can *I/you* tell me the time?
2  Could *I/you* open the door? I'm busy.
3  Can *I/you* help you?
4  Could *I/you* have a cup of tea, please?
5  Can *I/you* tell me your name, please?
6  Could *I/you* pass me the milk, please?
7  Can *I/you* give me £1 for the bus?
8  Could *I/you* listen to your new CD?

**6** Choose the correct word to complete each sentence.

1  Where were you *yesterday/last/ago* night?
2  Are you similar *to/at/on* your mother or your father?
3  Who *washes/cleans/does* the laundry in your house?
4  Is she married *with/to/of* your brother?
5  I was on holiday in Colombia six months *yesterday/last/ago*.
6  What was she famous *on/to/for*?
7  Where were you *yesterday/last/ago* afternoon?
8  Can you *wash/vacuum/iron* the house today?
9  He's friends *of/with/to* Mark Heller.
10 Are you good *on/to/at* tennis?

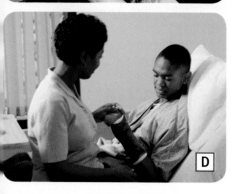

# 10 | Stories

## Lead-in

**1**  **a** Complete each situation with a verb from the box.

> win   arrests   get   meet   ~~lose~~   steals   find   break   stay   move

   1  You *lose* your wallet/purse.
   2  A thief _____ your mobile phone.
   3  You _____ in bed all day.
   4  You _____ the lottery.
   5  You _____ married.
   6  You _____ €10 on the street.
   7  A police officer _____ you.
   8  You _____ to a new house.
   9  You _____ your arm.
  10  You _____ your favourite actor.

  **b** `10.1` Listen and check.

  **c** Look at the pictures. Match a phrase to each picture.

**2**  **a** Are the experiences in Ex. 1a good or bad? Complete the table.

| GOOD EXPERIENCES | BAD EXPERIENCES |
|---|---|
|  | *You lose your wallet/purse.* |

  **b** Change the sentences in Ex. 1a. Tell your partner. Your partner responds with an adjective.

A: *You lose your camera.*     B: *That's bad.*
A: *You move to a new city.*     B: *That's exciting.*

### The Story of the *Mona Lisa* (PART 1)

Every day, 15,000 people visit the Louvre museum in Paris. Most of them want to see the *Mona Lisa*. But what is the story of this painting?

The artist was, of course, Leonardo da Vinci. He started the painting in 1503 and he finished it about four years later. Leonardo was Italian but in 1516, he moved to France with the painting. The King of France liked it and the *Mona Lisa* stayed in France.

## Speaking

1   Work in pairs. Look at the painting. Answer the questions.

1   Who is the artist?
2   Who are your favourite artists?
3   What are your favourite paintings?

## Reading

2   **a** Look at *The Story of the Mona Lisa (Part 1)*. Read the text aloud.

**b** Read again. Complete the information below.

Place (now): *The Louvre, Paris*
Artist: _____
Started painting: _____
Finished painting: _____
Moved to France: _____

## Grammar 1 | Past Simple affirmative: regular verbs

3   **a** Underline the verbs in *The Story of the Mona Lisa (Part 1)*.

**b** Which verbs are in the Past Simple?

**c** How do you make the Past Simple of regular verbs?

4   Complete the Active grammar box with the correct form of the verb.

**Active grammar**

| Present Simple | Past Simple |
|---|---|
| I like the painting. | I *liked* the painting. |
| She stays with her friends. | She _____ with her friends. |
| They start work early. | They _____ work early. |

**Add *-ed* to make the Past Simple of regular verbs.**

see Reference page 107

5   Complete the texts with a verb from the box in the Past Simple.

finish   ~~want~~   start   ask

Pope Julius II (1) *wanted* a new ceiling in the Sistine Chapel. He (2) _____ Michelangelo to paint the ceiling of the Sistine Chapel. Michelangelo (3) _____ it in 1508. He (4) _____ it in 1512.

live   work   play   move (x2)

Marcel Duchamp was an artist. He was born in 1887. He (5) _____ in Paris and he (6) _____ chess with his brothers. In 1914, he (7) _____ to New York. He (8) _____ in a library in New York. In 1918, he (9) _____ to Argentina.

## Pronunciation

**6**  **a**  **10.2** Listen and repeat the Past Simple of the verbs in the box.

> want   ask   move   start
> finish   live   play   work
> cook   close   talk   arrest
> listen   walk

**b** How how do you pronounce the *-ed* ending of each verb? Copy the table and put the verbs in the correct column.

| /t/ | /d/ | /ɪd/ |
|------|------|--------|
| ask<u>ed</u> | mov<u>ed</u> | want<u>ed</u> |

**7**  **a** Read the texts in Ex. 5 aloud.

**b**  **10.3** Listen and check your pronunciation.

## Listening

**8**  **10.4** Listen to *The Story of the Mona Lisa (Part 2)*. Mark these sentences true (T) or false (F).

  **a** The *Mona Lisa* moved to the Louvre.

  **b** It stayed in Napoleon's bedroom.

  **c** The Louvre closed in 1910.

  **d** The police talked to Picasso.

  **e** The police talked to Vincenza Peruggia.

## Grammar 2 | Past Simple: negatives and questions

**9**  **a** Read and answer the questions.

  1  Did Napoleon like the *Mona Lisa*?     *Yes, he did.*

  2  Did the *Mona Lisa* stay in Napoleon's bedroom?   *No, it didn't.*

  3  Did the police talk to Picasso?

  4  Did the police talk to Vencenzo Peruggia?

  **b** Complete the Active grammar box with *did* or *didn't*.

> ### Active grammar
>
> | ⊖ | I/You/He/She/ It/We/They | *didn't* stay _____ talk | in Italy. to the police. |
> |---|---|---|---|
> | ❓ | _____ | I/you/he/she/it/ we/they | stay   in Italy? talk   to the police? |
>
> Yes, I/you/he/she/it/we/they _____ .
> No, I/you/he/she/it/we/they _____ .

see Reference page 107

**10**  **a** Make negative sentences.

  1  (Picasso/not like/the *Mona Lisa*)
  *Picasso didn't like the Mona Lisa.*

  2  (Leonardo da Vinci/not live/Spain)

  3  (the *Mona Lisa*/not stay/Italy)

  4  (Picasso/not move to/New York)

  **b** Make questions and answers.

  1  (Marcel Duchamp/play chess?)
  **A:** *Did Marcel Duchamp play chess?*   **B:** *Yes, he did*.

  2  (the police/arrest/Picasso?)
  **A:** _____ ?   **B:** No, _____ .

  3  (Andy Warhol/work for/*Vogue*?)
  **A:** _____ ?   **B:** Yes, _____ .

  4  (Van Gogh/move to/London?)
  **A:** _____ ?   **B:** Yes, _____ .

  **c** Work in pairs. Write six questions about Leonardo da Vinci and the *Mona Lisa*. Ask your questions to another pair.

## Speaking

**11**  **a** Work in pairs. What do you think?

  1  Who was the thief?

  2  Where was the *Mona Lisa* for two years?

  3  How did the thief steal the *Mona Lisa*?

  **b** Read the last part of the story on page 114. Answer the questions above.

## Reading

**1** **a** Who or what is in the news? Write a list.

*Orlando Bloom*

*Real Madrid Football Club*

**b** Was it a good week or a bad week for each person/thing in your list?

**2** **a** Read the magazine page below. Complete the gaps with *good* or *bad*.

**b** **10.5** Listen and check.

**c** Read again. Are these statements true (T) or false (F)?

1 Romero Cline got married last week. ☐ T
2 Monica Hawkins works in a restaurant. ☐
3 Emiliana Rotman doesn't have €14 million. ☐
4 Emiliana Rotman is very sad. ☐
5 Gilt's concert was on Saturday. ☐
6 Sia Kahn bought a T-shirt. ☐
7 Mr and Mrs Blatt found the coins under the fish. ☐
8 Mr and Mrs Blatt bought three fish. ☐

**3** Close your books. What can you remember about the four stories?

**MONDAY**
**12th JUNE**

# Good week, bad week

**1** It was a _____ week for ... actor Romero Cline, 43. He went to Las Vegas last week and he met Monica Hawkins, a waitress in a fast food restaurant. Three days later, they got married.

**2** It was a ____ week for ... Mr and Mrs Blatt from the UK. They had fish for dinner and they found three gold coins inside the fish. 'The fish was £3.50,' said Mrs Blatt, 'but the gold coins are £1,000 each!'

**3** It was a _____ week for ... Emiliana Rotman from Sweden. She won £14 million on the Euro lottery but she lost her ticket. 'Never mind,' said Emiliana, 'That's life!'

**4** It was a _____ week for ... pop group *Gilt*. *Gilt's* concert was last Friday but the tickets said 'Saturday'. 'Only five people came and saw the concert,' said Sia Kahn, *Gilt's* singer. 'They took photos and bought a T-shirt but it wasn't a good day.'

**CROSSWORD**

## Grammar | Past Simple: irregular verbs

**4**   **a** Look at the magazine page in Ex. 2a again. <u>Underline</u> all the verbs in the Past Simple.

**b** Complete the Active grammar box with *take* or *took*.

---

### Active grammar

**Some verbs are irregular in the Past Simple (but only in affirmative sentences).**

| ⊕ | I/You/He/She/We/They | went to Paris. |
| | | _____ a lot of photos. |
| ⊖ | I/You/He/She/We/They | didn't go to Paris. |
| | | didn't _____ a lot of photos. |
| ❓ | Did | I/you/he/she/we/they | go to Paris? |
| | | | _____ a lot of photos? |

Yes, I/you/he/she/we/they did.
No, I/you/he/she/we/they didn't.

---

*see Reference page 107*

**5**   **a** Complete the magazine crossword on page 102 with the Past Simple of the verbs below. Some are regular, some are irregular.

ACROSS   **3** come   **5** play   **8** see   **9** buy
**12** finish   **14** have   **15** move   **16** go

DOWN   **1** meet   **2** ask   **4** listen   **6** get
**7** win   **10** find   **11** say   **13** lose

**b** Complete the text with the verb in brackets.

Yesterday, Emiliana Rotman (1) <u>*found*</u> (find) her lottery ticket and (2) _____ (win) £14 million. 'I (3) _____ (not find) the ticket,' Emiliana (4) _____ (say). 'My brother (5) _____ (come) to my house for dinner and he (6) _____ (see) it under my sofa. So we (7) _____ (not have) dinner at home. I (8) _____ (take) him to a nice restaurant.'

**6**   Look at the phrases below. What did/didn't you do last week? Write sentences then tell your partner.

> take a photo   go to a supermarket
> come to class late   lose something
> have fish for dinner   find some money
> buy some new clothes

*I bought some new clothes last week.*

## Vocabulary | high numbers

**7**   **a** Read the How to ... box. When is *and* used?

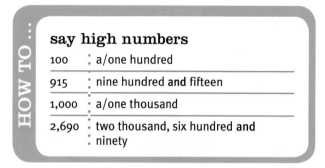

**HOW TO ...**

**say high numbers**

| 100 | a/one hundred |
| 915 | nine hundred **and** fifteen |
| 1,000 | a/one thousand |
| 2,690 | two thousand, six hundred **and** ninety |

**b** **10.6** Listen and write the prices.

**Lovely ELECTRONICS**

was €149
sale price €199

was _____
sale price _____

was _____
sale price _____

was _____
sale price _____

was _____
sale price _____

was _____
sale price _____

**8**   Now write new prices in the advert. Tell your partner the prices.

*The DVD player was €179. Now it's €105.*

## Speaking

**9**   **a** Ask five people 'How was last week for you?' Make notes.

**b** Tell your partner about the people you talked to.

*It was a good week for Dario and Rikka. Dario started a new job and Rikka went to Paris.*

## Writing

**10** Look at your list from Ex. 1a. Choose one person or thing. Write a short good week/bad week news story.

| Grammar | *going to* |
|---|---|
| Can do | talk about immediate and long-term plans |

Orla

Charlie

Nick

Abby

## Listening

1　Ask and answer the questions below with a partner.

　1　How was your week?

　2　What happened in the last seven days?

2　a　**10.7** Look at the photo above and listen. Match a person in the photo to their week below:

　1　an exciting week　2　an interesting week　3　busy week (x2)

　b　Listen again. Complete the chart below with notes.

|  | What happened? | What are his/her plans? |
|---|---|---|
| **Nick** | *talked to manager* | *find a new job* |
| **Abby** |  |  |
| **Charlie** |  |  |
| **Orla** |  |  |

## Grammar | *going to*

3　Complete the Active grammar box with *'s, is, not* and *are*. Look at tapescript 10.7 on page 151 to help you.

### Active grammar

| ➕ | I'm <br> She__ | going to | get married. <br> find a new job. |
|---|---|---|---|
| ➖ | He's <br> They're | <u>not</u> going to <br> ___ going to | move to Ireland. <br> get married soon. |
| ❓ | ___ you <br> ___ she | going to | have a party? <br> see Daniel tonight? |
| ❓ | What ___ you <br> Where ___ he | going to | do tomorrow? <br> stay? |

*see Reference page 107*

4　a　Write sentences for your answers to Ex. 2b.

　1　*Nick is going to find a new job.*

　b　Look at Nick, Orla and Daniel's plans for next week. Write complete sentences.

|  | Nick | Orla and Daniel |
|---|---|---|
| tomorrow | ~~play football~~ <br> play tennis | ~~eat out~~ <br> stay at home |
| next Sunday | ~~write a report~~ <br> stay in bed all day | ~~go for a walk~~ <br> have lunch with friends |
| next Monday | ~~work from home~~ <br> visit a customer | ~~work~~ <br> have a holiday |

　1　*Nick's not going to play football tomorrow. He's going to play tennis.*

　c　Work in pairs. Ask questions from the chart in Ex. 4b.

A: *Is Nick going to play football tomorrow?*

B: *No, he isn't.*

　d　Tell your partner your plans for next week.

## Pronunciation

**5** **a** `10.8` Listen and write the four questions and answers.

1 A: *Are you going to buy her a present?*
 B: *Yes, I am.*

**b** Listen again. How do you pronounce *going to*? Repeat the questions and answers with a partner.

## Speaking

**6** What are your plans for this year/next year? Make notes and then tell your partner.

*I'm going to move to a new flat next year.*

## Vocabulary | future plans

**7** **a** Match a phrase in the box to a picture 1–6 below.

> get fit   go to university   retire
> learn to drive   start a business
> have a child/children

**b** Which of the phrases did you/your friends/your family do in the past? Tell your partner.

A: *My brother started a business three years ago.*

**c** Which of these things are you going to do in the future? Tell your partner.

*When I'm forty, I'm going to start a business.*

*In ten years' time, I'm going to retire.*

## Listening

**8** **a** `10.9` Listen. Charlie tells a story about a fisherman and his grandson. Put the grandson's phrases in the correct order.

[  ]  start a business      [  ]  enjoy my life
[  ]  go fishing            [ 1 ]  go to university
[  ]  make a lot of money   [  ]  be rich

**b** Listen again. The fisherman asks three questions. What are they?

**9** Look at the prompts in Ex. 8a. Can you remember the conversation between the fisherman and his grandson?

A: *What are you going to do in life?*

B: *I'm going to go to university.*

## Speaking

**10** Imagine. You win €3 million on the lottery. What are you going to do? Make notes and then tell your partner.

**1  a** Look at the photos of holidays A–D. Put them in order for you (1 = favourite, 2 = second favourite, etc). Compare with a partner.

**b** Think about your favourite holiday from your past. Complete the questionnaire below.

When was it? .....................

Where did you go? ......................

Who did you go with? ......................

How long did you stay? ......................

Where did you stay (hotel, *B&B*, etc)? ......................

What did you do in the morning and afternoon? ......................

What did you do in the evening? ......................

**c** Work in pairs. Use your notes to tell your holiday stories to your partner.

*My favourite holiday was in 1999. I went to South Africa with my wife and we went on a Safari. We stayed for two weeks and ...*

**2  a** Make a list of cities/places you want to go to on holiday. Compare with your partner.

**b** Imagine. You and your partner win a holiday of a lifetime. Read the rules below.

## The Rules

1 It is a two-week holiday.

2 You can fly to three different places.

3 You always fly from west to east around the world.

4 You always travel together.

**c** Work in pairs. Plan your holiday. Choose three destinations and make notes:

1 where (e.g. Marrakech in Morocco); 2 how long (e.g. four days); 3 plans (e.g. go to the markets, see the Atlas mountains)

A: *How about Marrakech?*

B: *Yes, good idea. I want to go there. How long are we going to stay?*

**3**  Find a new partner. Explain your holiday plans to your new partner.

*First, we're going to fly to Marrakech in Morrocco. We're going to stay there for four days. We're going to see the Atlas mountains and we're going to go to the markets. Then we're going to fly to ...*

## The Past Simple
### Regular verbs

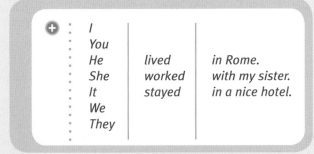

| ⊕ | I<br>You<br>He<br>She<br>It<br>We<br>They | lived<br>worked<br>stayed | in Rome.<br>with my sister.<br>in a nice hotel. |
|---|---|---|---|

To make the Past Simple of regular verbs, add *-ed* to the end of the verb.

### Irregular verbs

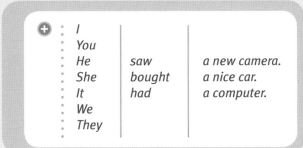

| ⊕ | I<br>You<br>He<br>She<br>It<br>We<br>They | saw<br>bought<br>had | a new camera.<br>a nice car.<br>a computer. |
|---|---|---|---|

A lot of verbs are irregular in the Past Simple affirmative; for example:

| | | |
|---|---|---|
| buy—bought | come—came | do—did |
| eat—ate | find—found | get—got |
| give—gave | go—went | have—had |
| make—made | read /riːd/—read /red/ | |
| say—said | see—saw | speak—spoke |
| win—won | write—wrote | |

| ⊖ | I<br>You<br>He<br>She<br>It<br>We<br>They | didn't talk<br>didn't listen<br>didn't go | to Cynthia.<br>to the pop star.<br>out. |
|---|---|---|---|

Use *didn't* + verb to make the negative. Do not use the past form in the negative.

~~She didn't went to the cinema.~~

*She didn't go to the cinema.*

| ? | Did | I<br>you<br>he<br>she<br>it<br>we<br>they | move<br>walk<br>go<br>come | to work?<br>to school?<br>to London? |
|---|---|---|---|---|

Use *Did* + subject + verb to make questions. Do not use the past form in the question.

~~Did they moved to Paris?~~

*Did they move to Paris?*

## Going to

Use *going to* + verb to talk about plans for the future.

| ⊖ | I | 'm | | |
|---|---|---|---|---|
| | You | 're | | |
| | He<br>She<br>It | 's | going to<br>not going<br>to | get fit.<br>retire.<br>get married. |
| | We | 're | | |
| | They | 're | | |

| ? | Am | I | | |
|---|---|---|---|---|
| | Are | you | | |
| | Is | he<br>she<br>it | going to | take the bus?<br>visit my sister? |
| | Are | we | | |
| | Are | they | | |

### Key vocabulary

**Verbs + nouns**
lose your wallet    steal a mobile phone
stay in bed    win the lottery
find some money
move to a new house    break your arm
meet a famous person

**Future plans**
get fit    go to university
have a child/children    learn to drive
retire    start a new business

# 10 Review and practice

**1** Complete the email with the verbs in the box in the Past Simple.

> watch  talk  cook  ~~work~~  visit  stay  play

Hi Felicia,
How was your weekend? I (1) _worked_ on Saturday ☺ – I have a lot of work at the moment. In the evening, my friend (2) _____ dinner for me and we (3) _____ a film. That was nice! On Sunday morning, I (4) _____ tennis with my friends and in the afternoon, my cousin (5) _____ me. He lives in Ireland. We (6) _____ at home and (7) _____ about our lives. He's very happy in Ireland.
Hope you're ok. Send me an email soon!
Kiera

**2** Write complete sentences in the Past Simple.

1 (my friend/start/a new job)
   _My friend started a new job._
2 (Louise/move/to America?)
   _____ ?
3 (I/not talk/to my boss)
   _____ .
4 (you/play chess/with Michelle?)
   _____ ?
5 (Quentin and I/cook/dinner)
   _____ .
6 (Pietro/not like/his present)
   _____ .
7 (The artist/start/a new painting/in 1994)
   _____ .
8 (they/want/eat out tonight?)
   _____ ?

**3** Find the Past Simple of the following verbs in the Word grid.

| | | | |
|---|---|---|---|
| 1 | have | 5 | give |
| 2 | find | 6 | steal |
| 3 | take | 7 | go |
| 4 | meet | 8 | say |

| e | y | u | b | f | l |
|---|---|---|---|---|---|
| m | e | t | o | o | k |
| s | a | i | d | u | k |
| t | a | z | g | n | m |
| o | g | h | a | d | v |
| l | j | f | v | d | f |
| e | s | w | e | n | t |

**4** Complete each sentence with the correct form of the verb in brackets in the Past Simple.

1 How _did_ you _break_ your arm? (break)
2 They _____ a lot of money. (win)
3 Why _____ the police _____ them? (arrest)
4 I _____ _____ any clothes today. (not buy)
5 Your mother _____ to the supermarket for some bread. (go)
6 My wife _____ your dog in the park an hour ago. (see)
7 What _____ you _____ for dinner? (have)
8 They _____ married last year. (get)

**5** Write questions to find the missing information.

1 ___?___ 's going to retire.
   _Who's going to retire?_
2 I'm going to buy a ___?___ .
   _What are you going to buy?_
3 They're going to ___?___ .
   _____ ?
4 We're going to see ___?___ at the cinema.
   _____ ?
5 ___?___ 's going to get fit.
   _____ ?
6 I'm going to call ___?___ .
   _____ ?
7 Lucy's going to go to ___?___ University.
   _____ ?
8 Tom and Minnie are going to move to ___?___ .
   _____ ?

**6** Match the start of each sentence 1–8 to the end of each sentence a–h.

| | | | |
|---|---|---|---|
| 1 | The police officer | a | your leg? |
| 2 | It was two thousand, | b | ten euros. |
| 3 | He wants to start | c | arrested him. |
| 4 | When did they get | d | children? |
| 5 | It's five thousand and | e | a business. |
| 6 | How did you break | f | did she go to? |
| 7 | Which university | g | two hundred dollars. |
| 8 | Do you want to have | h | married? |

# Communication activities

## Lesson 2.2 | Ex. 7a, page 23

**You are Terri**

**Name:** Terri Nielson
**Age:** 42
**From:** the UK
**Address:** 19 Filamore Street, London
**Phone №:** 020 3890 3124
**Mobile №:** 07933 348 672

**You are Vittoria**

**Name:** Vittoria Lombardi
**Age:** 42
**From:** Italy
**Address:** 60 Bishop Road, Hampstead, London
**Phone №:** 020 8110 4455
**Mobile №:** 07146 993 381

**You are Sanjay.**

**Name:** Sanjay Naveen
**Age:** 28
**From:** India
**Address:** 16 Davis Street, Ealing, London
**Phone №:** 020 7440 1005
**Mobile №:** 07881 442901

**You are Hans.**

**Name:** Hans Melo
**Age:** 34
**From:** Germany
**Address:** 90 Clapton Road. Clapton, London
**Phone №:** 020 8169 7197
**Mobile №:** 07225 893223

## Lesson 3.3 | Ex. 6, page 35

**Student B**

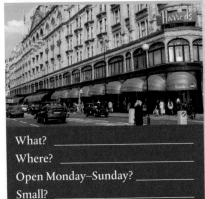

Harrods

What? _____
Where? _____
Open Monday–Sunday? _____
Small? _____
Old? _____
Beautiful? _____
Entrance free? _____

# LOUVRE

The Louvre is a museum and a gallery. It's in Paris and it's open from Monday to Sunday. The Louvre is big, beautiful and old but the 'pyramid' is modern. Entrance is €8.50.

## Lesson 4.3 | Ex. 2b, page 44

A

B

C

D

E

F

# Communication activities

## Communication 4 | Ex. 2b, page 46

### Student B

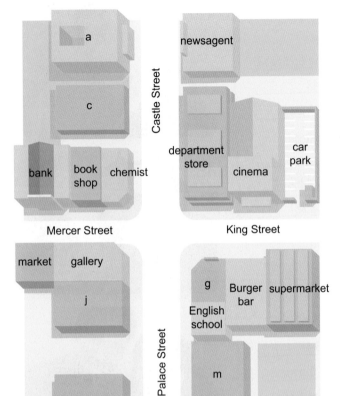

Ask for:
- the sports shop
- the Blue Café
- the bus stop
- the museum
- the shoe shop

## Lesson 9.1 | Ex. 5b, page 91

**Answer:** John Lennon

## Lesson 8.3 | Ex. 2a, page 84

### Student C

The Top Restaurants in the World.

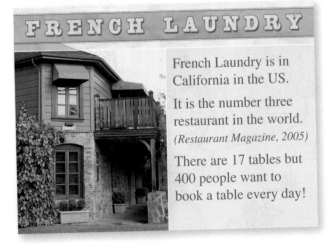

FRENCH LAUNDRY

French Laundry is in California in the US.

It is the number three restaurant in the world. *(Restaurant Magazine, 2005)*

There are 17 tables but 400 people want to book a table every day!

## Lesson 8.2 | Ex. 3c, page 82

A present for Paul's sister: money

## Lesson 6.2 | Ex. 9, page 63

### Student A

| | |
|---|---|
| Name | Ingrid Young |
| From | Scotland |
| Live in | Vancouver, Canada |
| Holiday or business | business |
| Job | Sales rep |
| Do | sell suitcases and backpacks to shops |
| Work for | The Big Bag Company |
| Work where | near Vancouver |
| Husband | William Young (Student B) |

### Student B

| | |
|---|---|
| Name | William Young |
| From | Australia |
| Live in | Vancouver, Canada |
| Holiday or business | business |
| Job | Sales rep |
| Do | sell tea and coffee to supermarkets |
| Work for | Coffee Love |
| Work where | in Vancouver |
| Wife | Ingrid Young (Student A) |

## Lesson 7.1 | Ex. 8c, page 71

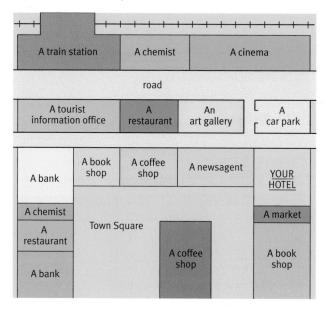

See page 112 for answers.

## Lesson 5.2 | Ex. 8, page 53

### Student A

You are a hotel receptionist.

| A train station | A chemist | A cinema |
|---|---|---|
| road | | |

| A tourist information office | A restaurant | An art gallery | A car park |
|---|---|---|---|

| A bank | A book shop | A coffee shop | A newsagent | YOUR HOTEL |
| A chemist | Town Square | | | A market |
| A restaurant | | A coffee shop | | A book shop |
| A bank | | | | |

## Lesson 8.3 | Ex. 2a, page 84

### Student A

The Top Restaurants in the World.

The Fat Duck is near London in the UK.

"It's the number one restaurant in the world"
*Restaurant Magazine, 2005*

It serves very unusual food, for example bacon and egg ice cream.

The Fat Duck
heston blumenthal

## Communication 8 | Ex. 2, page 86

### Student A

| Person | Address |
|---|---|
| Mr M. Haddon | 14d Brooklyn Road |
| Mrs A. Walker | 14c Brooklyn Road |
| Miss Z. Smith | 16b Brooklyn Road |
| Mr J. Heller | 14a Brooklyn Road |
| Mr G. Dyer | 12a Brooklyn Road |

## Communication 4 | Ex. 2b, page 46

### Student A

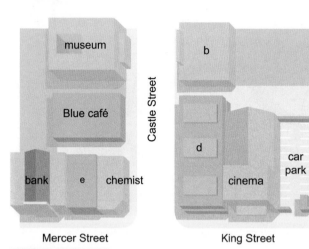

Ask for:
- the burger bar
- the department store
- the newsagent
- the English school
- the bookshop

## Lesson 6.1 | Ex. 6a, page 61

### Student B

1 big cities
2 John Lennon's music
3 Prince Charles and Camilla Parker Bowles
4 museums
5 Julia Roberts
6 Bill Gates
7 the countryside

## Lesson 7.1 | Ex. 8c, page 71

Answers:  1 April   2 January   3 October   4 July

## Lesson 8.2 | Ex. 3c, page 82

A present for Paul's sister: money

## Lesson 6.2 | Ex. 9, page 63

### Student C

| Name | Pamela Price | |
|---|---|---|
| From | the US | |
| Live in | Liverpool, the UK | |
| Holiday or business | | holiday |
| Job | designer | |
| Do | design bags | |
| Work for | Bags R Us | |
| Work where | | in Liverpool |
| Husband | Ron Price (Student D) | |

### Student D

| Name | Ron Price | |
|---|---|---|
| From | the UK | |
| Live in | Liverpool, the UK | |
| Holiday or business | | holiday |
| Job | teacher | |
| Do | teach English | |
| Work for | an English school in Liverpool | |
| Work where | | in Liverpool |
| Wife | Pamela Price (Student C) | |

## Communication 6 | Ex. 3c, page 66

findanicepresent chart

---

http://www.findanicepresent.com

my account | track order | quick order | help

# Find a nice present

Search [          ] GO!

for him | for her | for children | best sellers | special offers

### Who for?

| work long hours? | [    ] |
| married? | [    ] |
| have children? | [    ] |
| travel a lot? | [    ] |
| can cook? | [    ] |
| watch a lot of films? | [    ] |
| listen to a lot of music? | [    ] |

### For him

a tie

a book

an MP3 player

a travel iron

a set of saucepans

a DVD

a CD

### For her

a pen

candles

flowers

a suitcase

a cookery book

a DVD

a CD

---

## Lesson 8.2 | Ex. 8a, page 83

Read the quiz questions. Tick (✓) A, B or C.
**A** = Yes, I have.   **B** = No, but I want one.
**C** = No, and I don't want one.

| Technology Quiz | A | B | C |
|---|---|---|---|
| 1 Have you got a computer? | | | |
| 2 Have you got an MP3 player? | | | |
| 3 Have you got a digital camera? | | | |
| 4 Have you got a camera-phone? | | | |
| 5 Have you got a DVD player? | | | |
| 6 Have you got a camcorder? | | | |
| 7 Have you got a LCD TV? | | | |
| 8 Have you got a GPS device? | | | |
| 9 Have you got a CD player in your car? | | | |

## Lesson 8.3 | Ex. 2a, page 84

### Student B

The Top Restaurants in the World

# elBulli

**El Bulli** is near Barcelona in Spain.

It is the number two best restaurant in the world.
*(Restaurant Magazine 2005)*

Normal restaurants have three courses: starter, main course and dessert… El Bulli has 27 courses!

## Lesson 8.3 | Ex. 11, page 85
**Students B and C**

### Salt and Pepper
#### Menu

**STARTERS**
*Chicken salad*
*Vegetable soup*
*Fruit salad*

**MAIN COURSES**
*Beef and vegetables with rice*
*Lamb curry*
*Fruit salad*

**DESSERTS**
*Chocolate ice cream*
*Fruit cake*
*Cheese and buscuits*

## Lesson 10.1 | Ex. 11b, page 101

(PART 3)
### The Story of the Mona Lisa

Two years later, the police arrested Vencenzo Peruggia. He was the thief. But how did he steal the Mona Lisa? Vencenzo was in the Louvre on August 21, 1911. The museum was very quiet. When Vencenzo walked out, the Mona Lisa was under his coat. The painting stayed in Vencenzo's apartment, near the Louvre, for two years. In 1913, Vencenzo wanted to sell the painting. He wanted to sell it in Italy. The police arrested him in Milan.

## Lesson 5.2 | Ex. 8, page 53
**Student B**

You are a hotel guest. Ask questions with *Is there a ... near here?* or *Are there any ... near here?* Complete the chart.

| What? | Yes/No | Where? |
|---|---|---|
| Restaurant | Yes (2) | 1= next to the gallery 2=next to the bank |
| Market | | |
| Bookshop | | |
| Tourist information office | | |
| Coffee shop | | |
| Train staiton | | |
| Bank | | |
| Chemist | | |

## Communication 8 | Ex. 2, page 86
**Student B**

| | |
|---|---|
| Mrs M. Atwood | 16a Brooklyn Road |
| Mr J. Coe | 14b Brooklyn Road |
| Miss T. Morrison | 12b Brooklyn Road |
| Mr O. Pamuk | 16c Brooklyn Road |
| Mrs A Levy | 12c Brooklyn Road |

## Lesson 9.2 | Ex. 1ob, page 93

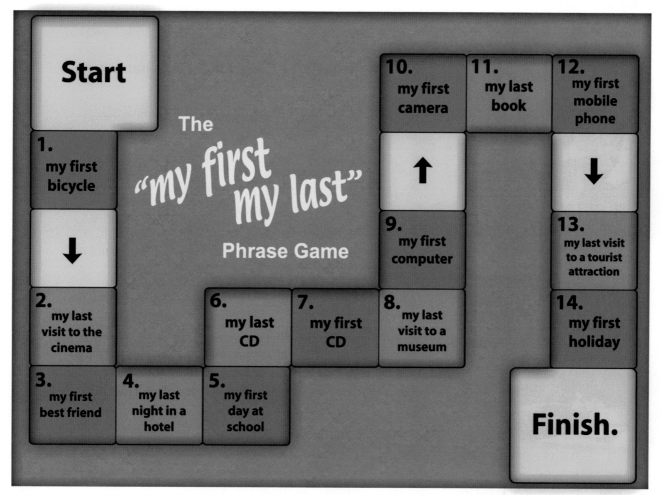

**Start**

The **"my first my last"** Phrase Game

1. my first bicycle

2. my last visit to the cinema

3. my first best friend

4. my last night in a hotel

5. my first day at school

6. my last CD

7. my first CD

8. my last visit to a museum

9. my first computer

10. my first camera

11. my last book

12. my first mobile phone

13. my last visit to a tourist attraction

14. my first holiday

**Finish.**

## Film stills

1 Look at the pictures. Match a conversation A–F below to a picture 1–6.

**A** *3*

**Conversation A**

A: Mitsuru?

B: Yes?

A: Good to meet you. I'm Andy.

B: Good to meet you, too.

**Conversation B**

A: This is Rosi Bates. She's from our head office in the US.

B: Hi.

C: Hi.

**Conversation C**

A: ... and John Cooper. Managing Director of Omega.

B: How do you do, Miss Valdez.

C: I'm very pleased to meet you all. But please call me Ana.

**Conversation D**

A: Hi, John.

B: Oh, hi, Keira. How are you?

A: I'm fine, thanks. And you?

B: Fine, fine. Keira, this is Laurence.

A: Hi. Nice to meet you.

C: Nice to meet you, too.

**Conversation E**

A: Hi, Tommy. How are you?

B: I'm fine, thanks.

**Conversation F**

A: How are you doing?

B: Great, thank you.

2 Watch the film. Check your answers.

3 Work in pairs. Choose a picture and write a new conversation.

4 Read your conversation to the class. Can they guess which picture?

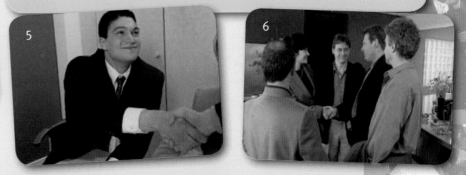

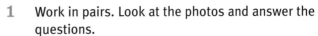

1

2

3

4

1 Work in pairs. Look at the photos and answer the questions.
   **Photo 1:** Who is the actor?
   **Photo 2:** Who is the writer?
   **Photo 3:** What city is it?
   **Photo 4:** What TV programme is it?

2 Complete the table with the cities, actors, books and TV programmes in the box.

> Mr Bean   The Picture of Dorian Gray   Robert de Niro
> ~~London~~   Oliver Twist   Renee Zellweger   Doctor Who
> Jane Fonda   Auckland   Murder on the Orient Express
> Toronto   The Blue Planet

| City | Actor | Book | TV programme |
|------|-------|------|--------------|
| *London* | | | |
| | | | |
| | | | |
| | | | |
| | | | |

3 Watch the film and check your answers.

4 Ask your partner the questions from the film.

FILM
BAN

PACIFIC
OCEAN

C A N A D A

ATLANTIC
OCEAN

**1** Work in pairs. Write some words connected to Canada.

*The Rockies*

*Montreal*

**2** Look at the map of Canada. Mark these places on the map.

1 Vancouver

2 Victoria

3 Nova Scotia

4 The Rockies

5 Montreal

**3** Watch the film and check your answers. Mark Gill William's journey on the map.

**4** Match the phrases below to the places 1–5 in Ex 2.

a) '… [it's] on Vancouver Island'

b) '… the mountains here are great'

c) '… it's very cold here in winter'

d) '… a beautiful city near the mountains'

e) '… on the Atlantic Ocean'

**5** Which place is your favourite?

A

B

C

D

E

F

**1** Match a phrase 1–6 in the table to a photo a–f above.

| | | | |
|---|---|---|---|
| 1 A bunch of flowers | | | your mother. |
| 2 A bottle of perfume | | | your new boyfriend. |
| 3 A pair of trainers | is | a good present for | your new girlfriend. |
| 4 A T-shirt | isn't | | a 10 year-old boy. |
| 5 A book | | | your boss. |
| 6 A vase | | | a colleague. |

**2** Make sentences about the photos. Use the table above.

*A bunch of flowers is a good present for your new girlfriend.*
*A bottle of perfume isn't a good present for a 10 year-old boy.*

**3** Look at the photos below, read the sentences and then watch the film.
Put the phrases in the order that you hear them.

Steve

Mike

Lisa

| | | |
|---|---|---|
| Steve: | Can I have a cappuccino, please? | ☐ |
| Steve: | They're for my mother. It's her birthday. | ☐ |
| Mike: | Nice to meet you, too. | ☐ |
| Lisa: | Oh, Steve, they're lovely. Thank you. | ☐ |
| Steve: | How much are those pink flowers? | ☐ |
| Mike: | Can I help you? | ☑ |
| Lisa: | This is Steve, my new boyfriend. | ☐ |
| Mike: | Are these for your mother, too? | ☐ |

**4** Work in pairs. Can you remember the conversation in the flower shop?

Mike: *Good morning.*
Steve: *Good morning.*
Mike: *Can I help you?*
Steve: *Yes, please. How much are these flowers?*

The Valley of the Kings, Luxor, Egypt

Murawhai, New Zealand

The Amazon rainforest, Brazil

San Antonio, Ibiza, Spain

A cruise ship, the Mediterranean

1   Work in pairs. Look at the photographs. Are they good places for a holiday? Give reasons.

*I think the Valley of the Kings is a good place for a holiday. It's hot, there are good hotels and the Valley of the Kings is amazing*

2   Look at the table below. Before you watch the film, match a sentence 1–9 to a place a–c.

| | |
|---|---|
| 1  There are really good shops. | |
| 2  There aren't any big hotels. | |
| 3  It's quiet and there aren't a lot of people. | a)  Cornwall |
| 4  There are great hotels. | |
| 5  The coast is amazing, too. | b)  New York |
| 6  It's very beautiful and very romantic. | c)  Murawhai in New Zealand |
| 7  There are miles and miles of sandy beaches. | |
| 8  The buildings are fantastic. | |
| 9  There are some fantastic tourist attractions there. | |

1 *b*

3   Watch the film and check your answers..

4   Work in pairs. What is your favourite place for a holiday from the film. Give reasons.

*New York is my favourite place for a holiday from the film. There are really good hotels and a lot of shops.*

a guitar

Aretha Franklin

Queen

Jazz musician

1   Put the words in the photos in the correct column below.

| bands | singers | instruments | kinds of music |
|-------|---------|-------------|----------------|
| *Queen* | | | |

2   Work in pairs. Add more words to each column. Use your dictionary if you want to.

3   Ask your partner questions with the words in the table. Use the questions below:

Do you like ...?

Can you play ...?

**NOTE:** use *the* for instruments: *Can you play the guitar?*

4   Watch the video and complete Emma's questions below.

1   Where are you from?

2   What kind of music do you like?

3   Who are your favourite _____ and _____ ?

4   Do you listen to a lot of music?

5   What _____ do you play?

6   Do you _____ long hours?

7   Can you _____ ?

8   Do you _____ a lot?

5   Can you remember Andy's answers?

6   Ask your partner the questions in Ex. 4.

Sarah/Receptionist

Michael/Chef

Yemi/Designer

Derek/Post-room worker

1 Work in pairs. Add more ideas to the two lists below. Use your dictionary if you want to.

**A good job**      **A good salary**
*A bad job*      *A poor salary*

2 Look at the photos and the sentences below. Who do you think says each sentence: Sarah, Michael, Yemi or Derek?

1 I work with lots of people. _____
2 I don't like the early start. It's awful. _____
3 I never take work home with me. _____
4 I don't like the early mornings. _____
5 I make cakes for the morning coffee break. _____
6 I design books and book covers. _____
7 I answer the phone and I greet visitors to the company. *Sarah*
8 I see lots of people and I like that. _____

3 Watch the film and check your answers. Then complete the information about each person in the table.

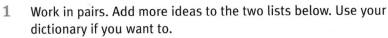

| Sarah | Michael | Yemi | Derek |
|---|---|---|---|
| Starts work: *10 o' clock* | Starts work: | Starts work: | Starts work: |
| Finishes work: | Finishes work: | Finishes work: | Finishes work: |

4 Put the four jobs in order of preference for you. Show your partner. Give reasons.

*Michael's job is number one on my list. I like food and he finishes work early.*

1 Windsurfing

2 _____

3 _____

4 _____

5 _____

6 _____

7 _____

8 _____

9 _____

10 _____

1 Look at the photos 1–10. Match a word/ phrase from the box below to each photo.

> climbing   scuba diving   in-line skating
> windsurfing   bungee jumping
> canoeing   snowboarding   BMX racing
> parascending   skateboarding

2 Complete the sentences below with one or more of the words/phrases in the box. Then read your sentences to your partner.

*I want to try …*

*I don' t want to try …*

3 Work in pairs. Read the phrases below from the film. Which activity do you think they refer to?

1 'exciting'   *BMX racing*

2 'quiet … the colours are amazing' _____

3 'fun but it isn't always easy' _____

4 'very difficult but very exciting' _____

5 'exciting – you can see for miles' _____

6 'cheap and easy to learn' _____

7 'great fun' _____

8 'fast and exciting' _____

9 'easy but it isn't boring' _____

10 'great' _____

4 Watch the film and check your answers.

5 Work in pairs. Choose a title below and write a list. Give reasons.

The top five exciting holiday activities

The top five relaxing holiday activities

The top five activities for a rainy weekend at home

*The top five relaxing holiday activities*

1 *lying in the sun*

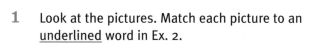

**1** Look at the pictures. Match each picture to an <u>underlined</u> word in Ex. 2.

**2** Read the sentences below. Which sentences do you think are true?

100 years ago in the UK …

a) most men were in a <u>suit</u> and hat.
b) there weren't any <u>horses</u> on the street.
c) there were <u>cows</u> on the street.
d) there weren't any football teams.
e) there wasn't any free time for most people.
f) there were a lot of old people.
g) there were <u>exercise classes</u> for school children.
h) all ten year old children were at school.
i) there were a lot of cars on the roads.
j) there were <u>trams</u> on the roads.
k) there weren't any <u>bicycles</u>.
l) walks in the park were popular.
m) <u>funfairs</u> were popular.
n) <u>days at the sea</u> were popular.
o) rugby was popular.
p) there were <u>shows</u> and concerts at the beach.

**3** Watch the film and check your answers.

**4** Work in pairs. Discuss the questions.

1 What can you remember about the film?
2 What was surprising in the film?
3 What do you think was similar to your country in the film?

1 Work in pairs. Look at the photos. Do you know how to play any of these games? Can you play them? Tell your partner.

2 Read the article on bowls then close your books. What can you remember about bowls? Tell your partner.

Bowls

Croquet

Darts

Petanque

## Bowls

Bowls is a very, very old game. There is a famous bowling green in Southampton in England – it is over 700 years old. Some people say that the Egyptians played bowls 7000 years ago. In the UK, bowls is very popular with old people. They often play. So how do you play? It's very easy. There are two teams with one or two people in each team. A player rolls the jack to the other end of the green. Each player rolls their bowl towards the jack. The team with the bowl or bowls closest to the jack is the winner. But there are a lot of other do's and don'ts for behaviour during the game.

bowl

roll

green

jack

### Do's and don'ts

1 Don't touch or kick the bowls during a game.
2 Wear white clothes.
3 Don't walk across other games on the green.
4 Don't make a noise when someone is bowling.
5 Don't get angry when you lose.
6 Be polite to the other team.
7 You can take a tea-break in the middle of the game.
8 Be polite to the referee.
9 Don't shout.
10 Don't throw your bowl on the ground.
11 Be polite to your team-mate.
12 Accept the referee's decision.

3 Watch the film. Which do's and don'ts did they break? Make sentences.

1 *They touched and kicked the bowls during the game.*

4 Work in pairs. What activities are popular with old people in your country?

# Writing bank

## A holiday email

Write a subject for your email

Begin the email: *Hi* or *Hello* + name

Talk about the place: your hotel/the town, etc. Use contractions: *we're, it's, ...*

Explain any attachments

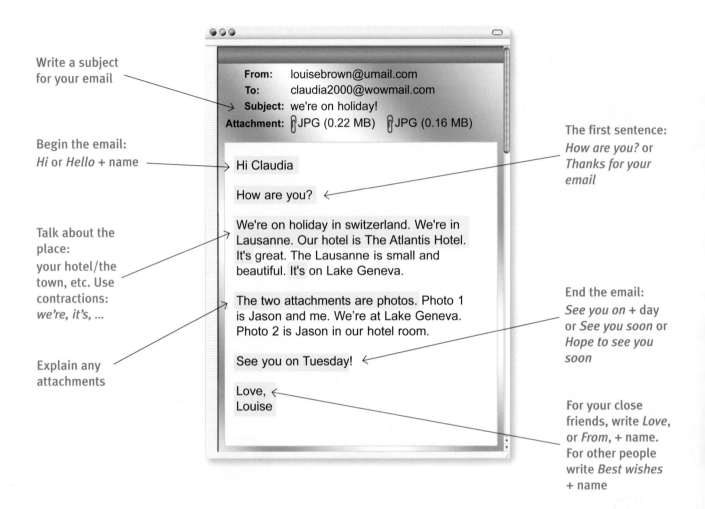

The first sentence: *How are you?* or *Thanks for your email*

End the email: *See you on* + day or *See you soon* or *Hope to see you soon*

For your close friends, write *Love*, or *From*, + name. For other people write *Best wishes* + name

From: louisebrown@umail.com
To: claudia2000@wowmail.com
Subject: we're on holiday!
Attachment: JPG (0.22 MB) JPG (0.16 MB)

Hi Claudia

How are you?

We're on holiday in switzerland. We're in Lausanne. Our hotel is The Atlantis Hotel. It's great. The Lausanne is small and beautiful. It's on Lake Geneva.

The two attachments are photos. Photo 1 is Jason and me. We're at Lake Geneva. Photo 2 is Jason in our hotel room.

See you on Tuesday!

Love,
Louise

## Writing tip | punctuation

. = a full stop
A, B, C, etc = **ca**pital **let**ters
, = a **com**ma
? = a **ques**tion mark
' = an **apos**trophe

### Full stops

- Use a full stop at the end of a sentence.
  *Our hotel is The Atlantis Hotel.*

### Capital letters

- Use a capital letter at the beginning of a sentence.
  *The two attachments are photos.*
- Use capital letters for the names of people, places, days, months, books and films:
  *My favourite author is Hemingway.*
  *See you on Thursday.*
- Use a capital letter for the pronoun I.
  *Can I have a coffee, please?*

- Use capital letters for countries, nationalities and languages.
  *She's from Spain. She's Spanish.*

### Commas

- Use commas in lists.
  *It's small, old and beautiful.*
  *The attachment is a photo of Laura, Adam and Sarah.*
- Use a comma before *please* and after *yes* and *no*.
  *What's your name, please?*
  **A:** *Coffee?*  **B:** *No, thank you.*

### Apostrophe

- Use an apostrophe to show a contraction.
  *We are on holiday.* → *We're on holiday.*
- Use an apostrophe + *s* to show possession.
  *Do you like Jason's car.*
  *They are Susan's books*

## A description | my favourite place for a holiday

Where is it? *It's in the north/south/east/west/centre of* + country
Use capital letters for places: *London, Berlin, Austria, Poland, ...*

Use apostrophe + *s* ('*s*) to show possession: *London's parks, the Queen's palace, ...*

Use adjectives to describe a place: *popular, great, modern, beautiful, old, ...*

Talk about location: *in, on, near, next to, ...*

My favourite place for a holiday is London. It's the capital of the UK and it's in the south-east of England. There are a lot of museums, shops, restaurants and other tourist attractions.

London's parks are great. Hyde Park is in the centre of London. It's very big and in summer there are concerts in the park. Hampstead Heath is beautiful, too. It's a big park in the north of London.

The British Museum is very popular. It's very big and the building is quite old. But I think The Science Museum is London's top attraction. It's in South Kensington, near the centre of London. The exhibitions are great!

The London Eye is a new tourist attraction. It's a big wheel. It's on the River Thames, near Big Ben. It's expensive but the views of London are amazing.

## Writing tip | and, but

- Use *and* before the last item in a list.

  *There are a lot of museums, shops, restaurants and other tourist attractions.*
  *The British Museum is very big, very old and very popular.*
  *He's an actor and a teacher.*

- Use *and* to join two similar sentences.

  *The countryside is beautiful. The beaches are great.*
  → *The countryside is beautiful and the beaches are great.*

  *Hyde Park is very big. There are concerts in the park.*
  → *Hyde Park is very big and there are concerts in the park.*

- Use *but* to join two different (contrasting) sentences.

  *The countryside is beautiful. The beaches are awful.*
  → *The countryside is beautiful but the beaches are awful.*

  *There's a museum in the town. There isn't a gallery.*
  → *There's a museum in the town but there isn't a gallery.*

## A letter to a friend

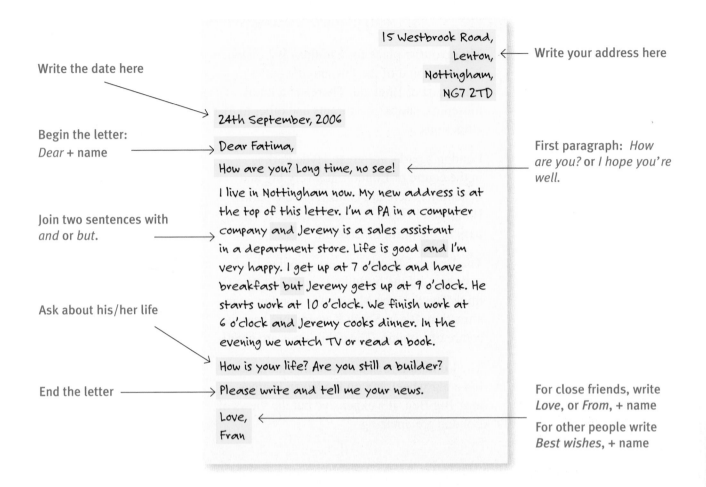

Write your address here

15 Westbrook Road,
Lenton,
Nottingham,
NG7 2TD

Write the date here

24th September, 2006

Begin the letter:
*Dear* + name

Dear Fatima,

First paragraph: *How are you?* or *I hope you're well.*

How are you? Long time, no see!

I live in Nottingham now. My new address is at the top of this letter. I'm a PA in a computer company and Jeremy is a sales assistant in a department store. Life is good and I'm very happy. I get up at 7 o'clock and have breakfast but Jeremy gets up at 9 o'clock. He starts work at 10 o'clock. We finish work at 6 o'clock and Jeremy cooks dinner. In the evening we watch TV or read a book.

Join two sentences with *and* or *but*.

Ask about his/her life

How is your life? Are you still a builder?

End the letter

Please write and tell me your news.

Love,
Fran

For close friends, write *Love,* or *From,* + name

For other people write *Best wishes,* + name

**Writing tip** | spelling of verbs in the Present Simple with *he/she/it*

- With *he, she* and *it* add *-s* to the verb.
  *I get up early. He gets up late.*
  *I start work at 9 o'clock. She starts work at 10 o'clock.*

- With verbs ending in *-ch, -sh, -s, -x, -z* and *-o*, add *-es* to the verb with *he, she* and *it*.
  *They watch TV. She watches TV.*
  *We do exercise every day. He does exercise every day.*
  *I finish work at 5 o'clock. She finishes work at 6 o'clock.*

- For verbs ending in consonant + *-y*, remove the *-y* and add *-ies*.
  *I carry the big bags and my brother carries the small bags.*

  **NOTE:** For verbs ending in vowel + *-y*, add *s*.
  *I play tennis and my sister plays basketball.*

  **NOTE:** *have* is irregular.
  *We have a small house but she has a big house.*

# A formal email

Write a subject for your email

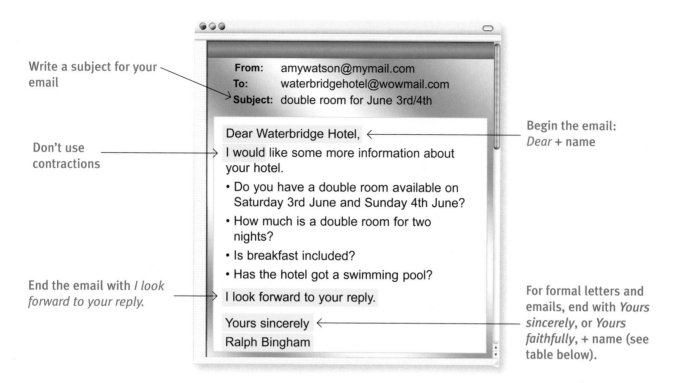

Begin the email: *Dear + name*

Don't use contractions

End the email with *I look forward to your reply.*

For formal letters and emails, end with *Yours sincerely*, or *Yours faithfully*, + name (see table below).

**From:** amywatson@mymail.com
**To:** waterbridgehotel@wowmail.com
**Subject:** double room for June 3rd/4th

Dear Waterbridge Hotel,

I would like some more information about your hotel.

• Do you have a double room available on Saturday 3rd June and Sunday 4th June?
• How much is a double room for two nights?
• Is breakfast included?
• Has the hotel got a swimming pool?

I look forward to your reply.

Yours sincerely

Ralph Bingham

## Writing tip | formal English and informal English

These are the main differences between formal English and informal English in writing.

| Informal<br>e.g. an email to a friend | Formal<br>e.g. a business letter |
|---|---|
| Start with:<br>• *Hi* + first name.<br>  **NOTE:** we don't use<br>  • ~~*Dear Friend,*~~<br>  • ~~*Hi Friend,*~~ | Start with:<br>• *Dear* + *Mr/Mrs/Miss/Ms.* + surname.<br>  **NOTE:** When you don't know the person's name, start with:<br>• *Dear Sir or Madam.* |
| Before you end the email use:<br>• *See you soon.*<br>• *Speak to you soon.* | Before you end the email, use:<br>• *I look forward to your reply.*<br>• *I look forward to hearing from you soon.* |
| End with:<br>• *Best wishes,*<br>• *From,*<br>• *Love,*<br>• *All the best,*<br>When you don't know the person very well, end with:<br>• *Regards,*<br>• *Kind regards,* | When you start with *Dear* + name, end with:<br>• *Yours sincerely,*<br>  **NOTE:** When you start with *Dear Sir or Madam*, end with:<br>• *Yours faithfully,* |
| Use contractions:<br>• e.g. *I'm, you're, they're, etc.* | Do not use contractions. Use:<br>• *I am, you are, they are, etc.*<br>  **NOTE:** it is OK to use *don't.* |
| Use *would like*, not *want*.<br>• *I would like some information about …*<br>• ~~*I want some information about …*~~ | |

# Pronunciation bank

## Part 1 | English phonemes

| Symbol | Key word | Symbol | Key word |
|--------|----------|--------|----------|
| d | **d**ate | ŋ | goi**ng** |
| b | **b**ed | s | **s**ofa |
| t | **t**en | z | **z**ero |
| p | **p**ark | ʃ | **sh**op |
| k | **c**ar | ʒ | televi**si**on |
| g | **g**ame | h | **h**at |
| tʃ | **ch**ild | m | **m**enu |
| dʒ | **j**ob | n | **n**ear |
| f | **f**our | l | **l**ike |
| v | **v**isit | r | **r**ide |
| θ | **th**ree | j | **y**oung |
| ð | **th**is | w | **w**ife |

| Symbol | Key word | Symbol | Key word |
|--------|----------|--------|----------|
| iː | b**e** | eɪ | d**ay** |
| ɪ | s**i**t | əʊ | g**o** |
| e | r**e**d | aɪ | **wh**y |
| æ | c**a**t | aʊ | h**ou**se |
| ɑː | c**ar** | ɔɪ | b**oy** |
| ɒ | d**o**g | ɪə | h**ere** |
| ɔː | f**our** | eə | th**ere** |
| ʊ | b**oo**k | eɪə | pl**ayer** |
| uː | sh**oe** | aɪ | t**ired** |
| ʌ | b**u**t | aʊə | fl**ower** |
| ɜː | w**or**d | ɔɪə | l**awyer** |
| ə | moth**er** | | |

## Part 2 | Sound-spelling correspondences

| Sound | Spelling | Examples |
|-------|----------|----------|
| /ɪ/ | i | th**i**s l**i**sten |
| | y | g**y**m t**y**pical |
| | ui | b**ui**ld g**ui**tar |
| | e | pr**e**tty |
| /iː/ | ee | gr**ee**n sl**ee**p |
| | ie | n**ie**ce bel**ie**ve |
| | ea | r**ea**d t**ea**cher |
| | e | th**e**se compl**e**te |
| | ey | k**ey** mon**ey** |
| | ei | rec**ei**pt rec**ei**ve |
| | i | pol**i**ce |
| /æ/ | a | c**a**n m**a**n p**a**sta l**a**nd |
| /ɑː/ | a | c**a**n't d**a**nce* |
| | ar | sc**ar**f b**ar**gain |
| | al | h**al**f |
| | au | **au**nt l**au**gh |
| | ea | h**ea**rt |
| /ʌ/ | u | f**u**n s**u**nny h**u**sband |
| | o | s**o**me m**o**ther m**o**nth |
| | ou | c**ou**sin d**ou**ble y**ou**ng |
| /ɒ/ | o | h**o**t p**o**cket t**o**p |
| | a | w**a**tch wh**a**t w**a**nt |
| /ɔː/ | or | sh**or**t sp**or**t st**or**e |
| | ou | y**our** c**our**se b**ou**ght |
| | au | d**au**ghter t**au**ght |
| | al | b**al**d sm**al**l **al**ways |
| | aw | dr**aw** jigs**aw** |
| | ar | w**ar**den w**ar**m |
| | oo | fl**oo**r ind**oo**r |
| /aɪ/ | i | l**i**ke t**i**me **i**sland |
| | y | dr**y** sh**y** c**y**cle |
| | ie | fr**ie**s d**ie** t**ie** |
| | igh | l**igh**t h**igh** r**igh**t |
| | ei | h**ei**ght |
| | ey | **ey**es |
| | uy | b**uy** |
| /eɪ/ | a | l**a**ke h**a**te sh**a**ve |
| | ai | w**ai**t tr**ai**n str**ai**ght |
| | ay | pl**ay** s**ay** st**ay** |
| | ey | th**ey** gr**ey** ob**ey** |
| | ei | **ei**ght w**ei**ght |
| | ea | br**ea**k |
| /əʊ/ | o | h**o**me ph**o**ne **o**pen |
| | ow | sh**ow** thr**ow** **ow**n |
| | oa | c**oa**t r**oa**d c**oa**st |
| | ol | c**o**ld t**o**ld |

\* In American English the sound in words like *can't* and *dance* is the /æ/ sound, like *can* and *man*.

## Part 3 | Pron1 Minimal pairs

| | Phonetic symbol | Example | Phonetic symbol | Example | Sentence |
|---|---|---|---|---|---|
| 1 | /ɪ/ | big | /æ/ | bag | It's a big bag. |
| 2 | /ɪ/ | sit | /iː/ | seat | Can I sit in this seat? |
| 3 | /æ/ | map | /ɒ/ | mop | That's my map and my mop. |
| 4 | /ɪ/ | live | /ʌ/ | love | I love living in London. |
| 5 | /ʌ/ | cup | /æ/ | cap | The cup is under your cap. |
| 6 | /iː/ | me | /ɔː/ | more | Please give me more. |
| 7 | /ɪ/ | ship | /ɒ/ | shop | There's a shop on the ship. |
| 8 | /ɪ/ | lift | /e/ | left | The lift is on the left. |
| 9 | /ɑː/ | car | /iː/ | key | Where's my car key? |
| 10 | /ɒ/ | box | /ʊ/ | books | Look at the box of books. |
| 11 | /iː/ | he | /ɜː/ | her | He hates her. |
| 12 | /iː/ | Sophie | /ə/ | sofa | Sophie's on the sofa. |
| 13 | /e/ | let | /eɪ/ | late | Let's get up late. |
| 14 | /aɪ/ | kite | /eɪ/ | Kate | This is Kate's kite. |
| 15 | /iː/ | she | /əʊ/ | show | She's at the show. |
| 16 | /iː/ | eat | /eɪ/ | eight | Did Jane eat eight cakes? |
| 17 | /aʊ/ | how | /aɪ/ | Hi | Hi. How are you? |
| 18 | /iː/ | week | /eɪ/ | wake | I wake up at six in the week. |
| 19 | /p/ | Paul | /b/ | ball | Put Paul's ball in the bin. |
| 20 | /t/ | to | /d/ | do | What do you want to do? |
| 21 | /k/ | came | /g/ | game | He came and played a game. |
| 22 | /tʃ/ | chess | /dʒ/ | Jess | Jess plays chess. |
| 23 | /f/ | off | /v/ | of | Please get off of Fran's van. |
| 24 | /p/ | pink | /θ/ | think | I think it's pink. |
| 25 | /p/ | pay | /ð/ | they | Did they pay for the party? |
| 26 | /s/ | keeps | /z/ | keys | She keeps her keys in her bag. |
| 27 | /t/ | fit | /ʃ/ | fish | Is your fish fit? |
| 28 | /t/ | letter | /ʒ/ | leisure | This letter's about leisure. |
| 29 | /m/ | mice | /n/ | nice | Are your mice nice? |
| 30 | /l/ | collect | /r/ | correct | Did you collect the correct letter? |

## Part 4 | Pron2 Syllable stress

Words with more than one syllable have the stress on one of the syllables.

| 1–syllable words ● | 2–syllable words ●○ | 2–syllable words ○● |
|---|---|---|
| one  six  big  young  read  learn  friend  great  lake  house  beach  road  west | happy  seven  listen  morning  passport  father  website  surname  photo  awful  teacher  picture  modern  Sunday | Japan  address  between  today  return  behind  Chinese  design  July  explain  mistake  dessert  because |
| 3–syllable words ●○○ | 3–syllable words ○●○ | 3–syllable words ○○● |
| India  favourite  gallery  holiday  beautiful  Saturday  visitor  newsagent  medium  popular  opposite  interview  architect  hospital | eleven  computer  cathedral  espresso  attachment  important  piano  designer  reporter  together  September  tomorrow  exciting  potato | afternoon  engineer  introduce  magazine |

## Part 5 | Pron3 Sentence stress and weak forms

Some syllables are stressed in a sentence. Others are weak. Stressed syllables are usually in nouns, verbs and adjectives. Weak syllables often use the 'schwa' /ə/ or other short vowels.

**My bro**ther is in Aus**tra**lia.

**Thi**s is a **beau**tiful **cas**tle.

**Their house** is **very mo**dern.

The **che**mist is **next** to the **bank**.

**My fav**ourite **place** for a **ho**liday is **Corn**wall.

I **don't like** this **mu**sic.

**Cath**erine **works** in a **fac**tory.

**Paul** is my **bro**ther and **he's** a de**sign**er.

I **get up** at **eight** o'**clock**.

She **never ans**wers the **phone**.

I'd **like** a **cup** of **tea, please**.

They **want** to **go** to the **beach**.

**Kerry found** her **bag un**der the **chair**.

I'm **go**ing to **buy** a **new car**.  or  I'm going to **buy** a **new car**.

## Part 6 | Pron4 Questions

We often use weak forms at the beginning of questions.

| | |
|---|---|
| <u>Are you</u> at home? | /ə juː/ |
| <u>Are they</u> ready? | /ə ðeɪ/ |
| <u>Do you</u> like it? | /dʒə/ |
| <u>Do you</u> write reports? | /dʒə/ |
| What <u>do you</u> do? | /dʒə/ |
| Where <u>do they</u> work? | /də ðeɪ/ |
| <u>Are you going</u> to get married? | /ə juː gəʊɪn tə/ or /ə juː gənə/ |
| <u>Are you going</u> to call her? | /ə juː gəʊɪn tə/ or /ə juː gənə/ |
| <u>Were you</u> a good student? | /wɜː juː/ |
| <u>Were we</u> at school together? | /wɜː wiː/ |
| <u>Did you</u> see him? | /dɪ juː/ |
| <u>Did you</u> talk to her? | /dɪ juː/ |

# A–Z Vocabulary list

(a pair of) shoes [ʃuːz] *3.2* _____

(a pair of) trousers ['traʊzəz] *3.2* _____

(in) brackets ['brækɪts] *8.1* _____

(on the) floor [flɔː] *6 t/s, 7c/a* _____

(past) experience [ɪk'spɪəriəns] *9.2* _____

play chess [tʃes] *8 l/in* _____

ability [ə'bɪləti] *5.3* _____

about four years [əbaʊt ˌfɔː
  'jɪəz] *10.1* _____

above [ə'bʌv] *6.1* _____

abroad [ə'brɔːd] *7.2* _____

accountant [ə'kaʊntənt] *2.3, 6.2* _____

activity [æk'tɪvəti] *6.2* _____

actor ['æktə] *2.3* _____

Act out the conversation.
  [ˌækt aʊt ðə ˌkɒnvə'seɪʃən] *7.3* _____

a cup of tea [ə ˌkʌp əv 'tiː] *7.3* _____

add [æd] *6.2* _____

address [ə'dres] *2 l/in* _____

adult ['ædʌlt, ə'dʌlt] *4.3* _____

adverb ['ædvɜːb] *7.2* _____

advert ['ædvɜːt] *10.2* _____

afternoon [ˌɑːftə'nuːn] *1.1* _____

again [ə'gen, ə'geɪn] *6.1* _____

age [eɪdʒ] *2.1* _____

agree [ə'griː] *9.3* _____

airport ['eəpɔːt] *1.2* _____

all day [ˌɔːl 'deɪ] *10 l/in* _____

a lot of [ə 'lɒt əv, ɒv] *5.1* _____

always ['ɔːlweɪz, -wɪz] *7.2* _____

and [ənd, ən] *3.2* _____

and so on [ənd 'səʊ ɒn] *8 c/a* _____

announcement [ə'naʊnsmənt] *7.1* _____

another example [əˌnʌðər
  ɪg'zɑːmpəl] *6.2* _____

answer ['ɑːnsə] *6.1* _____

antique [ˌæn'tiːk] *4.2* _____

any ['eni] *5.2* _____

Anything else? [ˌeniθɪŋ 'els] *4.1* _____

a packet of aspirin [ə ˌpækɪt
  əv 'æsprɪn] *4.3* _____

a piece of cake [ə ˌpiːs əv
  'keɪk] *4.1* _____

appointment [ə'pɔɪntmənt] *7 c/a* _____

April ['eɪprəl] *7.1* _____

architect ['ɑːkɪtekt] *6.2* _____

Are you ready to order? [ɑː
  jʊ ˌredi tʊ 'ɔːdə] *8 t/s* _____

Argentina [ˌɑːdʒən'tiːnə] *1.2* _____

armchair ['ɑːmtʃeə] *8.2* _____

around [ə'raʊnd] *4.3* _____

arrest [ə'rest] *10 l/in* _____

arrival [ə'raɪvəl] *1 l/in* _____

art [ɑːt] *3.3* _____

artist ['ɑːtɪst] *2.3* _____

ask (for) [ɑːsk] *2.2* _____

attachment [ə'tætʃmənt] *3.1* _____

attractive [ə'træktɪv] *9 t/s* _____

August ['ɔːgəst] *7.1* _____

aunt [ɑːnt] *6.3* _____

Australia [ɒ'streɪliə] *1.2* _____

available [ə'veɪləbəl] *8.1* _____

awful ['ɔːfəl] *2.2* _____

babies ['beɪbiz] *4.3* _____

baby ['beɪbi] *4.3* _____

back [bæk] *10 t/s* _____

backpack ['bækpæk] *3.1* _____

bad [bæd] *2.2* _____

Bad luck. [ˌbæd 'lʌk] *9.2* _____

bag [bæg] *4.2* _____

bank [bæŋk] *4 l/in* _____

basic ['beɪsɪk] *2.1* _____

basin ['beɪsən] *8.2* _____

bath [bɑːθ] *8.2* _____

beach [biːtʃ] *5 l/in* _____

beautiful ['bjuːtɪfəl] *3.1* _____

bed [bed] *5 c/a* _____

bedroom ['bedrʊm, -ruːm] *8.2* _____

beef [biːf] *8.3* _____

beginner [bɪ'gɪnə] *5.3* _____

behind [bɪ'haɪnd] *5.2* _____

below [bɪ'ləʊ] *6.1* _____

Be quiet [bi 'kwaɪət] *7.1* _____

best friends [ˌbest 'frendz] *6.2* _____

between [bɪ'twiːn] *3.2* _____

bicycle ['baɪsɪkəl] *8.1* _____

big [bɪg] *3.1* _____

biker ['baɪkə] *6.3* _____

bill [bɪl] *8.3* _____

birthday ['bɜːθdeɪ] *4 t/s* _____

biscuit ['bɪskɪt] *7.3* _____

black [blæk] *4.1* _____

blanket ['blæŋkɪt] *5 c/a* _____

blue [bluː] *4.2* _____

board [bɔːd] *7.2* _____

book [bʊk] *2 c/a, 8.3* _____

bookshop ['bʊkʃɒp] *4 l/in* _____

boring ['bɔːrɪŋ] *8.1* _____

box [bɒks] *6 l/in* _____

bracelet ['breɪslɪt] *4.2* _____

Brazil [brə'zɪl] *1.2* _____

break [breɪk] *10 l/in* _____

breakfast ['brekfəst] *5 c/a, 6.3* _____

brother ['brʌðə] 2 l/in _____

brown [braʊn] 4.2 _____

brunch [brʌntʃ] 6.3 _____

build [bɪld] 6.2 _____

builder ['bɪldə] 6.2 _____

building ['bɪldɪŋ] 5 l/in _____

bus stop ['bʌs stɒp] 4 l/in _____

busy ['bɪzi] 10.3 _____

but [bət, bʌt] 10.1 _____

Bye. [baɪ] 3 c/a _____

café ['kæfeɪ] 4 l/in _____

calendar ['kæləndə] 7.1 _____

call centre ['kɔːl ˌsentə] 7 l/in _____

camcorder ['kæmˌkɔːdə] 8.2 _____

camera ['kæmərə] 3.2 _____

can [kən, kæn] 5.3 _____

Canada ['kænədə] 2.3 _____

candle ['kændl] 6 c/a _____

Can he call you back? [kən
 hi ˌkɔːl jʊ 'bæk] 7 t/s _____

Can I have an espresso, please?
 [ˌkæn aɪ hæv ən e'spresəʊ
 pliːz] 4.2 _____

Can I help you? [kæn aɪ 'help
 jʊ] 3 t/s _____

Can I speak to Mr Flynn, please?
 [kən aɪ ˌspiːk tə ˌmɪstə 'flɪn ˌ
 pliːz] 7 t/s _____

canteen [ˌkæn'tiːn] 7.3 _____

capital ['kæpɪtl] 3.1 _____

car [kɑː] 3.1 _____

car park ['kɑː pɑːk] 4 l/in _____

carry ['kæri] 9.3 _____

cashpoint ['kæʃpɔɪnt] 4 l/in _____

castle ['kɑːsəl] 3 l/in _____

category ['kætəgəri] 6.1 _____

cathedral [kə'θiːdrəl] 3 l/in _____

ceiling ['siːlɪŋ] 10.1 _____

celebrate ['seləbreɪt] 8.3 _____

centre ['sentə] 5 l/in _____

century ['sentʃəri] 9.1 _____

Certainly./Sure ['sɜːtnli, ʃɔː] 4.1 _____

change [tʃeɪndʒ] 6.3 _____

chapel ['tʃæpəl] 6.3 _____

chart [tʃɑːt] 6 l/in _____

check [tʃek] 6 l/in _____

check in to a hotel [ˌtʃek ɪn
 tʊ ə həʊ'tel] 1.1 _____

cheese [tʃiːz] 8.3 _____

chef [ʃef] 8.2 _____

chemist ['kemɪst] 4 l/in _____

chicken ['tʃɪkən] 4.1, 8.3 _____

child [tʃaɪld] 4.3 _____

childcare ['tʃaɪldkeə] 9.3 _____

childhood ['tʃaɪldhʊd] 9.1 _____

children ['tʃɪldrən] 4.3 _____

China ['tʃaɪnə] 1 c/a _____

Chinese [ˌtʃaɪ'niːz] 5.2 _____

chocolate ['tʃɒklɪt] 4.1 _____

choose [tʃuːz] 8 t/s _____

chop [tʃɒp] 8.3 _____

cinema ['sɪnəmə] 4 l/in _____

city ['sɪti] 1.2 _____

classroom ['klɑːs-rʊm, -ruːm] 7.1 _____

clean [kliːn] 9.3 _____

close [kləʊz] 6 c/a _____

closed [kləʊzd] 3.3 _____

clothes [kləʊðz, kləʊz] 4.2 _____

coast [kəʊst] 5 l/in _____

coat [kəʊt] 4.2 _____

coffee ['kɒfi] 4.1 _____

coffee table ['kɒfi ˌteɪbəl] 8.2 _____

coin [kɔɪn] 10.2 _____

cold [kəʊld] 3 c/a _____

colleague ['kɒliːg] 7.3 _____

colour ['kʌlə] 4.2 _____

column ['kɒləm] 10.1 _____

Come in. [kʌm 'ɪn] 7.1 _____

Come on. [kʌm 'ɒn] 8 t/s _____

common ['kɒmən] 1.3 _____

communication [kəˌmjuːnɪ'keɪʃən] 1 c/a _____

company ['kʌmpəni] 6 c/a _____

complete [kəm'pliːt] 6.1 _____

computer [kəm'pjuːtə] 2 l/in _____

concert ['kɒnsət] 10.2 _____

continue [kən'tɪnjuː] 6.2 _____

cook [kʊk] 5.3 _____

cooker ['kʊkə] 8.2 _____

cookery book ['kʊkəri bʊk] 6 c/a _____

correct [kə'rekt] 6 l/in _____

Could you pass the milk?
 [kʊd jʊ ˌpɑːs ðə 'mɪlk] 9.3 _____

country, countries ['kʌntri,
 'kʌntriz] 1.2 _____

countryside ['kʌntrisaɪd] 5 l/in _____

course [kɔːs] 5.3 _____

crazy ['kreɪzi] 9.3 _____

crossword ['krɒswɜːd] 10.2 _____

customer ['kʌstəmə] 7.2 _____

Dad [dæd] 3 c/a _____

daily ['deɪli] 6.3 _____

dance [dɑːns] 5.3 _____

darling ['dɑːlɪŋ] 9 t/s _____

date [deɪt] 7.3 _____

daughter ['dɔːtə] 2 l/in _____

day of the week [ˌdeɪ əv ðə
'wiːk] 3.3 _____

dead [ded] 9 l/in _____

December [dɪ'sembə] 7.1 _____

department store [dɪ'pɑːtmənt
ˌstɔː] 3 l/in _____

describe [dɪ'skraɪb] 6.3 _____

description [dɪ'skrɪpʃən] 5.1, 9.2 _____

design [dɪ'zaɪn] 6.2 _____

designer [dɪ'zaɪnə] 6.2 _____

dessert [dɪ'zɜːt] 7.3 _____

dial ['daɪəl] 1 c/a _____

dictionary ['dɪkʃənəri] 6 c/a _____

different ['dɪfərənt] 6.2 _____

difficult ['dɪfɪkəlt] 8.1 _____

digital camera [ˌdɪdʒɪtl
'kæmərə] 8.2 _____

disaster [dɪ'zɑːstə] 9 l/in _____

dishes ['dɪʃɪz] 9.3 _____

do [duː] 6.2 _____

do an interview [ˌduː ən
'ɪntəvjuː] 6.1 _____

doctor ['dɒktə] 2.3 _____

do exercise [ˌduː 'eksəsaɪz] 8 l/in _____

Don't come in. [ˌdəʊnt kʌm
'ɪn] 7.1 _____

do the laundry [ˌduː ðə
'lɔːndri] 9.3 _____

double bed [ˌdʌbəl 'bed] 5 c/a _____

draw [drɔː] 6.1 _____

dream [driːm] 9 l/in _____

dreamer ['driːmə] 9.1 _____

dress [dres] 4.2 _____

drink [drɪŋk] 4.1, 7.3 _____

drive [draɪv] 5.3 _____

driver ['draɪvə] 9.1 _____

dry [draɪ] 4.3 _____

each [iːtʃ] 6.1 _____

early ['ɜːli] 6.3 _____

east [iːst] 5 l/in _____

easy ['iːzi] 8.1 _____

Eat in or take away? [ˌiːt 'ɪn
ɔː ˌteɪk ə'weɪ] 4.1 _____

eat out [ˌiːt 'aʊt] 8 l/in _____

eight [eɪt] 1.1 _____

eighteen [ˌeɪ'tiːn] 2.1 _____

eighty ['eɪti] 2.1 _____

eleven [ɪ'levən] 2.1 _____

email ['iːmeɪl] 2 l/in _____

en-suite [ˌɒn 'swiːt] 5 c/a _____

ending ['endɪŋ] 10.1 _____

engineer [ˌendʒɪ'nɪə] 2.3 _____

England ['ɪŋglənd] 5.2 _____

English ['ɪŋglɪʃ] 5.2 _____

enter ['entə] 4.3, 8.3 _____

entrance ['entrəns] 3.3 _____

etc. = et cetera [et 'setərə] 6.2 _____

evening ['iːvnɪŋ] 1.1 _____

event [ɪ'vent] 10.1 _____

every ['evri] 6.3 _____

every year [ˌevri 'jɪə] 3.3 _____

exciting [ɪk'saɪtɪŋ] 8.1 _____

Excuse me, ... [ɪk'skjuːz mi] 1.3 _____

expensive [ɪk'spensɪv] 9.3 _____

explain [ɪk'spleɪn] 7.1 _____

expression [ɪk'spreʃən] 9.2 _____

factory ['fæktəri] 7 l/in _____

false [fɔːls] 1.2, 6.2 _____

family ['fæməli] 2.1 _____

famous ['feɪməs] 5.1 _____

fashion ['fæʃən] 6.1 _____

fast [fɑːst] 6.3 _____

fat [fæt] 6 l/in _____

father ['fɑːðə] 2 l/in _____

February ['februəri, 'febjʊri] 7.1 _____

feel [fiːl] 9.1 _____

fifteen [ˌfɪf'tiːn] 2.1 _____

fifty ['fɪfti] 2.1 _____

fighter ['faɪtə] 9.1 _____

film [fɪlm] 2 c/a _____

find [faɪnd] 1 c/a _____

fine ['faɪn] 3 c/a _____

finish ['fɪnɪʃ] 6.3 _____

first name ['fɜːst neɪm] 2 l/in _____

fish [fɪʃ] 8.3 _____

fisherman ['fɪʃəmən] 10.3 _____

five [faɪv] 1.1 _____

five past six [ˌfaɪv pɑːst 'sɪks] 5 c/a _____

flat [flæt] 8.2 _____

flight [flaɪt] 9.2 _____

flight attendant [flaɪt ə'tendənt] 9 t/s _____

floor [flɔː] 6 t/s, 7 c/a _____

flower ['flaʊə] 6 c/a _____

food [fuːd] 3 c/a _____

football team ['fʊtbɔːl ˌtiːm] 6.1 _____

for example [fər ɪg'zɑːmpəl] 4 t/s _____

form [fɔːm] 6.3 _____

forty ['fɔːti] 2.1 _____

fountain ['faʊntən] 5.2 _____

four [fɔː] 1.1 _____

fourteen [ˌfɔː'tiːn] 2.1 _____

free [friː] 3.3 _____

French [frentʃ] *5.2* _____

frequency ['fri:kwənsi] *7.2* _____

Friday ['fraɪdi, -deɪ] *3.3* _____

fridge [frɪdʒ] *5 c/a, 8.2* _____

friend [frend] *2.1*

from Tuesday to Sunday
[frəm ˌtjuːzdi tə 'sʌndi] *3.3* _____

from two o'clock to four o'clock
[frəm ˌtuː əklɒk tə 'fɔːr
əˌklɒk] *5.3* _____

fruit [fruːt] *7.3* _____

funny ['fʌni] *9 t/s* _____

furniture ['fɜːnɪtʃə] *8.2* _____

gallery ['gæləri] *3 l/in* _____

game [geɪm] *9.1* _____

gap [gæp] *6.2* _____

general ['dʒenərəl] *5.3* _____

Germany ['dʒɜːməni] *1.2* _____

get fit [get fɪt] *10.3* _____

get married [get 'mærɪd] *10 l/in* _____

get up [get ʌp] *6.3* _____

give an opinion [gɪv ən
ə'pɪnjən] *5.1* _____

give information (about) [gɪv
ɪnfə'meɪʃən] *2.1* _____

go cycling [ˌgəʊ 'saɪklɪŋ] *8 l/in* _____

go for a walk [ˌgəʊ fər ə
'wɔːk] *8 l/in* _____

go to university [ˌgəʊ tə ˌjuːnɪˈʊːsɪti] *10.3* _____

gold [gəʊld] *10.2* _____

golf course ['gɒlf kɔːs] *8 t/s* _____

good-looking [ˌgʊd 'lʊkɪŋ] *6 l/in* _____

good [gʊd] *1.1* _____

Good morning. [gʊd 'mɔːnɪŋ] *1 l/in* _____

go out [gəʊ 'aʊt] *8.1* _____

go sightseeing [ˌgəʊ
'saɪtˌsiːɪŋ] *8 l/in* _____

go swimming [ˌgəʊ 'swɪmɪŋ] *8 l/in* _____

go to bed [ˌgəʊ tə 'bed] *6.3* _____

GPS device [ˌdʒiː piː 'es
dɪˌvaɪs] *8.2* _____

grammar ['græmə] *1.1* _____

grandson ['grændsʌn] *10.3* _____

great [greɪt] *2.2* _____

green [griːn] *4.2* _____

greeting ['griːtɪŋ] *1.1* _____

greet someone ['griːt
ˌsʌmwʌn] *1.2* _____

group [gruːp] *6.2* _____

guess [ges] *9 l/in* _____

guide [gaɪd] *4.1* _____

half past seven [ˌhɑːf pɑːst
'sevən] *5 c/a*

happy ['hæpi] *6 l/in* _____

hat [hæt] *4.2* _____

have a child/children
[hæv ə tʃaɪld/tʃɪldrən] *10.3* _____

have a shower [hæv ə 'ʃaʊə] *6.3* _____

He's from Russia. [ˌhiːz frəm
'rʌʃə] *1.1* _____

headline ['hedlaɪn] *9 l/in* _____

hear [hɪə] *6.3* _____

Hello./Hi. [hə'ləʊ, he-, haɪ] *1 l/in* _____

here [hɪə] *3.3* _____

He wants to go to the cinema.
[hi ˌwɒnts tə ˌgəʊ tə ðə
'sɪnəmə] *8.1* _____

He was born on 8th January.
[hi wəz ˌbɔːn ɒn ði ˌeɪtθ əv
'dʒænjuəri] *9.1* _____

He was married to Cynthia.
[hi wəz ˌmærɪd tə 'sɪnθɪə] *9 t/s* _____

high [haɪ] *10.2* _____

hill [hɪl] *5 l/in* _____

history ['hɪstəri] *9.1* _____

Hold the line. [ˌhəʊld ðə 'laɪn] *7.1* _____

holiday ['hɒlədi, -deɪ] *3.1* _____

home [həʊm] *6 t/s* _____

hospital ['hɒspɪtl] *7 l/in* _____

hot [hɒt] *3 c/a* _____

house [haʊs] *3.1* _____

househusband ['haʊsˌhʌzbənd] *9.3* _____

housewife ['haʊswaɪf] *9.3* _____

housework ['haʊswɜːk] *9.3* _____

How about...? ['haʊ əbaʊt] *8 t/s* _____

How are you? [haʊ 'ɑː jʊ] *3.1* _____

How do you spell that? [ˌhaʊ
dʊ jʊ 'spel ðæt] *2.2* _____

How many people? [ˌhaʊ
meni 'piːpəl] *8.3* _____

How much are they? [haʊ
'mʌtʃ 'ɑː ðeɪ] *4.2* _____

How much is it? [haʊ 'mʌtʃ
'ɪz ɪt,] *4.2* _____

how often [ˌhaʊ 'ɒfən, 'ɒftən] *7.2* _____

How old is she? [haʊ 'əʊld
ɪz ʃi] *2.1* _____

How was your day? [ˌhaʊ
wəz jɔː 'deɪ] *9.3* _____

husband ['hʌzbənd] *2 l/in* _____

ice cream [ˌaɪs 'kriːm] *8.3* _____

iced coffee [ˌaɪst 'kɒfi] *4.1* _____

icon ['aɪkɒn] *9.1* _____

idea [aɪ'dɪə] *8.2* _____

I'm afraid he's in a meeting this morning. [aɪm əˌfreɪd
hiz ɪn ə 'miːtɪŋ ðɪs ˌmɔːnɪŋ] *7 t/s* _____

I'm from ... ['aɪm frəm] *1.3* _____

I'm sorry. [aɪm 'sɒri] *4 c/a* _____

immediate [ɪ'miːdiət] *10.3* _____

immediately [ɪ'miːdiətli] *3 t/s* _____

important [ɪm'pɔːtənt] *5.1* _____

in [ɪn] *5.2* _____

in a lot of ways [ɪn ə 'lɒt əv weɪz] *6.2* _____

in bold [ɪn 'bəʊld] *9.1* _____

in class [ɪn 'klɑːs] *7.1* _____

India ['ɪndiə] *1.2* _____

Indian ['ɪndiən] *5.2* _____

in front of [ɪn 'frʌnt əv, ɒv] *5.2* _____

in the afternoon/morning/evening [ɪn ði ˌɑːftə'nuːn, 'mɔːnɪŋ, 'iːvnɪŋ] *5.3* _____

in the north of [ɪn ðə 'nɔːθ əv] *5 l/in* _____

inside [ɪn'saɪd, 'ɪnsaɪd] *10.2* _____

instant coffee [ˌɪnstənt 'kɒfi] *4.1* _____

instruction [ɪn'strʌkʃən] *7.1* _____

intelligent [ɪn'telɪdʒənt] *6 l/in* _____

interesting ['ɪntrəstɪŋ] *8.1* _____

interview ['ɪntəvjuː] *6.1* _____

introduce someone [ˌɪntrə'djuːs ˌsʌmwʌn] *1.3* _____

Ireland ['aɪələnd] *5.2* _____

Irish ['aɪərɪʃ] *5.2* _____

iron ['aɪən] *9.3* _____

irregular [ɪ'regjʊlə] *4.3* _____

Is there a bank near here? [ɪz ðeər ə 'bæŋk nɪə ˌhɪə] *5.2* _____

It's called ... [ɪts kɔːld] *5.1* _____

It's four pounds fifty. [ɪts ˌfɔː paʊndz 'fɪfti] *4.2* _____

It's OK. [ɪts ˌəʊ 'keɪ] *2.1* _____

Italian [ɪ'tæliən] *5.2* _____

italics [ɪ'tælɪks] *6.1* _____

Italy ['ɪtəli] *1.2* _____

January ['dʒænjuəri, -njʊri] *7.1* _____

Japan [dʒə'pæn] *1.2* _____

job [dʒɒb] *2.3* _____

July [dʒʊ'laɪ] *7.1* _____

jumper ['dʒʌmpə] *4.2* _____

June [dʒuːn] *7.1* _____

kettle ['ketl] *5 c/a* _____

king [kɪŋ] *10.1* _____

kitchen ['kɪtʃən] *8.2* _____

know [nəʊ] *4 c/a, 6.2* _____

lake [leɪk] *3 l/in* _____

lamb [læm] *8.3* _____

lamp [læmp] *5 c/a, 8.2* _____

language ['læŋgwɪdʒ] *5.2* _____

large [lɑːdʒ] *4.1* _____

last month [ˌlɑːst 'mʌnθ] *9.2* _____

last night/week [ˌlɑːst 'naɪt, 'wiːk] *9.2* _____

last year [ˌlɑːst 'jɪə] *9.2* _____

later ['leɪtə] *10.1* _____

learn [lɜːn] *1.2* _____

learn to drive [lɜːn tə draɪv] *10.3* _____

lecturer ['lektʃərə] *7 l/in* _____

leisure activity ['leʒər ækˌtɪvəti] *8 l/in* _____

lesson ['lesən] *7.1* _____

Let's play. [lets 'pleɪ] *9 t/s* _____

letter ['letə] *1.2, 6.3* _____

level ['levəl] *5 t/s* _____

library ['laɪbrəri, -bri] *10.1* _____

life [laɪf] *2 l/in, 6.3, 9.1* _____

lifelong ['laɪflɒŋ] *1.2* _____

lifetime ['laɪftaɪm] *10.3* _____

lift [lɪft] *7 c/a* _____

like [laɪk] *6.1* _____

line [laɪn] *6.3* _____

list [lɪst] *6.1, 8.2* _____

listen ['lɪsən] *1.1, 6 l/in* _____

living room ['lɪvɪŋ ruːm, -rʊm] *8.2* _____

local ['ləʊkəl] *8.3* _____

location [ləʊ'keɪʃən] *5 c/a* _____

long-term [lɒŋ-'tɜːm] *10.3* _____

look (after) [lʊk] *9.3* _____

look at ['lʊk ət, æt] *6.1* _____

lose [luːz] *10 l/in* _____

lottery ['lɒtəri] *10 l/in* _____

Love ... [lʌv] *3.1* _____

low prices [ˌləʊ 'praɪsɪz] *10 t/s* _____

magazine [ˌmægə'ziːn] *8.2* _____

magazine article [ˌmægə'ziːn ˌɑːtɪkəl] *6.2* _____

main course [ˌmeɪn 'kɔːs] *7.3* _____

make [meɪk] *3.2* _____

make friends [meɪk 'frendz] *6.2* _____

man [mæn] *4.3* _____

manager ['mænɪdʒə] *2.3* _____

Many thanks. [ˌmeni 'θæŋks] *7.2* _____

map [mæp] *3.1* _____

March [mɑːtʃ] *7.1* _____

mark [mɑːk] *6.2* _____

market ['mɑːkɪt] *3 l/in* _____

marriage ['mærɪdʒ] *9.1* _____

married ['mærid] *6 c/a* _____

match [mætʃ] *6.2* _____

May [meɪ] *7.1* _____

meal [miːl] *9.2* _____

mean [miːn] *7 c/a* _____

meaning ['miːnɪŋ] *9.1* _____

medium ['miːdiəm] *4.1* _____

member ['membə] *6.3* _____

men [men] *4.3* _____

menu ['menjuː] *8.3* _____

Mexico ['meksɪkəʊ] *1 c/a* _____

microwave oven [,maɪkrəweɪv
'ʌvən] *8.2* _____

midnight ['mɪdnaɪt] *6.3* _____

milk [mɪlk] *4.1, 7.3* _____

mineral water ['mɪnərəl
,wɔːtə] *4.1* _____

mirror ['mɪrə] *8.2* _____

Miss Jones [mɪs 'dʒəʊnz] *1.1* _____

mistake [mɪ'steɪk] *7.2* _____

mobile phone [,məʊbaɪl 'fəʊn] *2 l/in* _____

model ['mɒdl] *9.1* _____

modern ['mɒdn] *3.1* _____

Monday ['mʌndi, -deɪ] *3.3* _____

more [mɔː] *6.1* _____

morning ['mɔːnɪŋ] *1.1* _____

most of them ['məʊst əv ðəm] *10.1* _____

mother ['mʌðə] *2 l/in* _____

mountain ['maʊntən] *3 l/in* _____

move [muːv] *10 l/in* _____

MP3 player [,em piː 'θriː
,pleɪə] *3.2* _____

Mrs/Ms Jones [,mɪsɪz 'dʒəʊnz,
,mɪz] *1.1* _____

Mr Smith [,mɪstə 'smɪθ] *1.1* _____

Mum [mʌm] *3 c/a* _____

museum [mjuː'ziəm] *3 l/in* _____

music ['mjuːzɪk] *5.2* _____

musician [mjuː'zɪʃən] *6.3* _____

my favourite ... [maɪ 'feɪvərɪt] *2 c/a* _____

narrative ['nærətɪv] *10.1* _____

nationality [,næʃə'næləti] *5.2* _____

near [nɪə] *3.3* _____

negative ['negətɪv] *9.2* _____

never ['nevə] *7.2* _____

Never mind. [,nevə 'maɪnd] *4 c/a* _____

new [njuː] *3 c/a* _____

news [njuːz] *5.2, 10.2* _____

newsagent ['njuːz,eɪdʒənt] *4 l/in* _____

newspaper ['njuːs,peɪpə] *8.2* _____

next to ['nekst tə, tʊ] *4 c/a* _____

next weekend [,nekst wiːk'end,
'wiːkend] *8 t/s* _____

Nice to meet you. [,naɪs tə
'miːt jʊ] *1 l/in* _____

Nice to meet you, too. [,naɪs
tə ,miːt juː 'tuː] *1 l/in* _____

night [naɪt] *1.1* _____

nine [naɪn] *1.1* _____

nineteen [,naɪn'tiːn] *2.1* _____

ninety ['naɪnti] *2.1* _____

No, thank you. [,nəʊ 'θæŋk
jʊ] *1.3* _____

north [nɔːθ] *5 l/in* _____

note [nəʊt] *7.2, 10 c/a* _____

notice ['nəʊtɪs] *7.1,* _____

November [nəʊ'vembə, nə-] *7.1* _____

now [naʊ] *6.3* _____

number ['nʌmbə] *1.1* _____

nurse [nɜːs] *7 l/in* _____

occupation [,ɒkjʊ'peɪʃən] *6 c/a* _____

October [ɒk'təʊbə] *7.1* _____

of course [əv 'kɔːs] *10.1* _____

office building ['ɒfɪs ,bɪldɪŋ] *6.2* _____

often ['ɒfən, 'ɒftən] *7.2* _____

Oh dear. [,əʊ 'dɪə] *6 t/s* _____

old [əʊld] *3.1* _____

on [ɒn] *5.2* _____

on business [ɒn 'bɪznəs] *6.2* _____

on holiday [ɒn 'hɒlədi, -deɪ] *6.2* _____

on King Street [ɒn 'kɪŋ striːt] *4 c/a* _____

on Mondays [ɒn 'mʌndiz] *3.3* _____

on the right/left [ɒn ðə 'raɪt,
'left] *7 t/s* _____

on the River Thames [ɒn ðə
,rɪvə 'temz] *3.3* _____

one [wʌn] *1.1* _____

one pound [,wʌn 'paʊnd] *4.1* _____

only ['əʊnli] *4.2* _____

open ['əʊpən] *3.3* _____

opposite ['ɒpəzɪt] *4 c/a, 6 l/in* _____

or [ə, ɔː] *4.3* _____

orange ['ɒrəndʒ] *4.2* _____

orange juice ['ɒrəndʒ dʒuːs] *4.1* _____

order ['ɔːdə] *4.1* _____

ordinal number ['ɔːdɪnəl nʌmbə] *7.3* _____

other ['ʌðə] *2.3* _____

outdoors [,aʊt'dɔːz] *7.2* _____

outdoor theatre [,aʊtdɔː 'θɪətə] *5.1* _____

over sixty [,əʊvə 'sɪksti] *6.2* _____

PA (personal assistant)
[,pɜːsənəl ə'sɪstənt] *7 l/in* _____

page [peɪdʒ] *1.2* _____

painting ['peɪntɪŋ] *10.1* _____

pair [peə] *6.1* _____

palace ['pæləs] *3 l/in* _____

paper ['peɪpə] *8.2* _____

Pardon? ['pɑːdn] 1.3 _____

parents ['peərənts] 9.1 _____

park [pɑːk] 8.2 _____

part [pɑːt] 6 c/a _____

partner ['pɑːtnə] 6 c/a _____

passport ['pɑːspɔːt] 2 l/in _____

past [pɑːst] 9 l/in _____

pasta ['pæstə] 8.3 _____

pay by credit card [ˌpeɪ baɪ
'kredɪt kɑːd] 4.3 _____

pen [pen] 6 c/a _____

people ['piːpəl] 1.3 _____

pepper ['pepə] 8.3 _____

permission [pə'mɪʃən] 9.3 _____

person ['pɜːsən] 4.3 _____

personal details [ˌpɜːsənəl
'diːteɪlz] 2.2 _____

phone [fəʊn] 2 l/in _____

phone call ['fəʊn kɔːl] 7.1 _____

phone number ['fəʊn ˌnʌmbə] 1 c/a _____

photo ['fəʊtəʊ] 2 l/in _____

phrase [freɪz] 1.3 _____

pianist ['piːənɪst] 9.1 _____

picture ['pɪktʃə] 2.3 _____

place [pleɪs] 3.1 _____

place of work [ˌpleɪs əv 'wɜːk] 7.3 _____

plan [plæn] 7 c/a _____

plans [plænz] 10.3 _____

plants from all over the world
[plɑːnt frəm ˌɔːl əʊvə ðə
'wɜːld] 5.1 _____

play [pleɪ] 5.3 _____

play chess [ˌpleɪ tʃes] 8 l/in _____

play golf [ˌpleɪ 'gɒlf] 5.3 _____

play the piano [ˌpleɪ ðə
pi'ænəʊ] 5.3 _____

point [pɔɪnt] 8.2 _____

Poland ['pəʊlənd] 1.2 _____

police officer [pə'liːs ˌɒfɪsə] 2.3 _____

polite [pə'laɪt] 7.1 _____

poor [pɔː] 6 l/in _____

popular ['pɒpjʊlə] 4.2 _____

possess [pə'zes] 8.2 _____

postman ['pəʊstmən] 8 c/a _____

potato(es) [pə'teɪtəʊs] 8.3 _____

practise ['præktɪs] 7.1 _____

prawns [prɔːnz] 8.3 _____

prepare [prɪ'peə] 7.2 _____

present ['prezənt] 6.1, 6.3 _____

presentation [ˌprezən'teɪʃən] 7.2 _____

president ['prezɪdənt] 9 L/in _____

price [praɪs] 4.1 _____

prince [prɪns] 9.1 _____

princess [ˌprɪn'ses] 9.1 _____

problem ['prɒbləm] 8.1 _____

pronounce [prə'naʊns] 7.2 _____

pronunciation [prəˌnʌnsi'eɪʃən] 1.2 _____

purse [pɜːs] 10 l/in _____

put [pʊt] 6 l/in _____

quarter past four [ˌkwɔːtə
pɑːst 'fɔː] 5 c/a _____

question ['kwestʃən] 1.3 _____

quite [kwaɪt] 6 l/in _____

quiz [kwɪz] 8.2 _____

quote [kwəʊt] 9.1 _____

read [riːd] 1.2 _____

Read the conversation aloud.
[ˌriːd ðə kɒnvəˌseɪʃən ə'laʊd] 7.3 _____

ready ['redi] 9 t/s _____

really ['rɪəli] 6.2 _____

reason ['riːzən] 7.1 _____

receive [rɪ'siːv] 5.2 _____

receptionist [rɪ'sepʃənɪst] 7 c/a _____

red [red] 4.2 _____

regular ['regjʊlə] 3.2 _____

remember [rɪ'membə] 9.2 _____

repeat [rɪ'piːt] 6.1 _____

report [rɪ'pɔːt] 7.2 _____

reporter [rɪ'pɔːtə] 6.2 _____

request [rɪ'kwest] 7.2 _____

reservation [ˌrezə'veɪʃən] 8.3 _____

respond [rɪ'spɒnd] 10 l/in _____

restaurant ['restərɒnt] 2 c/a _____

retire [rɪ'taɪə] 10.3 _____

return [rɪ'tɜːn] 4.3 _____

rice [raɪs] 8.3 _____

rich [rɪtʃ] 6 l/in _____

river ['rɪvə] 3.3 _____

road [rəʊd] 5 l/in _____

room [ruːm, rʊm] 1.1 _____

routine [ruː'tiːn] 6.3 _____

royal ['rɔɪəl] 9 l/in _____

salad ['sæləd] 4.1 _____

sales assistant ['seɪlz əˌsɪstənt] 2.3 _____

sales rep. ['seɪlz rep] 6.2 _____

salt [sɔːlt] 8.3 _____

same [seɪm] 6.2 _____

sandwich ['sænwɪdʒ] 4.1 _____

Saturday ['sætədi, -deɪ] 3.3 _____

saucepan ['sɔːspən] 6 c/a _____

say [seɪ] 1.1 _____

school [skuːl] 7 l/in _____

science ['saɪəns] 9 c/a _____

score [skɔː] 8.2 _____

Scotland ['skɒtlənd] 5.2 _____

Scottish ['skɒtɪʃ] 5.2 _____

sea [siː] 5 l/in _____

seafood ['siːfuːd] 8.3 _____

second ['sekənd] 6.1 _____

See you on Friday. [ˌsiː jʊ ɒn
'fraɪdi] 3 c/a, 8 t/s _____

sell [sel] 6.2 _____

sentence ['sentəns] 6 l/in _____

September [sep'tembə] 7.1 _____

serve [sɜːv] 8.3 _____

seven ['sevən] 1.1 _____

seventeen [ˌsevən'tiːn] 2.1 _____

seventy ['sevənti] 2.1 _____

She's sixty-two years old.
[ʃiz ˌsɪksti tuː jɪəz 'əʊld] 2.1 _____

She is called Cynthia. [ˌʃiː ɪz
kɔːld 'sɪnθiə] 6.1 _____

She was born in 1963. [ʃi
wəz ˌbɔːn ɪn ˌnaɪntiːn sɪksti
'θriː] 9.1 _____

She was good at horse-riding and painting.
[ʃi wəz ˌgʊd ət ˌhɔːs raɪdɪŋ
ən 'peɪntɪŋ] 9 t/s _____

shirt [ʃɜːt] 4.2 _____

shop [ʃɒp] 3.3 _____

shopping ['ʃɒpɪŋ] 4.3 _____

short [ʃɔːt] 2.3, 6 l/in _____

show [ʃəʊ] 4.3 _____

shower ['ʃaʊə] 5 c/a _____

show interest [ˌʃəʊ 'ɪntrəst] 6.2 _____

sign [saɪn] 4.3, 7.1 _____

similar (to) ['sɪmələ] 9 t/s _____

simple ['sɪmpəl] 3.1 _____

sing [sɪŋ] 5.3 _____

singer [' sɪŋə] 2 c/a _____

single ['sɪŋgəl] 4.3 _____

sink [sɪŋk] 8.2 _____

sister ['sɪstə] 2 l/in _____

Sit down. [ˌsɪt 'daʊn] 7.1 _____

six [sɪks] 1.1 _____

sixteen [ˌsɪk'stiːn] 2.1 _____

sixty ['sɪksti] 2.1 _____

skirt [skɜːt] 3.2 _____

small [smɔːl] 3.1, 4.1 _____

Smoking or non-smoking?
[ˌsməʊkɪŋ ɔː 'nɒn ˌsməʊkɪŋ] 8 t/s _____

snack [snæk] 7.3 _____

sofa ['səʊfə] 8.2 _____

some [səm, sʌm] 5.1 _____

someone ['sʌmwʌn] 6.2 _____

something ['sʌmθɪŋ] 4 c/a, 7.2 _____

son [sʌn] 2 l/in _____

song [sɒŋ] 6.3 _____

soon [suːn] 10.3, 10 t/s _____

Sorry. ['sɒri] 1.3 _____

soup [suːp] 7.3 _____

south [saʊθ] 5 l/in _____

space [speɪs] 9 l/n _____

Spain [speɪn] 9 c/a _____

speak [spiːk] 1.1 _____

spell [spel] 2.2 _____

spice [spaɪs] 5.1 _____

spoken ['spəʊkən] 7.1 _____

square [skweə] 5.2 _____

staff [stɑːf] 7.3 _____

start a business [ˌstɑːt ə 'bɪznɪs] 10.3 _____

start a conversation [ˌstɑːt ə
ˌkɒnvə'seɪʃən] 1.3 _____

starter ['stɑːtə] 7.3 _____

start work [ˌstɑːt 'wɜːk] 6.3 _____

statement (about) ['steɪtmənt] 9.1 _____

stay [steɪ] 9.3 _____

steal [stiːl] 10 l/in _____

still/sparkling mineral water
[ˌstɪl 'mɪnərəl ˌwɔːtə, ˌspɑːklɪŋ] 8.3 _____

story ['stɔːri] 10.1 _____

stranger ['streɪndʒə] 9.3 _____

street [striːt] 3.3 _____

strong [strɒŋ] 9.1 _____

student ['stjuːdənt] 2.3 _____

subject ['sʌbdʒɪkt] 9 c/a _____

succeed [sək'siːd] 7.1 _____

sugar ['ʃʊgə] 4.1, 7.3 _____

suggest [sə'dʒest] 8.3 _____

suggestion [sə'dʒestʃən] 8.2 _____

suitcase ['suːtkeɪs, 'sjuːt-] 3.1 _____

summary ['sʌməri] 10.2 _____

Sunday ['sʌndi, -deɪ] 3.3 _____

sunny ['sʌni] 9 t/s _____

supermarket ['suːpəˌmɑːkɪt] 4 l/in _____

surname ['sɜːneɪm] 2 l/in _____

survive [sə'vaɪv] 4/3 _____

swim [swɪm] 5.3 _____

T-shirt ['tiː ʃɜːt] 4.2 _____

take (home) [teɪk] 7.2 _____

talk (about) ['tɔːk] 2.1 _____

talk (to) [tɔːk] 6.2 _____

tall [tɔːl] 6 l/in _____

taste [teɪst] 8.3 _____

teach [tiːtʃ] 7.1 _____

teacher ['tiːtʃə] 2.3, 7 l/in _____

technology [tek'nɒlədʒi] 8.2 _____

television ['teləˌvɪʒən,
ˌtelə'vɪʒən] 5 c/a _____

tell [tel] *6.1* _____

ten [ten] *1.1* _____

tennis court ['tenɪs kɔːt] *8 t/s* _____

ten to nine [ˌten tə 'naɪn] *5 c/a* _____

test [test] *6 l/in* _____

text [tekst] *9.1* _____

Thanks. [θæŋks] *7.2* _____

Thank you. ['θæŋk juː] *1 l/in* _____

That's forty-two thirty, please.
[ðæts ˌfɔːti tuː 'θɜːti ˌpliːz] *4.1* _____

That's life. [ðæts 'laɪf] *10.2* _____

theatre ['θɪətə] *8 l/in* _____

the first of September [ðə
ˌfɜːst əv sep'tembə] *7.3* _____

the ninth of February [ðə
ˌnaɪnθ əv 'februəri, 'febjʊri] *7.3* _____

then [ðen] _____

the second of July [ðə ˌsekənd
əv dʒʊ'laɪ] *7.3* _____

the third of April [ðə ˌθɜːd
əv 'eɪprəl] *7.3* _____

the twentieth of May [ðə
ˌtwentiəθ əv 'meɪ] *7.3* _____

the UK [ðə juː 'keɪ] *1.2* _____

the US [ðə juː es] *1.2* _____

there [ðeə] *3.3* _____

There are nice hotels in New York.
[ðeər ə ˌnaɪs həʊˌtelz ɪn
njuː 'jɔːk] *5.1* _____

They got married. [ðeɪ gɒt
'mærid] *10.2* _____

They were poor. [ðeɪ wə 'pɔː] *9.1* _____

thief [θiːf] *10 l/in* _____

thin [θɪn] *6 l/in* _____

thing [θɪŋ] *3.2* _____

think [θɪŋk] *5.1* _____

thirteen [ˌθɜː'tiːn] *2.1* _____

thirty ['θɜːti] *2.1* _____

This is fun. [ðɪs ɪz 'fʌn] *8.1* _____

This is Paul. [ðɪs ɪz 'pɔːl] *1.3* _____

thousand ['θaʊzənd] *10.2* _____

three [θriː] *1.1* _____

three euros [ˌθriː 'jʊərəʊz] *4.1* _____

Thursday ['θɜːzdi, -deɪθɜːzdi,
-deɪ] *3.3* _____

tick [tɪk] *6 c/a* _____

ticket (to) ['tɪkɪt] *3.2, 10.2* _____

tie [taɪ] *6 c/a* _____

time [taɪm] *5 c/a* _____

Time's up. [ˌtaɪmz 'ʌp] *9.2* _____

Time is up. [ˌtaɪm ɪz 'ʌp] *6 t/s* _____

time of day [ˌtaɪm əv 'deɪ] *6.1* _____

today [tə'deɪ] *3.3* _____

toilet ['tɔɪlət] *7 c/a* _____

tomorrow [tə'mɒrəʊ] *7.2* _____

top [adj] [tɒp] *3.3* _____

top [tɒp] *3.2* _____

tourist ['tʊərɪst] *4.2* _____

tourist attraction ['tʊərɪst
əˌtrækʃən] *3 l/in* _____

tourist information [ˌtʊərɪst
ɪnfə'meɪʃən] *3.3* _____

towel ['taʊəl] *5 c/a* _____

town [taʊn] *4 l/in* _____

train station ['treɪn ˌsteɪʃən] *4 l/n* _____

travel ['trævəl] *3 l/in* _____

tree [triː] *5 l/n* _____

true [truː] *6.2* _____

Tuesday ['tjuːzdi, -deɪ] *3.3* _____

Turkey ['tɜːki] *1.3* _____

Turn off your mobile phone.
[ˌtɜːn ɒf jɔː ˌməʊbaɪl 'fəʊn] *7.1* _____

Turn right/left [ˌtɜːn 'raɪt, 'left] *7 t/s* _____

twelve [twelv] *2.1* _____

twenty ['twenti] *2.1* _____

two [tuː] *1.1* _____

two dollars [ˌtuː 'dɒləz] *4.1* _____

two kilometres [ˌtuː 'kɪləmiːtəz,
kɪˈɒmɪtəz] *4.2* _____

two o'clock [ˌtuː ə'klɒk] *5.3* _____

two years ago [ˌtuː 'jɪəz əˌgəʊ] *9.2* _____

ugly ['ʌgli] *3.1* _____

under ['ʌndə] *5.2* _____

underlined [ˌʌndə'laɪnd] *6.3* _____

understand [ˌʌndə'stænd] *4.2* _____

unhappy [ʌn'hæpi] *6 l/in* _____

university [ˌjuːnə'vɜːsəti] *7 l/in* _____

use [juːz] *5.3* _____

usually ['juːʒuəli, 'juːʒəli] *7.2* _____

vacuum ['vækjuəm, -kjʊm] *9.3* _____

vegetable ['vedʒtəbəl] *7.3* _____

very ['veri] *3 c/a* _____

visit ['vɪzɪt] *7.3* _____

visitor ['vɪzɪtə] *3.3, 7.3* _____

vocabulary [və'kæbjʊləri, vəʊ-] *6.2* _____

waiter ['weɪtə] *7 l/in* _____

Wales [weɪlz] *5.2* _____

wallet ['wɒlət] *6 c/a* _____

wardrobe ['wɔːdrəʊb] *8.2* _____

washing machine ['wɒʃɪŋ
məˌʃiːn] *8.2* _____

watch TV [ˌwɒtʃ tiː 'viː] *6.3* _____

we are fine ['weː ɑː faɪn] *3.1* _____

weather ['weðə] *9 t/s* _____

website ['websaɪt] *2 l/n* _____

wedding ['wedɪŋ] **8.2** _____

Wednesday ['wenzdi, -deɪ] **3.3** _____

Welcome to ... ['welkəm tə,
  tʊ] **5.3** _____

Welcome to Easton Hotel.
  [ˌwelkəm tʊ ˌiːstən həʊˈtel] **1 l/in, 5.3** _____

Well done! [ˌwel ˈdʌn] **9.2** _____

Welsh [welʃ] **5.2** _____

west [west] **5 l/in** _____

What about...? ['wɒt əbaʊt] **8 t/s** _____

What are you going to do? ['wɒt ə jʊ ˈgəʊɪŋ
  tʊ duː] **10.3** _____

What food ...? [ˌwɒt ˈfuːd] **8.3** _____

What happened? [ˌwɒt ˈhæpənd] **10.3** _____

What is on sale? [ˌwɒt ɪz ɒn ˈseɪl] **4.2** _____

What kind of ...? ['wɒt kaɪnd
  əv] **4.2** _____

What time? [wɒt ˈtaɪm] **8.3** _____

What would you like to drink?
  [ˌwɒt wʊd jʊ ˌlaɪk tə ˈdrɪŋk] **7.3** _____

What's his job? [ˌwɒts hɪz
  ˈdʒɒb] **2.3** _____

What's the matter? [ˌwɒts ðə
  ˈmætə] **9 t/s** _____

What's your address? [ˌwɒts
  jɔːr əˈdres] **2.2** _____

What's your name? [ˌwɒts jɔː
  ˈneɪm] **1 l/in** _____

when [wen] **5.3** _____

When is your birthday? [ˌwen
  ɪz jɔː ˈbɜːθdeɪ] **7.3** _____

Where are you from? [ˌweər
  ə jʊ ˈfrɒm] **1.3** _____

Which restaurant ...? [ˌwɪtʃ
  ˈrestərɒnt] **8.3** _____

white [waɪt] **4.1** _____

Who's she? [ˌhuːz ˈʃiː] **2.1** _____

why [waɪ] **8.1** _____

wife [waɪf] **2 l/in** _____

win [wɪn] **10 l/in** _____

wine [waɪn] **4.3** _____

winner ['wɪnə] **8 c/a** _____

with [wɪð, wɪθ] **3.1** _____

without [wɪðˈaʊt] **8 l/in** _____

wives [waɪvz] **4.3** _____

woman ['wʊmən] **3.2** _____

women ['wɪmɪn] **4.3** _____

word [wɜːd] **6 l/in** _____

work long hours [ˌwɜːk lɒŋ
  ˈaʊəz] **6 c/a** _____

world [wɜːld] **3 l/n** _____

write [raɪt] **2.3** _____

written ['rɪtn] **7.1** _____

wrong [rɒŋ] **9 t/s** _____

yellow ['jeləʊ] **4.2** _____

Yes, please. [jes ˈpliːz] **1.3** _____

yesterday ['jestədi, -deɪ] **9.2** _____

yoga ['jəʊgə] **6.3** _____

young-at-heart [ˌjʌŋ ət ˈhɑːt] **6.2** _____

young [jʌŋ] **6 l/in** _____

Your go. [jɔː ˈgəʊ] **9.2** _____

You're welcome. [jɔː ˈwelkəm] **4 c/a** _____

zero ['zɪərəʊ] **1.1** _____

# Irregular verbs

| Verb | Past Simple | Past Participle |
|---|---|---|
| be | was/were | been |
| become | became | become |
| begin | began | begun |
| break | broke | broken |
| bring | brought | brought |
| build | built | built |
| buy | bought | bought |
| can | could | been able |
| catch | caught | caught |
| choose | chose | chosen |
| come | came | come |
| cost | cost | cost |
| dig | dug | dug |
| do | did | done |
| draw | drew | drawn |
| drink | drank | drunk |
| drive | drove | driven |
| eat | ate | eaten |
| fall | fell | fallen |
| feed | fed | fed |
| feel | felt | felt |
| find | found | found |
| fly | flew | flown |
| forget | forgot | forgotten |
| get | got | got |
| give | gave | given |
| go | went | gone/been |
| grow | grew | grown |
| have | had | had |
| hear | heard | heard |
| hold | held | held |
| hurt | hurt | hurt |
| keep | kept | kept |
| know | knew | known |
| learn | learned/learnt | learned/learnt |

| Verb | Past Simple | Past Participle |
|---|---|---|
| leave | left | left |
| let | let | let |
| lose | lost | lost |
| make | made | made |
| mean | meant | meant |
| meet | met | met |
| pay | paid | paid |
| put | put | put |
| read /riːd/ | read /red/ | read /red/ |
| ride | rode | ridden |
| ring | rang | rung |
| run | ran | run |
| say | said | said |
| see | saw | seen |
| sell | sold | sold |
| send | sent | sent |
| shine | shone | shone |
| show | showed | shown |
| sing | sang | sung |
| sit | sat | sat |
| sleep | slept | slept |
| speak | spoke | spoken |
| spend | spent | spent |
| stand | stood | stood |
| steal | stole | stolen |
| swim | swam | swum |
| take | took | taken |
| teach | taught | taught |
| tell | told | told |
| think | thought | thought |
| throw | threw | thrown |
| understand | understood | understood |
| wear | wore | worn |
| win | won | won |
| write | wrote | written |

# Tapescripts

## Do you know? Recording 1
1 supermarket  2 restaurant  3 cinema
4 camera  5 doctor  6 football  7 bus
8 television  9 pizza  10 tennis  11 taxi
12 police  13 university  14 telephone
15 hotel

## Do you know? Recording 2
zero, one, two, three, four, five, six, seven,
eight, nine,

## Do you know? Recording 3
a, b, c, d, e, f, g, h, l, j, k, l, m, n, o, p, q, r, s, t,
u, v, w, x, y, z

## Do you know? Recording 4
1 listen  2 read  3 write  4 speak
5 match  6 repeat  7 look

## Do you know? Recording 5
Sorry, I don't understand
What's 'Hola' in English?
Can you say that slowly, please?
Excuse me, can you help me?

## Unit 1 Recording 1
R=Receptionist  G=Guest
R: Good morning.
G: Good morning.
R: Welcome to Easton Hotel.
G: Thank you.
**Photo A**

A=Alonzo  C=Camila
A: Hello. I'm Alonzo Moreno.
C: Hello. I'm Camila Diaz. Nice to meet you.
A: Nice to meet you, too.
**Photo D**

J=James  N=Nina
J: Hi Nina.
N: Hi James.
**Photo B**

M=Maria  H=Helga
M: Hello. I'm Maria Hofmann. What's your
name?
H: I'm Helga Peters.
**Photo C**

## Unit 1 Recording 2
1 Good morning.
2 Welcome to Leonard Hotel.
3 Hello.
4 Nice to meet you.
5 Hello. What's your name?

## Unit 1 Recording 3
zero, one, two, three, four, five, six, seven,
eight, nine

## Unit 1 Recording 4
R=Receptionist  C=Cristina
R: Hello.
C: Hello. I'm Cristina Branco.
R: Welcome to Bally Hotel, Miss Branco.
You're in room 329.
C: Thank you.
R: Thank you.

## Unit 1 Recording 5
1
A=Auguste  B=Betty
A: Good morning.
B: Good morning.
2
A=Auguste  C=Camilla
A: Good afternoon.
C: Good afternoon.
3

A=Auguste  D=Daniel
A: Good evening.
D: Good evening.
4
A=Auguste  P=People
A: Good night.
P: Good night.

## Unit 1 Recording 6
a, b, c, d, e, f, g, h, i, j, k, l, m, n, o, p, q, r, s, t,
u, v, w, x, y, z

## Unit 1 Recording 7
a h j k / b c d e g p t v / f l m n s x z / i y /
o / q u w / r

## Unit 1 Recording 8
1 India  2 Australia  3 Argentina
4 Japan  5 the US  6 Brazil  7 the UK
8 Germany  9 Italy  10 Poland

## Unit 1 Recording 9
1
M=Martin  S=Sunny
M: Sunny Deva?
S: Yes.
M: Hello, Mr Deva. I'm Martin. Welcome to
the UK.
S: Thank you.
2
R=Rachel  A=Ana
R: Ana Goncalvez?
A: Yes.
R: Hello, Mrs Goncalvez. I'm Rachel.
Welcome to Germany.
A: Thank you.
3
A=Abby  N=Nicole
A: Nicole Redman?
N: Yes.
A: Hello, Ms Redman. I'm Abby. Welcome to
the US.
N: Thank you.

## Unit 1 Recording 10
1
A: Coffee?
B: Yes, please.
2
W=Waiter  C=Customer
W: Black pepper?
C: No, thank you.
3
P=Peter  D=David
P: Hello. I'm Peter.
D: I'm David. Nice to meet you.
4
Woman: Excuse me, ...
5
Man: Oh! Sorry!
6
A: He's Ronaldinho. He's from Brazil.
B: Pardon?
A: He's from Brazil.

## Unit 1 Recording 11
1
Woman: You're in room 829.
2
T=Todd  J=Janice
T: Hello. I'm Todd Williams.
J: I'm Janice Simpson ...
3
K=Karen  J=Janice
K: Hi Janice.
J: Hi Karen. Come in.
K: Thank you.
J: Coffee?

## Unit 1 Recording 12
L=Luisa  B=Boris  A=Andy
A: Hi Boris.
B: Hi, Andy. This is Luisa.
A: Nice to meet you, Luisa.
L: Nice to meet you, too.

## Unit 1 Recording 13
A=Andy  L=Luisa
L: Where are you from, Andy?
A: I'm from the US.
L: Where are you from in the US?
A: I'm from New York. Where are you from?
L: I'm from Argentina.
A: Where are you from in Argentina?
L: I'm from Rosario.

## Unit 1 Recording 14
1 Where are you from?
2 Where are you from in Poland?
3 I'm from Warsaw.

## Unit 1 Recording 15
Australia: six, one.
Brazil: double five.
China: eight, six.
Japan: eight, one.
Mexico: five, two.
Russia: seven.
Spain: three, four.
Turkey: nine, o.
The UK: double four.
The US: one.

## Unit 1 Recording 16
1
M=Man  W=Woman
M: Directory enquiries.
W: The Lamden Hotel, please.
M: Where is it?
W: It's in Rome, in Italy.
M: Thank you.
**Machine:** The number is: double o – three
– nine – six – eight – one – two – nine – four
– one.
I repeat: double o – three – nine – six – eight
– one – two – nine – four – one.

## Unit 2 Recording 1
1 mother  son  2 father  daughter
3 sister  brother  4 father  son
5 wife  husband  6 mother  daughter

## Unit 2 Recording 2
1 mobile phone  2 phone
3 phone number  4 email address
5 computer  6 website  7 photo
8 passport  9 first name  10 surname
11 address

## Unit 2 Recording 3
L=Liz  S=Sabrina
L: Ooh! Who's he?
S: Carl? He's my brother. He's 26 years old.
L: Twenty-six? I'm twenty-six.
S: You're thirty-six!
L: Oh, yes.
S: She's my sister, Anna. She's thirty-two.
And he's my father, Marek. He's from
Poland. He's sixty.
L: Who's she?
S: She's my mother, Sofia. She's from Italy.
She's fifty-seven. And my daughter, Sarah.
She's one. And my son, Tom. He's three.
L: Ooh! Who's he?
S: He's my husband, James.
L: Oh! How old is he?
S: He's forty.

## Unit 2 Recording 4

ten, eleven, twelve, thirteen, fourteen, fifteen, sixteen, seventeen, eighteen, nineteen, twenty.

## Unit 2 Recording 5

twenty, twenty-one, thirty, thirty-three, forty, forty-nine, fifty, fifty-six, sixty, sixty-seven, seventy, seventy-four, eighty, eighty-eight, ninety, ninety-nine

## Unit 2 Recording 6

1 He's my brother. He's 13.
2 Carol's my sister. She's 40.
3 She's Helen. She's 80.
4 My son's 15.
5 He's my husband. He's 60.
6 Roberto's 17.

## Unit 2 Recording 7

1 59 Princes Street, Edinburgh
2 31 Globe Road, London
3 80 Boulevard de Clichy, Paris
4 46 Lower Abbey Street, Dublin
5 70 Brook Street, Boston

## Unit 2 Recording 8

B=Ben J1=Judge 1 J2=Judge 2
B: Hello.
J1/J2: Hello.
J1: What's your name?
B: Ben Gibson.
J1: How do you spell that?
B: Gibson. G – I – B – S – O – N
J1: Where are you from, Ben?
B: I'm from Australia.
J1: How old are you, Ben?
B: I'm twenty-nine.
J2: What's your address?
B: Seventeen, Kings Road, Angel, London.
J1: What's your phone number?
B: My home number is 0 – two – 0 – eight, three – nine – one, double two – four. And my mobile number is 0 – seven – eight, seven – two – four, nine – one.
J1/J2: Thank you.
J2: OK, Mr Gibson!
B: Oh! OK! Yes ...
B: Every morning, she's on my train, where is she from, and what's her name ...

## Unit 2 Recording 9

J1=Judge 1 J2=Judge 2 J3=Judge 3
J4=Judge 4 J5=Judge 5
T=Terri V=Vittoria H=Hans S=Sanjay
1
J1: Thank you. Ben. Goodbye. He's awful.
J2: Yes, awful.
2
J3: Thank you, Terri.
T: OK. Thank you. Goodbye.
J3: Goodbye. She's good.
J4: Yes, she's good.
3
J1: Thank you Vittoria.
V: Oh, thank you.
J1: Goodbye.
V: Goodbye.
J1: She's OK.
J5: Yes, she's OK.
4
J3: Thank you Hans. Thank you.
H: OK. Thank you. Goodbye.
J3: He's great!
J2: Yes, he's great.
5
J4: Thank you Sanjay.
S: OK, thank you.
J4: Goodbye.
S: Goodbye.

J4: He's bad.
J1: Yes, he's bad.

## Unit 2 Recording 10

1
S=Simon
A: What's your name, please?
S: Simon Ambrose.
A: How do you spell that?
S: Ambrose. A – M – B – R – O – S – E.
2
A: What's your address, please?
B: 82 via Speranza, Rome.
A: How do you spell that, please?
B: Via: V – I – A. Speranza: S – P – E – R – A – N – Z – A.

## Unit 2 Recording 11

A: What's the website?
B: www.emailfriends.net
A: Uh-huh. Who's she?
B: Her name's Frieda Lang.
A: What's her job?
B: She's a teacher.
A: What's her email address?
B: frieda@teachernet.de
A: What's his name?
B: Tom Mackinstosh.
A: What's his job?
B: err ... He's an accountant.
A: What's his email address?
B: It's tom@mackintosh.com
A: Hmmm ... What's her name?
B: Her name's Junko Nakamura.
She's a student.
A: Oh! I'm a student. What's her email address?
B: junura@jmail.jp
A: How do you spell that?
B: Junura: J – U – N – U – R – A, at jmail: J – M – A – I – L dot J – P.
A: Thank you!

## Unit 2 Recording 12

1 doctor  2 artist  3 teacher
4 student  5 actor  6 police officer
7 engineer  8 accountant
9 sales assistant  10 manager

## Unit 2 Recording 13

1 He's a teacher  2 She's an actor
3 He's a student  4 She's an engineer

## Unit 3 Recording 1

a castle, a cathedral, a palace, a museum, a gallery, a department store, a market, a mountain, a lake

## Unit 3 Recording 2

1 They're from Spain.
2 Their mother is Tina.
3 Their hotel is in Vienna.
4 They're students.
5 They're in Istanbul.
6 Where is their camera?

## Unit 3 Recording 3

1 a suitcase  2 a map  3 a top
4 a camera  5 a pair of shoes  6 a book
7 a pair of trousers  8 a skirt
9 a backpack  10 an MP3 player

## Unit 3 Recording 4

R=Ravi  D=Diane  E=Eva
1
A: Hello, sir. What's in your suitcase, please?
R: What's in my suitcase? Um, a map, a camera, two books, a top and two pairs of trousers. Oh, and a pair of shoes.

2
A: Hello Madam. What's in your suitcase?
D: Oh, err. Let me see. A camera – no! Two cameras, an MP3 player, a pair of shoes, two skirts, three tops, three books and a backpack.
3
A: Hello Madam. What's in your suitcase, please?
E: What's in my suitcase? Umm, a camera, two maps, two books, three tops, an MP3 player, a pair of trousers and a skirt and ... err ... five pairs of shoes.

## Unit 3 Recording 5

a two suitcases  b five maps
c seven tops  d three cameras
e two pairs of shoes  f four books
g eight pairs of trousers  h six skirts

## Unit 3 Recording 6

MB=Mr Boyle J=Jane Miles
MB: Excuse me.
J: Yes?
MB: I'm Mr Boyle. What's your name?
J: Jane Miles.
MB: What's in your suitcase, Miss Miles.
J: I'm not Miss Miles. I'm Mrs Miles.
MB: Sorry. OK, a camera ...
J: It isn't a camera. It's an MP3 player.
MB: Oh! Sorry. An MP3 player ... and two books ...
J: They aren't books. They're maps.
MB: Yes, of course. Sorry ...

## Unit 3 Recording 7

Monday, Tuesday, Wednesday, Thursday, Friday, Saturday, Sunday

## Unit 3 Recording 8

1
A=Assistant B=Man
A: Good morning.
B: Good morning. Is [beep] near here?
A: No, it isn't. It isn't in London. Are you in a car?
B: Yes, I am.
A: It's about twelve kilometres from here. Here's a map. We are ... here. And it is ... there.
B: OK. Is it free?
A: No, it isn't.
B: And is it open today?
A: Yes, it is.
B: OK, great. Thank you. Goodbye.
A: Goodbye.

2
A=Assistant B=Woman
A: Good morning.
B: Good morning.
A: Can I help you?
B: Yes. Is [beep] open today?
A: Yes, it is.
B: Good. Is it near here?
A: Yes, it is. Here's a map. We are ... here. And it is ... there. It's near Oxford Street.
B: Great. Thank you. Are museums in London free?
A: Yes, they are.
B: OK, great. Thank you. Goodbye.
A: Goodbye.

3
A=Assistant B=Man
A: Good morning. Can I help you?
B: Yes. Is [beep] open today?
A: No, it isn't. It's closed on Mondays.
B: Oh.
A: Sorry.
B: OK. Goodbye.
A: Goodbye.

# Tapescripts

## Unit 3 Recording 9
**L=Louis  S=Sara**
L: Hello.
S: Hi, Louis. It's Sara.
L: Hi Sara. How are you and Paul?
S: Fine thanks. And you?
L: Fine thanks. Where are you?
S: We're in Morocco.
L: Are you in Casablanca?
S: No, we aren't. We're in Marakesh.
L: Is it beautiful?
S: Yes, it is. It's very beautiful.
L: Is it hot?
S: Yes, it is. It's very hot.
L: Is your hotel nice?
S: No, it isn't. It's very small and very old.
L: Oh dear! Is the food nice?
S: Yes. It's very nice. Are Mum and Dad OK?
L: Yes, they are. They're fine.
S: OK – see you on Friday.
L: See you on Friday. Bye.
S: Bye.

## Unit 4 Recording 1
**A** café  **B** cashpoint  **C** train station
**D** newsagent  **E** cinema  **F** car park
**G** bookshop  **H** bank  **I** chemist
**J** restaurant  **K** supermarket
**L** bus stop  **M** market

## Unit 4 Recording 2
1 This is an instant coffee. It's very popular in the UK with milk and sugar.
2 This is a black coffee or a filter coffee. It's very popular in the US.
3 This is a white coffee. It's a black coffee with milk.
4 This is an espresso. It's very popular in a lot of countries, for example Spain.
5 This is a cappuccino. It's an espresso with hot milk. It's very popular in a lot of countries, for example Italy.
6 This is an iced coffee. It's very popular in hot countries, for example Greece.

## Unit 4 Recording 3
1
A: Yes, madam. Can I help you?
B: Yes. Can I have a chicken salad, please.
A: Certainly. Anything else?
B: Yes. Can I have a large mineral water, please.
A: Of course.
2
A: Good afternoon.
B: Good afternoon.
A: So, a cheese sandwich and a small orange juice. Anything else?
B: No, thank you.
A: Eat in?
B: Pardon?
A: Eat in or take away?
B: Take away, please.
3
A: Yes, sir. Can I help you?
B: Yes, can I have a cup of tea and a piece of chocolate cake, please?
A: Certainly. Anything else?
B: No, thank you.
A: So, one cup of tea and one piece of chocolate cake.
B: Yes, thank you.
A: No problem ...

## Unit 4 Recording 4
Can I ...?
Can I have a ...?
Can I have a small coffee?

## Unit 4 Recording 5
1
A: Can I help you?
B: Yes. Can I have an espresso please, to go.
A: Anything else?
B: No, thank you.
A: That's one pound ten please.
2
A: Can I help you?
B: Can I have a cappuccino and a mineral water, please.
A: Anything else?
B: No, thank you.
A: That's three eighty-nine, please.
3
A: Good morning. Can I help you?
B: Coffeeeeee!
A: Coffee. Err, black.
B: Coffeeeeee!
A: OK. One large black coffee. That's one dollar nineteen cents.
4
A: Bonjour.
B: Hello. Can I have a cappuccino, please?
A: With sugar?
B: No, thank you.
A: Anything else?
B: A piece of chocolate cake, please.
A: Certainly. That's four euros thirty-four.
5
A: Can I help you.
B: Can I have an iced coffee, please.
A: An iced coffee and ... is that a chicken sandwich?
B: Yes.
A: That's three thirty-nine, please.

## Unit 4 Recording 6
1 a green T-shirt  2 a white pairs of shoes
3 an orange dress  4 a red coat
5 a yellow hat  6 a black pair of trousers
7 a blue bag  8 a brown skirt
9 a pink shirt

## Unit 4 Recording 7
**S=Seller  C=Claudia  A=Adam**
S: Hello. Can I help you?
C: Yes, how much is this blue hat?
A: It isn't blue. It's green!
C: No, it isn't! It's blue.
S: It's three pounds fifty.
C: Ooh! And how much are these beautiful dresses?
A: They aren't beautiful. They're ugly!
C: No, they're not. They're ...
S: They're twelve pounds eighty-five.
C: How much is that yellow skirt?
A: Yuk!
S: It's seventeen ninety-nine.
A: Seventeen ninety-nine? How much are those white shirts?
S: They're eight pounds forty-five. The orange shirts are nine pounds.
A: Hmm – it's my birthday on Wednesday, Claudia ...  Claudia? ... Claudia? Where is she?

## Unit 4 Recording 8
1
**T=Tony  W=Woman**
T: Can I have three tickets to Bristol, please. Two adults and one child.
W: Single or return?
T: Return, please.
W: That's forty-two thirty, please. ... Thank you. ... Here you are.
2
**M=Man  S=Shula**
M: Can I help you?
S: Yes, please. Can I have a packet of aspirin, please.
M: Twenty-four or forty-eight?
S: Twenty-four, please.
M: That's one forty-nine, please. ... Thank you.
3
**J=Jack  W= Woman**
J: Can I have two tickets for *ChickenMan Returns*, please.
W: That's fifteen pounds ninety, please.
J: Can I pay by credit card?
W: Sure. ... Sign here, please ... Thank you. Here you are.
J: Thanks.
4
**W=Woman  M=Man**
W: Thirty-one pounds and seven pence, please.
W: Here you are.
W: Thank you. Enter your PIN number, please. ... Thank you.

## Unit 4 Recording 9
1
A: Excuse me. Where is the gallery?
B: Err ... Ah yes, it's next to the market on Mercer Street.
A: Great. Thank you.
B: You're welcome.
2
A: Excuse me. Where's the train station?
B: I'm sorry, I don't know.
A: OK. Never mind. Thank you. *[Asking someone else]* Excuse me, where's the train station?
C: The train station? ... It's on Palace Street, opposite the White Café.
A: Great. Thank you.
C: You're welcome.
3
A: Excuse me. Where's the nearest supermarket?
B: The nearest supermarket is opposite the car park, on King Street.
A: Great. Thank you.
B: You're welcome.

## Unit 5 Recording 1
1 Darwin is in the north of Australia.
2 Perth is in the west of Australia.
3 Brisbane is in the east of Australia.
4 Adelaide is in the south of Australia.
5 Alice Springs is in the centre of Australia.

## Unit 5 Recording 2
A: City
B: Buildings and a road
A: Countryside
B: Trees and a river
A: Coast
B: The sea and a beach

## Unit 5 Recording 3
**S=Speaker**
S: My favourite place for a holiday is Cornwall. Cornwall is in the south-west of ... England. The coast and the countryside are very beautiful and the beaches are ... great. There are two famous castles in Cornwall. Tintagel Castle is in the north of Cornwall and Pendennis Castle is in the ... south. There is a great gallery in the west of Cornwall. It's called Tate St. Ives. There is a new tourist attraction in south-east Cornwall. It's called ... The Eden Project. There are plants and trees from all over the ... world. There is a beautiful outdoor ... theatre in the west of Cornwall. It's called the Minack Theatre.

## Unit 5 Recording 4
**Picture 1** There's one person in the theatre.
**Picture 2** There are some people in the theatre.
**Picture 3** There are a lot of people in the theatre.

## Unit 5 Recording 5
1 The newsagent is next to the hotel.
2 The café is in front of the train station.
3 The chemist is opposite the Italian restaurant.
4 The cinema is behind the town square.
5 The department store is near the chemist.

## Unit 5 Recording 6
**R=Receptionist  M=Man  W=Woman**
R: Hello sir, madam. Can I help you?
M: Yes. Is there a café near this hotel?
R: Yes, sir, there is. There's a café next to this hotel and there's another café in front of the train station.
W: Are there any good restaurants near here?
R: There's a good Chinese restaurant next to the chemist. There's an Indian restaurant behind this hotel. That's very good. And there's an Italian restaurant next to the newsagent.
M: Great. And, is there a bank near here?
R: Yes, sir, there is. There's a bank next to the department store but it isn't open today. It's Saturday.
M: Oh no!
R: But there's a cashpoint in this hotel. It's over there.
M: Oh! Great!
W: Are there any tourist attractions near here?
R: Yes, madam, there are. There's a good museum behind the Italian restaurant and a there's a famous cathedral near here. Here's a map. We're here … the cathedral is here … and the museum is here.
W: Great. Thank you. And are there any galleries near here?
R: No, madam, there aren't.
W: Never mind. Come on George, let's go …

## Unit 5 Recording 7
Chez Pierre is a French restaurant.
The Taj Mahal is an Indian restaurant.
La Spiga is an Italian restaurant.
Wong Li is a Chinese restaurant.
King Henry's is an English restaurant.

## Unit 5 Recording 8
**P=Patricia  J=James**
P: Hi, James. How are you?
J: Fine, thanks, Patricia. And you?
P: I'm OK. What's that?
J: It's a brochure for Harefield College.
P: Harefield College? Is that the language school in the centre of town?
J: That's right. The *Language plus* courses are very popular.
P: *Language plus*? But your English is fine.
J: It's not for me. It's for my cousin, Vanda. She's from Augsburg in Germany.
P: Augsburg?
J: It's near Munich. Vanda's English level is A1.
P: Oh, I see. The course is for her!
J: Yes!

## Unit 5 Recording 9
P: Can she drive?
J: Yes, she can.
P: OK. So course 175 is not good for Vanda. Can she swim?
J: No, she can't.
P: Aha! So, perhaps course 174. Can she play golf?
J: No, she can't. And she can't cook. But she can use a computer.
P: So course 178 is not good for Vanda. Can she dance?
J: Yes, she can. And she can sing. She's very good.
P: Oh … I can't dance and I can't sing.
J: Never mind.
P: But I can play the piano.
J: Vanda can't play the piano. So course 173 is OK. But it's not a morning course.
P: So?
J: She's a waitress in a restaurant in the afternoon and evening.
P: Oh, I see.

## Unit 5 Recording 10
1 I can speak English.   2 I can't speak Italian.   3 Can you speak German?   4 He can speak Russian.   5 She can't speak Spanish.   6 Can they speak Portuguese?

## Unit 5 Recording 11
A Ten o'clock in the morning.
B Three o'clock in the afternoon.
C Seven o'clock in the evening.
D Eight o'clock in the morning.
E One o'clock in the afternoon.
F Eight o'clock in the evening.

## Unit 5 Recording 12
**T=Teresa  N=Nick  B=Brenda**
T: Welcome to my B&B. I'm Teresa. Nice to meet you.
N: Nice to meet you, too.
T: Where are you from?
N: Croydon. It's in south London.
T: Oh, yes. Great. OK. Come with me, please. This is your bedroom. There's an en-suite bathroom with a shower. There's a double bed and there are some towels on the bed.
B: Is there an extra blanket?
T: Yes. There's a blanket on the bed, next to the towels.
B: Great.
T: There's a kettle on the table.
N: Is there a fridge?
T: Yes, there is. It's under the table.
B: What time is breakfast?
T: It's from half past seven to half past ten.
N: And what's the checkout time?
T: Checkout time is quarter to twelve.
N/B: Great.
B: It's very nice.
N: Yes, beautiful.
T: Any questions, just ask.
N: Thanks. Bye.
N: This room is awful!
B: I know – awful!

## Unit 5 Recording 13
six o'clock, five past six, ten past six, quarter past six, twenty past six, twenty-five past six, half past six, twenty-five to seven, twenty to seven, quarter to seven, ten to seven, five to seven

## Unit 6 Recording 1
thin  good-looking  tall  fat  short  not intelligent  happy  ugly  young  rich  old  poor  sad  intelligent

## Unit 6 Recording 2
**DJ=Disk Jockey  CC=Cynthia Castro**
DJ: Now it's time for our 60-second interview. Today Cynthia Castro is in the studio. Welcome to *Radio Dublin* Cynthia.
CC: Thank you.
DJ: Cynthia … your 60-second interview starts … now.
DJ: What's your job?
CC: I'm a singer.
DJ: Where are you from?
CC: I'm from Rio but Dublin is my home now. My husband is Irish.
DJ: Do you like Dublin?
CC: Yes, I do.
DJ: Do you like me?
CC: Sorry?
DJ: It's a joke. Do you like Irish music?
CC: No, I don't. I like Brazilian music.
DJ: What's your favourite time of day?
CC: Half past nine in the morning. It's time for my first coffee.
DJ: Do you like football?
CC: Of course! I'm Brazilian.
DJ: What's your favourite football team?
CC: AC Milan.
DJ: Do you like American food?
CC: No, I don't. I like Indian food.
DJ: What are your favourite things in life?
CC: I like Brazilian music, German cars, Italian fashion …
DJ: Ah! Time is up. Thank you Cynthia Castro!
CC: You're welcome.
DJ: That was our 60-second interview!

## Unit 6 Recording 3
1 Do you like Italian food?
2 Do you like coffee?
3 Are you from Brazil?
4 Are you a student?
5 Do you like London?
6 Do you like Paris?
7 Are you happy?
8 Do you like this film?

## Unit 6 Recording 4
1 Do you like me?   2 I like you.
3 I don't like him.   4 I don't like her.
5 I like it.   6 I like them.

## Unit 6 Recording 5
1
A: What do architects do?
B: They design buildings, for example houses and shops.
2
A: What do sales reps. do?
B: They sell things, for example computers and books.
3
A: What do designers do?
B: They design things, for example clothes and shoes.
4
A: What do reporters do?
B: They write articles, for example newspaper articles.
5
A: What do chefs do?
B: They cook food, for example Chinese food and Italian food.
6
A: What do builders do?
B: They build buildings, for example houses and shops.

## Unit 6 Recording 6
**S=Sharon  C=Catherine**
**P=Pat  A=Anthony**
S: Excuse me. Your coat is on the floor.
C: Sorry?
S: Your coat. It's on the floor.
C: Oh! Thank you very much.
S: No problem! Are you on holiday?

# Tapescripts

C: Yes, I am. I'm here with my husband. He's in our room.  We really like this city.
S: Yes, it's great. Where are you from?
C: I'm from South Africa and my husband is from Canada.  We live in the UK. Where are you from?
S: We're from Ireland.
C: Are you on holiday?
S: No, we aren't. We're on business.
C: What do you do?
S: We're architects.
C: Great! What do you design?
S: We design houses and office buildings.
C: I'm a sales rep and my husband is a chef.
S: Oh really? What do you sell?
C: I sell towels and blankets to hotels.
P: And who do you work for?
C: It's a small company. It's called PDS HotelCare.
S: Great! My name's Sharon and this is my husband, Pat.
C: Nice to meet you. My name's Catherine. Ah! Here's my husband. Anthony, this is Sharon and Pat. They're from Ireland.
A: Nice to meet you.
P: Nice to meet you, too.
C: Sharon and Pat are architects. They design houses and office buildings.
A: Oh really? Where do you work?

## Unit 6 Recording 7
A=Adam  E=Emma
A: Hey, Emma. Listen. This song is for you.
E: What's it called?
A: It's called She's my soulmate.
E: Ahhh!
A: She gets up early – I get up late,
But that ok – she's my soulmate.
She eats a salad – I eat a pizza
But she's my soulmate – I love her, I need her
She finishes work – I watch TV
I don't do much – I just drink tea
But she still loves me – I love me too
We're a great team – yes it's true
Soulmate, soulmate,
I'm so happy we are together
Soulmate, soulmate,
My life with you, is so much better!
E: That's, err, yes, that's very ... nice.
A: Thank you. Do you really like it?
E: I like the music – I don't like the words ...

## Unit 6 Recording 8
J=Josef  N=Nadine
J: Oh dear. Oh dear! Oh dear, oh dear, oh dear.
N: What's the problem, Josef?
J: I can't find a present for Nisha.
N: Who's Nisha?
J: She's my friend. It's her birthday on Thursday.
N: Do you know www.findanicepresent.com
J: No. What is it?
N: It's a great website. It finds presents for you. Look. This is the website.
J: Is it free?
N: Yes, it is.

## Unit 6 Recording 9
J=Josef  N=Nadine
J: Is it free?
N: Yes, it is. OK, there are some questions about Nisha. How old is she?
J: She's twenty-nine.
N: What does she do?
J: She's a reporter.
N: Who does she work for?
J: Newstime Magazine.
N: So does she work long hours?
J: Yes, she does.

N: Is she married?
J: No, she isn't.
N: Does she have any children?
J: No, she doesn't.
N: Does she travel a lot?
J: Yes, she does. She travels all over the world.
N: Can she cook?
J: No, she can't.
N: Does she watch a lot of films?
J: No, she doesn't.
N: Does she listen to a lot of music?
J: Yes, she does.
N: OK – there are three presents.

## Unit 7 Recording 1
1  I'm a waiter. I work in a restaurant.
2  I'm a PA. I work in an office.
3  I'm a factory worker. I work in a factory.
4  I'm a nurse. I work in a hospital.
5  I'm a sales assistant. I work in a shop.
6  I'm a lecturer. I work in a university.
7  I'm a call centre worker. I work in a call centre.
8  I'm a teacher. I work in a school.

## Unit 7 Recording 2
M=Man  W=Woman
1
W: Yes, sir. Can I help you?
2
W: Good morning. Can I speak to Mr Jones, please?
M: This is Mr Jones.
W: Mr Jones, my name is Tina from The Great Mobile Phone Company. How are you today, Mr Jones? Oh!
3
M: OK children. Settle down, please. Kevin! Don't do that!
4
M: Here are your drinks. Are you ready to order?
5
W: Hello, TM Architects office. Can I help?
M: Can I speak to Mr Flynn, please?
W: I'm afraid he's in a meeting this morning. Can he call you back?
6
M: Good morning. This lecture is about Hamlet by Shakespeare. Hamlet is the Prince of Denmark. Hamlet's father, the king, is killed by ...
7
M: Hello, Bill. Are you ok? How is your wife? Good. OK, time to start work ...
8
W: Excuse me, doctor. That's his right leg. The problem is his left leg.
M: Oh yes, of course. Thank you nurse Taylor.

## Unit 7 Recording 3
1
PA=Personal Assistant  J=Jake  A=Alice
PA: Hello. Parkside School.
J: Can I speak to Mrs Fisher, please?
PA: Hold the line, please ...
A: Hello. Alice Fisher.
J: Hello Mrs Fisher. My name's Jake Parker. I'm interested in the advert for teachers. It's in today's newspaper ...
A: Oh, yes. Great.
2
A=Alice  J=Jake
A: Jake Parker?
J: Yes.
A: I'm Alice Fisher. nice to meet you.
J: Nice to meet you, too.
A: Come in Mr Parker. Please sit down.

J: Thank you.
3
J=Jake  S=Steven
J: OK class, be quiet. Look at page 32 in your books. Page 32. OK? Now listen to the conversation.
J: Steven. please turn off your mobile phone.
S: Sorry, sir.

## Unit 7 Recording 4
1
M: Please come with me. Your table is ready.
2
W: Taylor. Be QUIET.
3
W: This is a message for Dr. Morgan. Please go to A&E immediately.
4
M: This is a customer announcement. Visit our great kitchen sale on the ground floor. Saucepans for twelve ninety-nine, Cookery books for three ninety-nine. Thank you for shopping at Madisons.
5
W: This is a message for all passengers on flight FH453 to Madrid. Please go to gate 23 immediately. That's flight FH453. Please go to gate 23 immediately. Thank you.

## Unit 7 Recording 5
January, February, March, April, May, June, July, August, September, October, November, December

## Unit 7 Recording 6
H=Game show host  J=John
H: OK, John. Are you ready?
J: Yes, I'm always ready! I love this game.
H: Good. Let's start. Do you work from home?
J: No, I never work from home.
H: Do you have meetings?
J: Yes, but not often.
H: Do you give presentations?
J: Yes, I sometimes give presentations.
H: Do you call customers:
J: No, never. I don't have customers.
H: Do you write reports?
J: Yes, I do. I usually write three or four reports a week.
H: Do you take work home?
J: No, not usually.
H: Do you travel abroad?
J: No, I never travel abroad.
H: Do you answer the phone?
J: Yes, I quite often answer the phone.
H: Do you work outside?
J: Yes, very often.
H: Do you help people?
J: Yes, I always help people.
H: Are you a teacher?
J: No, I'm not.
H: Oh!! What is he?

## Unit 7 Recording 7
1  I usually have a meeting on Monday morning.
2  I often take work home.
3  I don't usually answer the phone.
4  I don't often give presentations.

## Unit 7 Recording 8
M=Michelle  S=Sarah
M: Good morning, Sarah!
S: Morning, Michelle. Nice weekend?
M: Yes, thank you. And you?
S: Good, thanks.
M: Oh, Sarah, when is Mr Wu's visit?
S: Let me see. Mr Wu's visit is the 8th of

June.
**M:** What's the date today.
**S:** It's the 6th of June.
**M:** Are there any other visits this month?
**S:** Yes, there are. There's Mrs King on the fourteenth of June.
**M:** Mrs King - the 14th of June.
**S:** And there's Miss Brown on the 24th of June.
**M:** The 24th of June. Is that all?
**S:** No, there's one more. It's Mr Rogers.
**M:** Mr Rogers – he's the BIG BOSS from the US! He's very important! When is his visit?
**S:** The 6th of June.
**M:** The 6th of Ju… But that's today.
**S:** Oh yes! Hello, Sarah Walker speaking. … Oh hello Mr Rogers. … You're in reception … That's lovely. … See you in five minutes … Goodbye. That's Mr Rogers. He's in reception.
**M:** Arrrghhhh!

## Unit 7 Recording 9

1 first, second, third, fourth, fifth, sixth, seventh, eighth, ninth, tenth
2 eleventh, twelfth, thirteenth, fourteenth, fifteenth, sixteenth, seventeenth, eighteenth, nineteenth, twentieth
3 twenty-first, twenty-second, twenty-third, twenty-fourth, twenty-fifth, twenty-sixth, twenty-seventh, twenty-eighth, twenty-ninth, thirtieth

## Unit 7 Recording 10

**M=Michelle  R=Mr Rogers  K=Ms. Khan**
**M:** Please, come in. Sit down. What would you like to drink? Tea? Coffee?
**R:** I'd like a coffee, please.
**K:** I'd like a cup of tea, please.
**M:** Would you like milk and sugar?
**R:** No, thank you.
**K:** Milk, no sugar, please.
**M:** Would you like a biscuit?
**R:** Yes, please.
**K:** No, thank you.

## Unit 7 Recording 11

**M=Michelle  R=Mr Rogers  A=Aisha Khan**
**M:** OK, this is the canteen. Are you hungry?
**R/A:** Yes.
**M:** Good. OK, the drinks are here on the right. There are snacks next to the drinks. There's mineral water, orange juice … etc. There are some starters next to the snacks. Would you like a starter?
**R:** Err, no thank you. I'd like a salad.
**M:** OK. There's a salad bar in the middle of the canteen.
**A:** I'd like some fruit.
**M:** The fruit is next to the salad. And there are some desserts next to the cash tills.
**R:** Great. Thank you.

## Unit 7 Recording 12

**R=Receptionist  D=Dodek**
**R:** Good morning.
**D:** Good morning. I'm here to see Martina Hafner.
**R:** What's your name, please?
**D:** Dodek Nowak.
**R:** How do you spell that?
**D:** N – O – W – A – K.
**R:** OK, Mr Nowak. Take the lift to the third floor. Turn right. Miss Hafner's office is the third door on the left.
**D:** Thank you.
**R:** You're welcome.

### R=Receptionist  J=Jennifer

**R:** Good morning.
**J:** Good morning. I have a meeting with

Lorda Romero.
**R:** What's your name, please?
**J:** Jennifer Wood.
**R:** Jennifer – Wood. OK, Mrs Wood. Take the lift to the third floor. Turn right. Mrs Romero's office is the second on the right.
**J:** Thank you. Where are the toilets, please?
**R:** There's a toilet on the third floor, next to the lift.

### R=Receptionist  J=Jemma

**R:** Good afternoon.
**J:** Good afternoon. I'm here to see Patrick Swinton.
**R:** Do you have an appointment?
**J:** Yes, I do.
**R:** What's your name, please?
**J:** My name's Jemma Hayes.
**R:** How do you spell Hayes?
**J:** H – A – Y – E – S.
**R:** OK, Ms Hayes. Mr Swinton's office is on the third floor. Take the lift and turn right. It's the first door on the left.
**J:** Thank you.

## Unit 8 Recording 1

1 go to the theatre  2 eat out
3 play chess  4 go swimming
5 play football  6 go for a walk
7 watch TV  8 go sightseeing
9 read a book  10 play tennis
11 go cycling  12 do exercise

## Unit 8 Recording 2

**G=Gary  A=Annie**
**A:** Gary.
**G:** Yes?
**A:** Are you happy?
**G:** Happy?
**A:** Yes. Are you happy?
**G:** Yes. I'm happy.
**A:** I'm not. We never go out.
**G:** Oh.
**A:** We never go to the cinema. We don't often eat in restaurants. We never do exercise. We always watch television.
**G:** But I like watching television.
**A:** Gary!

## Unit 8 Recording 3

**G=Gary  A=Annie**
**G:** OK. Turn the TV off. Come on – choose a hotel with me.
**A:** A hotel?
**G:** Yes, for next weekend.
**A:** Oh. OK.
**G:** Right. Look at this one. The Langston Hotel? There's a golf course and there are tennis courts. It's great! I like playing golf.
**A:** Hmm. I want to go sightseeing. Look! What do you think of this one? The New Metro Hotel. There's got a swimming pool. You like swimming and I like going sightseeing.
**G:** I don't like going sightseeing. I want to do some exercise. Now this is good. Blue Sea Hotel. You can swim in the sea and you can walk in the countryside. We like swimming and walking.
**A:** I can't swim.
**G:** But you want to learn.
**A:** That's true. OK. Blue Sea Hotel it is.
**G:** Great. Now, is there a television at the Blue Sea Hotel?

## Unit 8 Recording 4

**M=Man  W=Woman**
**M:** bedroom
**W:** a) mirror  b) bed  c) wardrobe
**M:** bathroom
**W:** d) bath  e) toilet  f) basin
**M:** kitchen

**W:** g) cooker  h) sink  i) washing machine j) fridge
**M:** living room
**W:** k) sofa  l) lamp  m) coffee table n) armchair
**M:** garage
**W:** o) car
**M:** garden
**W:** p) bicycle

## Unit 8 Recording 5

**P=Paul  J=Jo**
**P:** Hi Jo. How are you?
**J:** Oh hi Paul. I'm fine. How are you?
**P:** Oh, so-so. It's my sister's wedding next week. I want to buy her a really nice present but I can't find one.
**J:** I can help.
**P:** Really?
**J:** Sure. OK. What does she like doing?
**P:** Well, she likes doing things at home … she likes watching TV … she's likes cooking … Oh, and she like modern furniture. Her husband likes furniture, too.
**J:** Have they got an armchair?
**P:** Yes, they have.
**J:** Have they got a lamp?
**P:** Yes, they have.
**J:** Has your sister got a wardrobe for her clothes?
**P:** No, she hasn't.
**J:** Aha!
**P:** But my parents want to buy a wardrobe for her clothes.
**J:** Oh! Have they got a bed?
**P:** Yes, they have.
**J:** Has she got a bicycle?
**P:** No, she hasn't.
**J:** Aha!
**P:** But he's got a bicycle and she uses it.
**J:** Oh dear. I know!
**P:** What?
**J:** It's always a good wedding present.
**P:** What?
**J:** Give them …

## Unit 8 Recording 6

**M=Man  W=Woman 1**
**M:** I live with my wife in a small house. We've got a bedroom, a living room, a kitchen and a bathroom. We've got a small garden – it's beautiful. But we haven't got a garage. My husband's got a car. He drives to work every day. I haven't got a car. I can't drive. But I've got a bicycle.
**W:** I live in my sister's house. She's got four bedrooms and two living rooms. She's got a TV in her bedroom. She watches TV in bed. But she hasn't got a TV in the living room. She's got a sofa and a big armchair in the living room. She's got a big cooker in the kitchen – it's great. We like cooking. She hasn't got a microwave oven. She doesn't like them.

## Unit 8 Recording 7

**M:** Hi, Alda. How are you?
**A:** Fine thanks. And you?
**M:** Fine, thanks. I've got a new job!
**A:** Hey, that's great! How about dinner next Friday? We can celebrate.
**M:** Good idea. Which restaurant do you want to go to?
**A:** How about Sinatra's?
**M:** Where's that?
**A:** It's in Alderton.
**M:** Hmm, it's not very near. What about Wasabi?
**A:** What food do they serve at Wasabi?
**M:** Japanese food.

**A:** How big is it? I like small restaurants.
**M:** It's quite big.
**A:** What about Carlitto's? My friend is the manager there.
**M:** Who is your friend?
**A:** Thomas.
**M:** Oh yes. OK – Carlitto's is nice.

## Unit 8 Recording 8
**W=Waiter A=Alda**
**W:** Hello. Carlitto's Restaurant.
**A:** Hello. I'd like to book a table for Friday evening.
**W:** Certainly, madam. How many people?
**A:** Two.
**W:** What time?
**A:** 8 o'clock, please.
**W:** I'm sorry, we've only got 7 o'clock or 9 o'clock.
**A:** OK. 9 o'clock, please.
**W:** Smoking or non-smoking?
**A:** Non-smoking, please.
**W:** And what name, please?
**A:** Alda Pierce.
**W:** OK, that's fine Ms. Pierce. See you on Friday.
**A:** Thank you. Goodbye.

## Unit 8 Recording 9
1 chicken   2 chocolate   3 seafood
4 pasta   5 fish   6 beef   7 potatoes
8 lamb   9 cheese   10 rice

## Unit 8 Recording 10
**W=Waiter A=Alda M=Mark**
**W:** Hello, madam. Do you have a reservation?
**A:** Yes. My name is Alda Pierce.
**W:** Ms. Pierce. A table for two?
**A:** That's right.
**W:** Come with me, please.
**W:** Are you ready to order?
**M:** Yes. I'd like fish soup, please, and lamb chops.
**W:** Certainly, sir. And for you madam?
**A:** Can I have seafood cocktail, please, and vegetable pasta bake.
**W:** Certainly. What would you like to drink?
**M:** A mineral water, please.
**W:** Still or sparkling?
**M:** Still, please.
**A:** I'd like an orange juice, please.
**W:** Certainly, madam.
**M:** Look! It's 11:30.
**A:** Really? It's late.
**M:** Yes, it is. Excuse me. Can I have the bill, please?
**W:** Of course.

## Unit 9 Recording 1
1963  1946  1981  1977  1957  1912  2002
1990

## Unit 9 Recording 2
Sputnik in Space 1957
Charles and Di: Royal Wedding 1981
First ipod in Shops 2002
Titanic Disaster 1912
Nelson Mandela Free 1990
Martin Luther King: I have a dream 1963
Juan Peron: President of Argentina! 1946
Elvis Presley is dead 1977

## Unit 9 Recording 3
I was an actor.
You were a singer.
He was happy.
She was born in 1982.
It was great.
We were singers.

They were rich.

## Unit 9 Recording 4
**H=Host M=Mark T=Trudy J=Josh**
**H:** OK. This game is called 'Who am I?' This is how we play. I say sentences about a famous person from the past, but I don't say the name. You guess the name. But remember you've got just one guess so don't get it wrong. Are you ready Mark?
**M:** I'm ready.
**H:** Are you ready Trudy?
**T:** I'm ready.
**H:** Are you ready Josh?
**J:** I'm ready.
**H:** OK. Let's play 'Who am I?'
For 10 points: I was born in 1940 in the UK.
For 9 points: My parents were Julia and Alfred.
For 8 points: I was quite tall and very thin.
For 7 points: I was a singer and I was famous for my music.
For 6 points: I was friends with …
Yes, Josh. Do you know the answer?
**J:** Is it Sir Paul McCartney?
**H:** No Josh. It isn't Paul McCartney. You're out of this game.
**J:** Oh no!
**H:** OK. Let's continue.
For 6 points: I was friends with Paul McCartney.
For 5 points: I was from Liverpool.
For 4 points: I was married to Cynthia Powell in my twenties.
For 3 points: I was married to Yoko Ono in my thirties. Yes, Trudy.
**T:** Is it …

## Unit 9 Recording 5
**J=Jasmine C=Cristof I=Isabella**
**J:** OK. Your go, Cristof.
**C:** Four! One, two, three, four. My first teacher!
**I:** OK, Cristof, your first teacher. Forty-five seconds. Starting NOW!
**C:** OK, my first teacher was Mrs Lloyd. She was about fifty years old.
**J:** Was she a good teacher?
**C:** She was a good teacher but I wasn't a good student.
**I:** Were you her favourite student?
**C:** I wasn't her favourite student. Francoise was her favourite student.
**J:** Was Francoise your friend?
**C:** Yes, she … Oh no!
**J:** Bad luck, Cristof. OK, Isabella, your go.
**I:** Two! One, two. Your last meal at a restaurant.
**J:** OK, Isabella. Your last meal at a restaurant. Forty-five seconds. Starting NOW!
**I:** OK, my last meal at a restaurant was last week at Carluccio's.
**C:** Oh – that's great.
**I:** Yes, and Oh no!
**J:** Bad luck Isabella. OK, my go. Five! One, two, three, four, five. My last holiday.
**C:** OK, Jasmine. Your last holiday, forty-five seconds, starting NOW!
**J:** My last holiday was two years ago. It was a Greek island called Santorini.
**C:** Were you with your parents?
**J:** I wasn't with my parents. I was with my friend, Helen.
**I:** Was it a good holiday?
**J:** It was a very good holiday. The hotel was very nice.
**I:** Were there any tourist attractions? Castles, palaces, cathedrals?
**J:** There weren't any castles or palaces but there were some beautiful beaches.
**I:** Was the weather nice?

**J:** It was great. Sunny and hot …
**C:** Time's up! That's forty-five seconds. Well done Jasmine.
**I:** Yes, well done. Your go again.
**J:** Oh great! Six! One, two

## Unit 9 Recording 6
1 I was a **good stu**dent.
2 I **wasn't very** in**tel**ligent.
3 Was **she** a good **tea**cher?
4 **Who** was your **best friend**?

## Unit 9 Recording 7
1 You were my **best friend**.
2 You **weren't** a **good stu**dent.
3 Were you **happy** at **school**?
4 **Who** were your **favourite tea**chers?

## Unit 9 Recording 8
1 vacuum the house   2 clean the bathroom   3 wash the dishes   4 do the laundry   5 iron a shirt   6 cook dinner

## Unit 9 Recording 9
1
**AS=Aunt Sally J=Jeff**
**AS:** Hello Jeff. How are you?
**J:** Fine thank you, Aunt Sally.
**AS:** Look at you. You're so tall.
**J:** I'm thirty-nine Aunt Sally!
**AS:** Oh yes, of course.
**J:** How was your flight?
**AS:** Awful. Awful. There wasn't any coffee. There wasn't a film. And the flight attendants weren't attractive!
**J:** Aunt Sally!
**AS:** Now, Jeff. Could you carry my suitcases?
**J:** Oh dear …
2
**J=Jeff B=Billy**
**J:** So, how was school, Billy?
**B:** It was great!
**J:** Were you good for your teacher?
**B:** No! I was very bad! It was funny. Daddy, can I have chocolate for dinner?
**J:** No, you can't. Oh dear …
3
**K=Karen J=Jeff**
**K:** Hello Jeff.
**J:** Hello darling. How was your day?
**K:** It was OK. What's for dinner?
**J:** Spaghetti.
**K:** OK. Can I turn on the TV?
**J:** Oh dear …
4
**F=Friend J=Jeff**
**F:** So Jeff. How was your week?
**J:** It wasn't very good. My Aunt Sally is here, my son is …
**F:** Oh baby! What's the matter? Jeff, could you pass the milk?
**J:** Yes, of course. Oh dear …

## Unit 9 Recording 10
1 science   2 music   3 art   4 sport
5 maths   6 languages

## Unit 9 Recording 11
**Louise:** My school was called William Morris High School. It was in Oxford. I was there from 1981 to 1986. It was a good school but I wasn't a good student. I was good at sport and art but I was very bad at maths and science and languages. My favourite lesson was art. My teacher was Mr Little and he was great. My best friend was Sarah Jenkins. She was in my class and she was fun!

## Unit 10 Recording 1

1  You lose your wallet/purse.
2  A thief steals your mobile phone.
3  You stay in bed all day.
4  You win the lottery.
5  You get married.
6  You find €10 on the street.
7  A police officer arrests you.
8  You move to a new house.
9  You break your arm.
10 You meet your favourite actor.

## Unit 10 Recording 2

wanted  asked  started  finished
lived  played  worked  cooked  closed
talked  arrested  listened  walked

## Unit 10 Recording 3

1  Pope Julius II wanted a new ceiling in The Sistine Chapel. He asked  Michelangelo to paint the ceiling of the Sistine Chapel. Michelangelo started it in 1508. He finished it in 1512.

2  Marcel Duchamp was an artist. He was born in 1887. He lived in Paris and he played chess with his brothers. In 1914, he moved to New York.  He worked in a library in New York. In 1918, he moved to Argentina.

## Unit 10 Recording 4

**The story of the Mona Lisa (Part 2)**
The Mona Lisa **moved to** Versailles and then to the Louvre. In 1800, Napoleon **moved it** to his bedroom but it **didn't stay** there. Four years later, it was back in The Louvre. Then, on August the 21st, 1911, the Louvre **closed** its doors. There was a big problem. The Mona Lisa wasn't there! Who was the thief? The police **talked to** lots of people. They **talked to** Picasso. Was he the thief? He wasn't. But they **didn't talk** to Vencenzo Peruggia.

## Unit 10 Recording 5

1  It was a good week for … actor Romero Cline, 43. He went to Las Vegas last week and he met Monica Hawkins, a waitress in a fast food restaurant. Three days later, they got married.

2  It was a good week for … Mr and Mrs Blatt from the UK. They had fish for dinner and they found three gold coins inside the fish. 'The fish was £3.50' said Mrs Blatt, 'but the gold coins are £1,000 each!'

3  It was a bad week for … Emiliana Rotman from Sweden. She won €14 million on the Euro lottery but she lost her ticket. 'Never mind' said Emiliana, 'That's life.'

4  It was a bad week for … pop group *Gilt*. *Gilt's* concert was last Friday but the tickets said 'Saturday'. 'Only five people came and saw the concert' said Sia Kahn, *Gilt's* singer. 'They took photos and bought a T-shirt but it wasn't a good day.'

## Unit 10 Recording 6

Get down to LOVELY ELECTRONICS today. Low, low, low prices on hundred of items. A fantastic DVD player: was €149. Sale price €119!
A great laptop computer:was €1399. Sale price €1050!
A beautiful washing machine: was €625. Sale price €465!
Hurry, hurry, hurry. Sale ends soon.

A great LCD TV: was €2189. Sale price €1750!
A new fridge: was €505. Sale price €427!
And a fantastic cooker: was €469. Sale price €325!
Remember, our sale ends today so hurry, hurry, hurry down to Lovely Electronics.

## Unit 10 Recording 7

**Abby:** Hi, everyone. Sorry I'm late.
**Charlie:** No problem. Nice to see you.
**Abby:** You, too Charlie. Hi Orla. You look great.
**Orla:** You, too.
**Abby:** Thanks. Hi Nick.
**Nick:** Nice to see you, Abby.
**Abby:** So how was your week, Nick.
**Nick:** Well, it was quite interesting. I talked to my manager on Tuesday and he told me some news.
**Abby:** What?
**Nick:** My company is going to move to Ireland.
**Orla:** To Ireland! What are you going to do?
**Nick:** I'm not going to move to Ireland. I'm going to find a new job.
**Charlie:** Well I'm glad you're going to stay here.
**Nick:** Me, too, and I was bored in that job so it's OK really. How was your week, Abby?
**Abby:** Awful. Someone stole my mobile phone.
**Orla:** Where? When?
**Abby:** Yesterday. On the train I think.
**Nick:** Did you go to the police?
**Abby:** No, I didn't. I'm so busy. I'm going to go tomorrow.
**Charlie:** My week was busy, too. Louise and I moved to a new flat on Monday?
**Nick:** Oh great. How is it?
**Charlie:** It's OK but we're not going to stay there long. We're going to buy a house next year.
**Orla:** Well, my week was very exciting. Daniel asked me to marry him.
**Abby:** He asked you to marry him! I don't believe it!
**Nick:** What did you say?
**Orla:** I said yes!
**Charlie:** Wow! Congratulations.
**Abby:** That's really exciting. When are you going to get married?
**Orla:** Oh, next year, I think, maybe in the summer. And you're all going to come to my wedding, of course …

## Unit 10 Recording 8

1
**A:** Are you going to buy her a present?
**B:** Yes, I am.

2
**A:** Is he going to stay with us?
**B:** No, he isn't.

3
**A:** What are you going to do tonight?
**B:** We're going to watch a film.

4
**A:** Where is she going to live?
**B:** She's going to live in Ireland.

## Unit 10 Recording 9

**Charlie:** So what job are you going to do, Nick?
**Nick:** I don't know. I want to be rich but I want to be happy, too.
**Charlie:** I've got a great story about that. Do

you want to hear it?
**Nick:** Sure.
**Charlie:** OK. Once upon a time, there was an old fisherman. He lived in a small house on the beach. He went fishing in his small boat every day. He was poor but he was happy. One day, the fisherman's grandson visited him. They went fishing in the little boat.
'You are a boy now,' said the fisherman, 'but soon you're going to be a man. What are you going to do in life?'
'Grandfather,' said the boy, 'you are a fisherman but you are poor. I want to be rich. I'm going to go to university.'
'And then what are you going to do?' asked the fisherman.
'I'm going to start a business,' said the boy.
'And then what are you going to do?' asked the fisherman.
'I'm going to make a lot of money,' said the boy.
'And then what are you going to do?' asked the fisherman.
'I'm going to be rich and I'm going to have a lot of free time,' said the boy.
'And then what are you going to do?' asked the fisherman.
'I'm going to enjoy my life,' said the boy.
'And how are you going to do that?' asked the fisherman.
The boy thought for a while and then said, 'I'm going to buy a little boat and go fishing every day.'
'Welcome to my world,' said the fisherman.

## Pronunciation Bank
## Recording 1

1  /ɪ/, big, /æ/, bag, It's a big bag.
2  /ɪ/, sit, /iː/, seat, Can I sit in this seat?
3  /æ/, map, /ɒ/, mop, That's my map and my mop.
4  /ɪ/, live, /ʌ/, love, I love living in London.
5  /ʌ/, cup, /æ/, cap, The cup is under your cap.
6  /iː/, me, /ɔː/, more, Please give me more.
7  /ɪ/, ship, /ɒ/, shop, There's a shop on the ship.
8  /ɪ/, lift, /e/, left, The lift is on the left.
9  /ɑː/, car, /iː/, key, Where's my car key.
10 /ɒ/, box, /ʊ/, books, Look at the box of books.
11 /iː/, he, /ɜː/, her, He hates her.
12 /iː/, Sophie, /ə/, sofa, Sophie's on the sofa.
13 /e/, let, /eɪ/, late, Let's get up late.
14 /aɪ/, kite, /eɪ/, Kate, This is Kate's kite.
15 /iː/, she, /əʊ/, show, She's at the show.
16 /iː/, eat, /eɪ/, eight, Did Jane eat eight cakes?
17 /aʊ/, how, /aɪ/, Hi, Hi. How are you?
18 /iː/, week, /eɪ/, wake, I wake up at 6 in the week.
19 /p/, Paul, /b/, ball, Put Paul's ball in the bin.
20 /t/, to, /d/, do, What do you want to do?
21 /k/, came, /g/, game, He came and played a game.
22 /tʃ/, chess, /dʒ/, Jess, Jess plays chess.
23 /f/, off, /v/, of, Please get off of Fran's van.
24 /p/, pink, /t/, think, I think it's pink.
25 /p/, pay, /ð/, they, Did they pay for the party?
26 /s/, keeps, /z/, keys, She keeps her keys in her bag.
27 /t/, fit, /s/, fish, Is your fish fit?
28 /t/, letter, /ʒ/, leisure, This letter's about leisure.

**29** /m/, mice, /n/, nice, Are your mice nice?
**30** /e/, collect, /r/, correct, did you collect the correct letter?

## Recording 2

**One syllable words:** one  six  big  young  read  learn  friend  great  lake  house  beach  road  west

**Two syllable words:** stress on first syllable: happy  seven  listen  morning  passport  father  website  surname  photo  awful  teacher  picture  modern  Sunday

**Two syllable words:** stress on second syllable: Japan  address  between  today  return  behind  Chinese  design  July  explain  mistake  dessert  because

**3-syllable words:** stress on first syllable: India  favourite  gallery  holiday  beautiful  Saturday  visitor  newsagent  medium  popular  opposite  interview  architect  hospital

**3-syllable words:** stress on second syllable: eleven  computer  cathedral  espresso  attachment  important  piano  designer  reporter  together  September  tomorrow  exciting  potato

**3-syllable words:** stress on third syllable: afternoon  engineer  introduce  magazine

## Recording 3

**My bro**ther is in Australia.
**This** is a **beau**tiful **cast**le.
**Their house** is **very mo**dern.
The **chemist** is **next** to the **bank**.
**My favourite place** for a **holiday** is Cornwall.
I **don't like** this **music**.
**Catherine works** in a **factory**.
**Paul** is my **brother** and **he's** a **designer**.
I **get up** at **eight o'clock**.
She **never answers** the **phone**.
I'd **like** a **cup** of **tea, please**.
They **want** to **go** to the **beach**.
**Kerry found** her **bag under** the **chair**.
I'm **going** to **buy** a **new car**.  or  I'm gonna **buy** a **new car**.

## Recording 4

<u>Are you</u> at home?
<u>Are they</u> ready?
<u>Do you</u> like it?
<u>Do you</u> write reports?
What <u>do you</u> do?
Where <u>do they</u> work?
<u>Are you going to</u> get married? or <u>Are you gonna</u> get married?
<u>Are you going to</u> call her? or <u>Are you gonna</u> call her?
<u>Were you</u> a good student?
<u>Were we</u> at school together?
<u>Did you</u> see him?
<u>Did you</u> talk to her?